Beer Lover's
New England

Beer Lover's New England

First Edition

Norman Miller

Guilford, Connecticut

All the information in this guidebook is subject to change. We recommend that you call ahead to obtain current information before traveling.

gpp®

Photos on pp. 6, 7, 28, 31, 36, 83, 91, 92, 96, 129, 135, 137, 142, and 188 by Sean Browne.
Photos on pp. iv, 1, 48, 52, 58, 61, 64, 70, 71, 73, 107, 109, 112, 115, 117, 118, 122, 152, 170, 175, 203, 214, 218 licensed by Shutterstock.com.

Editor: Kevin Sirois
Project Editor: Meredith Dias
Layout Artist: Casey Shain
Text Design: Sheryl Kober
Maps: Alena Joy Pearce © Morris Book Publishing, LLC

ISBN 978-0-7627-7996-3

Printed in the United States of America

10 9 8 7 6 5 4 3 2 1

Contents

About the Author

Norman Miller grew up in the beer wasteland of Leominster, Massachusetts, where he still resides with his dog, Foxy, and his beer fridge, Beatrice. He writes the popular "Beer Nut" column that appears weekly in the *MetroWest Daily News* and the daily "Beer Nut" blog on Wickedlocal.com. He developed his love of craft beer at the now-defunct Stone Coast Brewery in Laconia, New Hampshire, and thinks New England has developed into one of the great brewing regions in the US.

Acknowledgments

Writing this book was a long process, and I have to thank a lot of people who made it possible. First, I want to thank my mother, Donna Miller, who convinced me, despite her not liking that I drink beer, to write this book.

I also need to thank my good friend, Charlie Breitrose. If it weren't for having him as a drinking buddy in the early exploration of the craft beer, I probably would never have developed a love for beer.

I also would like to thank my editors at the *MetroWest Daily News* in Framingham, first for giving me my weekly "Beer Nut" column and, despite the tough times in the industry, allowing me to continue it all these years.

Much appreciation has to go out to all of the brewers and brewery employees and owners who helped me with this book, none more so than Will Meyers of the Cambridge Brewing Company. Every time I needed any information, he responded quickly with what I needed. He helped me with many different aspects of the book, and I can't thank him enough.

A lot of thanks has to go out to all of the New England breweries that have brewed and continued to make some phenomenal beers. If it weren't for them creating great beer, there would not be a need for a book like this. They have truly made New England a hotbed of brewing that is getting better and better every day.

Also important are the craft beer fans in New England. Better beer lovers demand more than what mass-produced beers offer. They aren't willing to settle for less than the best, and that forces the New England breweries to continue to strive toward greatness.

And finally, many thanks have to go out to my liver. If it weren't for my liver, it would not have been possible to drink more than 1,000 different beers brewed in New England, and that would be sad because I would be missing out on some truly phenomenal beers.

Introduction

New England beer saved me from the mediocrity of flavorless, overpriced mixed drinks at bars. I hated beer while in college and wouldn't drink it. It wasn't snobbiness, it was flavor. Mass-produced beer didn't taste good to me, and why would I drink it? So I stuck to Captain Morgan's and Coke.

That was until I discovered the Stone Coast Brewery in Laconia, New Hampshire. I was working at a newspaper in the Granite State, and the Stone Coast, a brewpub, was the closest bar we could go to after deadline on Fridays. I remember looking at the beer list and seeing a beer called the Drunken Monkey Barleywine. I had no idea what a barleywine was, but I ordered it (how couldn't I, based on that name?) and tasted something I had never had before—a beer with flavor.

That started me on a journey of the exploration of the beer world. Sure, like all aspiring beer geeks, I fell in love with the California hop bombs, and the big, flavorful imperial stouts, but I always came back to New England breweries. Now, if you look in my beer fridge, most of it is New England beer. New England has truly turned into one of the great brewing regions in the country. You have the old standbys, such as Boston Beer Company (brewers of Samuel Adams Boston Lager) and Harpoon Brewery, both producing good solid beers, as well as branching out into more adventurous brews. And then you have exciting beer producers—Allagash Brewing Company in Maine that brews world class Belgian ales, Pretty Things Beer & Ale Project in Massachusetts that has some of the most exciting beers brewed anywhere in the US on the shelves, and the Narragansett Brewery of Rhode Island, which is trying to bring a classic New England brand back while introducing some of the best, easy-drinking seasonals on the market.

Don't forget about the brewpubs. Establishments throughout New England such as the Cambridge Brewing Company and the Perfect Pear Cafe combine quality beers brewed on the premises with delicious dishes, making them a one-stop destination for hungry craft beer lovers. Beer bars abound throughout the Northeast where you can get the latest and greatest local and imported beers on tap or in bottles.

Want to taste the best beer New England has to offer in one session? We're home to some of the best beer festivals in the country, from Beer Advocate's Extreme Beer Fest to the New England Real Ale Exhibition.

Ever thought about taking your love of craft beer to the next level and brewing your own? If you want to get your feet wet, stop by one of the handful of brew-on-premises establishments operating in New England to brew and bottle your own beer under the guidance of an expert. Go one step further and become a homebrewer, creating your own concoctions or trying one of the beer recipes available in this guide.

But the world of quality New England beer goes much further than brewing it and drinking it. Pair a dish with a good craft beer to take flavors to the next level, or better yet, cook with it! Try out some of the recipes on offer in the Food Recipes section to get a taste of classic New England food infused with its beer in your own kitchen.

This book is an exploration and celebration of New England beer from all angles. Maybe you'll find a brew you've never heard about, learn more about New England's proud brewing tradition, or be inspired to take a road trip to sample the best beer available in different regions, whether it's Massachusetts, Maine, Vermont, New Hampshire, Connecticut, or Rhode Island.

To us beer-loving New England natives and visitors alike: Cheers!

How to Use This Guide

The brewery, brewpub, and beer bar listings in *Beer Lover's New England* are organized alphabetically within each state: Massachusetts, Maine, Vermont, New Hampshire, Connecticut, and Rhode Island. Every brewery profile contains a **Beer Lover's Pick,** a spotlight on the most outstanding beer being produced by its respective brewery, complete with tasting notes. You can find a complete list of Beer Lover's Picks organized by alphabetical order at the back of this guide in the Appendix.

In addition to the brewery, brewpub, and beer bar profiles that make up the bulk of this guide, you'll also find sections on:

Beer Festivals: A 12-pack of annual beer events is listed by month, with themes ranging from extreme craft beer to your typical outdoor summer fest.

BYOB: Brew Your Own Beer: This section celebrates the homebrewer, whether you're slightly interested in brewing your own beer or you're an avid hobbyist who's turned parts of your home into your own personal craft brewery. We've provided listings for brew-on-premises establishments for beginners and clone beer recipes for the advanced homebrewer.

In the Kitchen: It goes without saying that if you fancy yourself a bit of a beer lover, you might appreciate good food, too. And what goes better with a delicious meal than a glass (or two) of quality beer? Learn all about pairing types of food with styles of craft beer—complete with specific New England beer examples—and try your hand cooking with beer with the food recipes submitted by local area chefs and beer enthusiasts.

Pub Crawls: In this itinerary-based section, we break down some of New England's greatest beer-centric cities into walkable tours where you can sample some of the best brew on offer throughout the region.

Glossary of Terms

ABV: Alcohol by volume—the percentage of alcohol in a beer. A typical domestic beer is a little less than 5 percent ABV.

Ale: Beer brewed with top fermenting yeast. Quicker to brew than lagers, and most every craft beer is a style of ale. Popular styles of ales include pale ales, amber ales, stouts, and porters.

Altbier: A German style of ale, typically brown in color, smooth, and fruity.

Barleywine: Not a wine at all but a high-ABV ale that originated in England and is typically sweet. American versions often have large amounts of hops.

Barrel of beer: Production of beer is measured in barrels. A barrel equals 31 gallons.

Beer: An alcoholic beverage brewed with malt, water, hops, and yeast.

Beer bar: A bar that focuses on carrying craft or fine imported beers.

Bitter: An English bitter is an English-style of ale, more hoppy than an English mild, but less hoppy than an IPA.

Bock: A German-style lager, typically stronger than the typical lager.

Bomber: Most beers are packaged in 12-ounce bottles. Bombers are 22-ounce bottles.

Brewpub: Typically a restaurant, but sometimes a bar, that brews its own beers on premises.

Cask: Also known as real ales, cask ales are naturally carbonated and are usually served with a hand pump rather than forced out with carbon dioxide or nitrogen.

Clone beer: A clone beer is a homebrew recipe based on a commericial beer.

Contract brewery: A company that does not have its own brewery and pays someone else to brew and bottle its beer.

Craft beer: High-quality, flavorful beer made by small breweries.

Double: Two meanings. Most often meant as a higher-alcohol version of a beer, most typically used in reference to a double, or imperial, IPA. Can also be used as an American translation of a Belgian dubbel, a style of Belgian ale.

Gastropub: A beer-centric bar or pub that exhibits the same amount of care selecting its foods as it does its beers.

Growler: A half-gallon jug of beer. Many brewpubs sell growlers of their beers to go.

Gypsy brewer: A company that does not own its own brewery, but rents space at an existing brewery to brew it themselves.

Hops: Hops are flowers used in beers to produce aroma, bitterness, and flavor. Nearly every beer in the world has hops.

IBU: International bittering units, which are used to measure how bitter a beer is.

Imperial: A higher alcohol version of a regular-strength beer.

IPA: India pale ale. A popular style of ale created in England that has taken a decidedly American twist over the years. Often bitter, thanks to more hops used than in other styles of beer.

Kolsch: A light, refreshing German-style ale.

Lager: Beer brewed with bottom fermenting yeast. Takes longer and is harder to brew than ales. Popular styles of lagers include black lagers, doppelbocks, pilsners, and Vienna lagers.

Malt: Typically barley malt, but sometimes wheat malt. Malt provides the fermentable sugar in beers. The more fermentable sugar, the higher the ABV in a beer. Without malt, a beer would be too bitter from the hops.

Microbrewery: A brewery that brews less than 15,000 barrels of beer a year.

Nanobrewery: A brewery that brews four barrels of beer per batch or less.

Nitro draft: Most beers that are served on draft use kegs pressurized with carbon dioxide. Occasionally, particularly with stouts, nitrogen is used, which helps create a more creamy body.

Pilsner: A style of German or Czeckolovian lager, usually light in color. Most mass-produced beers are based on this style.

Porter: A dark ale, similar to the stout but with less roasted characters.

Pounders: 16-ounce cans.

Quad: A strong Belgian-style ale, typically sweet and high in alcohol.

Regional brewery: A brewery that brews up to 6,000,000 barrels of beer a year.

Russian imperial stout: A stout is a dark, heavy beer. A Russian imperial stout is a higher-alcohol, thicker-bodied version of regular stouts.

Saison: Also known as a Belgian or French farmhouse ale. It can be fruity, and it can also be peppery. Usually refreshing.

Seasonal: A beer that is only brewed at a certain time of year to coincide with the seasons.

Session beer: A low-alcohol beer, one that you can have several of them in one long "session" of drinking.

Stout: A dark beer brewed with roasted malts.

Strong ale: A style of ale that is typically both hoppy and malty and can be aged for years.

Tap takeover: An event where a bar or pub hosts a brewery and has several of its beers on tap.

Triple (Tripel): A Belgian-style ale, typically lighter in color than a dubbel but higher in alcohol.

Wheat beer: Beers, such as hefeweizens and witbiers, are brewed using wheat malt along with barley malt.

Yeast: The living organism that is in beer that causes the sugars to ferment and become alcohol.

New England Beer News & Reviews

With the New England beer scene growing by leaps and bounds, the online beer community is keeping pace. There are numerous great beer blogs and websites worth checking out to get the latest news, information, reviews, and thoughts on beer. These eight are some of the best beer blogs out there, but search around and you may find your own favorite.

Andy Crouch's BeerScribe.com, www.beerscribe.com: Andy Crouch is one of the most knowledgeable people about beer in New England, and his articles are well written, informative, and entertaining. Crouch is a talented writer and has written two books, including *Great American Craft Beer*.

Beer Advocate, www.beeradvocate.com: There is simply not a better resource online anywhere for beer. Run by brothers Jason and Todd Alstrom, the site is a clearinghouse of beer news. Press releases about new beers are posted daily and every beer event—festivals, beer dinners, tastings—is listed. The Beer Fly is an essential tool when planning a beercation. There are also ample forums on numerous subjects where people get into debates, discuss new trends in beer, and share their latest beer hauls.

The Beer Babe, www.thebeerbabe.com: Meet Carla Companion, known in the beer world as the Beer Babe. This Maine-based blog is well organized and a fun read, with sections split up into different categories—reviews and beer adventures being two of them—so that it's easy to navigate.

Beer Nut, http://blogs.wickedlocal.com/beernut: Okay, self-promotion—this is my beer blog. It is updated daily with beer reviews, press releases, and information about upcoming events. Also features a weekly guest blog from Jack's Abby Brewing in Framingham and a weekly guest homebrewing blog.

Connecticut Beer, www.connbeer.com: If you want information about Connecticut beer, breweries, brewpubs, and bars, this is the place to go. Michael Walsh knows his stuff, and his passion for the local beer scene shows on his blog.

Here for the Beer, www.hereforthebeer.com: Here for the Beer is the brainchild of husband and wife Tim and Amy Brady of Vermont. The website is heavy on professional-quality videos of different bars and events the pair attend, as well as some of the most unique, and almost risqué, reviews on the web.

Lost in the Beer Aisle, www.lostinthebeeraisle.com: Blogger Josh Dion talks about beer from an everyman's perspective, posting honest reviews of what he thinks about craft beer. Numerous photos from different events and bars are always posted.

Seacoast Beverage Lab, http://seacoastbeveragelab.com: Brian Aldrich has one of the better-looking beer blogs in New England, and the content is pretty darn good, too. Heavy on reviews, it also has a calendar of events, a section on pub crawls, and beer news.

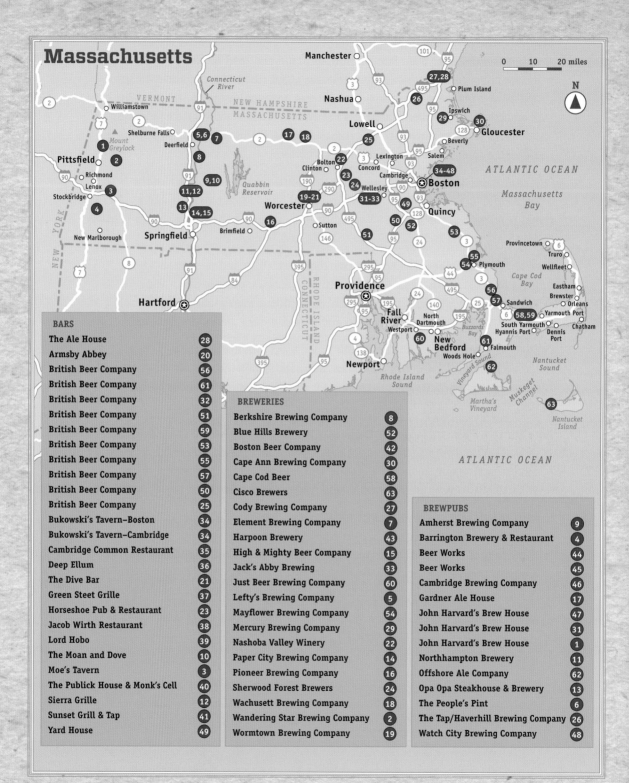

Massachusetts

Manchester

Williamstown
VERMONT
NEW HAMPSHIRE
MASSACHUSETTS
Connecticut River
Nashua
Lowell
Plum Island
Ipswich
Gloucester
Beverly
Salem

0   10   20 miles
N

Shelburne Falls
Deerfield
Mount Greylock
Pittsfield
Richmond
Lenox
Stockbridge
New Marlborough
Springfield
Brimfield
Sutton

ATLANTIC OCEAN
Massachusetts Bay

Quabbin Reservoir
Worcester
Bolton
Clinton
Concord
Cambridge
Lexington
Wellesley
Boston
Quincy

Provincetown
Truro
Wellfleet
Cape Cod Bay
Eastham
Brewster
Orleans
Sandwich
Yarmouth Port
Chatham
Dennis Port
South Yarmouth
Hyannis Port

Providence
Fall River
North Dartmouth
New Bedford
Westport
Woods Hole
Falmouth
Buzzards Bay
Vineyard Sound
Nantucket Sound
Newport
Rhode Island Sound
Martha's Vineyard
Muskeget Channel
Nantucket Island

Hartford

RHODE ISLAND
CONNECTICUT
NEW YORK

ATLANTIC OCEAN

BARS

The Ale House	28
Armsby Abbey	20
British Beer Company	56
British Beer Company	61
British Beer Company	32
British Beer Company	51
British Beer Company	59
British Beer Company	53
British Beer Company	55
British Beer Company	57
British Beer Company	50
British Beer Company	25
Bukowski's Tavern–Boston	34
Bukowski's Tavern–Cambridge	34
Cambridge Common Restaurant	35
Deep Ellum	36
The Dive Bar	21
Green Steet Grille	37
Horseshoe Pub & Restaurant	23
Jacob Wirth Restaurant	38
Lord Hobo	39
The Moan and Dove	10
Moe's Tavern	3
The Publick House & Monk's Cell	40
Sierra Grille	12
Sunset Grill & Tap	41
Yard House	49

BREWERIES

Berkshire Brewing Company	8
Blue Hills Brewery	52
Boston Beer Company	42
Cape Ann Brewing Company	30
Cape Cod Beer	58
Cisco Brewers	63
Cody Brewing Company	27
Element Brewing Company	7
Harpoon Brewery	43
High & Mighty Beer Company	15
Jack's Abby Brewing	33
Just Beer Brewing Company	60
Lefty's Brewing Company	5
Mayflower Brewing Company	54
Mercury Brewing Company	29
Nashoba Valley Winery	22
Paper City Brewing Company	14
Pioneer Brewing Company	16
Sherwood Forest Brewers	24
Wachusett Brewing Company	18
Wandering Star Brewing Company	2
Wormtown Brewing Company	19

BREWPUBS

Amherst Brewing Company	9
Barrington Brewery & Restaurant	4
Beer Works	44
Beer Works	45
Cambridge Brewing Company	46
Gardner Ale House	17
John Harvard's Brew House	47
John Harvard's Brew House	31
John Harvard's Brew House	1
Northhampton Brewery	11
Offshore Ale Company	62
Opa Opa Steakhouse & Brewery	13
The People's Pint	6
The Tap/Haverhill Brewing Company	26
Watch City Brewing Company	48

Massachusetts

This isn't the Massachusetts beer lovers from the 1990s and early 2000s remember. From a region that was once known for its traditional English-style pale ales, mild IPAs, and blueberry beers, Massachusetts has become an area exploding with experimentation.

Breweries—from those established in the mid-1980s like Harpoon to those just starting in the last couple of years such as Wormtown Brewing Company—are taking some serious chances with the beers they produce. And now pretty much every region in the state has a great beer bar to go out to and grab your local favorite or imported beer, all served in the proper glassware. Brewpubs aren't letting this experimentation pass them by, be it the barrel-aging process going on at Cambridge Brewing Company or brewing hopless beers or beers with bacon at the Watch City Brewing Company in Waltham.

Massachusetts has truly become one of the brewing hubs in the US.

Breweries

BERKSHIRE BREWING COMPANY

12 Railroad St., South Deerfield, MA; (413) 665-6600; www.berkshirebrewingcompany.com
Founded: 1994 **Founder:** Gary Bogoff and Chris Lalli **Brewer:** Gary Bogoff **Flagship Beer:** Steel Rail Pale Ale **Year-round Beers:** Berkshire Traditional Pale Ale, Dean's Beans Coffeehouse Porter, Drayman's Porter, Gold Spike German-Style Kolsch, Lost Sailor IPA, River Ale, Russian Imperial Stout, Shabadoo Black & Tan **Seasonals/Special Releases:** Cabin Fever Ale, Czech-Style Pilsner, Hefeweizen, Holidale, Maibock Lager, Oktoberfest Lager, Raspberry Barley Wine-Style Ale **Tours:** Sat, 1 p.m.

For years, Berkshire Brewing Company was western Massachusetts beer. It rarely got east of I-495. Now the secret is out. South Deerfield's Berkshire Brewing Company is available pretty much state-wide and people now know how good their beers are.

From their year-round beers to their seasonal beers, Berkshire does a great job with pretty much everything they brew. The **Steel Rail Pale Ale,** Berkshire's flagship beer, is a New England classic—a hoppy, well-balanced pale ale that is a treat to find on tap. **Dean's Beans Coffeehouse Porter** is a fantastic beer with strong coffee flavor from the use of real coffee beans, making it a perfect after-dinner drink. The **Drayman's Porter** (similar to the Coffeehouse Porter without the coffee) is a really good porter. The **Gold Spike Kolsch,** a year-round beer, is perfect to drink during the summer, and the **Lost Sailor IPA** is a quality IPA. The **Shabadoo Black & Tan** saves you the trouble of getting out a spoon and trying to do your own black and tan at home. The **Russian Imperial Stout** is an underrated beer. Drink this next to some of the nationally respected imperial stouts and it will hold up more than adequately.

Where Berkshire really excels is its seasonal beers. They have the best lineup of seasonal beers in all of New England. The **Czech-Style Pilsner** is excellent—nearly perfect for the style. It is a great summer beer, as is Berkshire's other summer beer, the **Hefeweizen.** The **Maibock Lager** is a German style brewed to be released in May. It's stronger than an average bock and has some heat from the alcohol—it's one of the best maibocks brewed in the US today. The **Oktoberfest Lager** is a slightly stronger version of the popular German style. It's one of the many quality Oktoberfest-style beers brewed in New England. Berkshire also brews three stupendous winter seasonals, the **Cabin Fever Ale, Holidale,** and the **Raspberry Barley Wine-Style Ale.** The Cabin Fever is a malty pale ale. The Holidale is a phenomenal barleywine. The Raspberry Barley Wine-Style Ale is not a traditional barleywine. It is actually a strong ale. Whatever style you call it, the raspberries make this a beer to

Coffeehouse Porter
Style: Coffee Porter
ABV: 6.2 percent
Availability: Year-round

A good porter can be an enjoyable beer to drink, but add real coffee and you have something special. Berkshire's Coffeehouse Porter is one of those special beers. The coffee flavors in this beer are incredible, yet it is still an easy-drinking beer. Great in a bottle, and on nitro draft. It is a perfect after-dinner drink.

seek out. Get a bottle of the Coffeehouse Porter and a bottle of the Raspberry Barley Wine-Style Ale. Pour a glass about three quarters full of the porter and then fill the rest with Raspberry. Yum.

Brewery tours are held on Saturday, and there are tastings in the Dick Schatz Tap Room. The tap room is named for a volunteer who died in 2006 and who left to Berkshire his large collection of beer memorabilia, which now adorns the walls at the brewery.

BLUE HILLS BREWERY

1020 Turnpike St., Canton, MA; (781) 821-2337; www.bluehillsbrewery.com
Founded: 2009 **Founders:** Peter Augis, Martin Grots, Andris Veidis **Brewer:** Andris Veidis **Flagship Beer:** IPA **Year-round Beers:** Black Hops, Imperial Red IPA, Wampatuck Wheat **Seasonals/Special Releases:** Antimatter, Dunkelweizen Wampatuck Winter Wheat, Oktobrau, Pumpkin, Watermelon Wampatuck Wheat **Tours:** Mon through Fri, 9 a.m. to 5 p.m.

What's better than spending the day on the slopes at the Blue Hills ski area and ending that day by a warm fire with a nice cup of hot cocoa? Ending the day cozied up to a bar with a good beer in your hand, that's what. And thanks to the nearby Blue Hills Brewery, there is plenty of fresh, locally brewed beer for the skiers and non-skiers alike.

Andris Veidis, a longtime brewer, brings years of experience to the brewery, brewing both traditional and newer styles of beer, giving local beer fans a wide variety to choose from. The **Black Hops** is a black India pale ale, or as some people call it, a Cascadian dark ale. Blue Hills incorporates the same malts into the Black Hops as they would for a German-style black lager. They then use the house ale yeast, and then lager it—fermenting it in the cold rather than in room temperature. This gives it a combination of chocolaty and citrus aroma and flavor. The **Imperial Red IPA** is basically an imperial red ale. It is a big beer (9 percent alcohol by volume). There's a lot of malt in it, typical of a red ale, and it's aggressively hopped like a double IPA. The regular **IPA** is a good, solid IPA. It leans toward the hoppy side, but has enough sweet malt to balance it out. The final year-round beer is the **Wampatuck Wheat,** a refreshing German-style hefeweizen. The Wampatucks were a local American Indian tribe, and Blue Hills honors them by naming several of their beers after them.

Their seasonals include the **Wampatuck Winter Wheat** and the **Watermelon Wampatuck Wheat,** which is a summer beer. The winter wheat is a heartier wheat beer, while the watermelon wheat is the original Wampatuck Wheat flavored with watermelon extract. The **Antimatter** is an interesting series of beers. Several breweries do what are called "single hop" beers. These are typically IPAs, all brewed exactly the same, except with different hops. The Antimatter alternates between being a single hop or single malt beer. It is cool to see how changing one ingredient changes the beer. The fall seasonals consist of the **Pumpkin** and the **OktoBrau.**

Beer Lover's Pick

OktoBrau
Style: Oktoberfest
ABV: 5.8 percent
Availability: Fall Seasonal
This is Blue Hill's best beer. The OktoBrau is a German-style Oktoberfest, and it's close to being spot on for the style, with a tad more sweetness than you would expect. There are caramel flavors, as well as the flavors of brown sugar. There is a graininess present, but it does not detract from the beer.

Pumpkin beer fans will enjoy the pumpkin ale and the OktoBrau is a traditional German-style Oktoberfest.

Blue Hills hosts tours on Friday from 3:30 p.m. to 6:30 p.m. and on Saturday from 2 p.m. to 6 p.m. with complimentary beer tastings. The tasting room manager typically leads the tour, but occasionally one of the brewers will take part.

BOSTON BEER COMPANY

30 Germania St., Jamaica Plain, MA; (617) 368-5080; www.samueladams.com
Founded: 1984 **Founder:** Jim Koch **Brewer:** Jim Koch **Flagship Beer:** Samuel Adams Boston Lager **Year-round Beers:** Sam Adams Light, Boston Ale, Pale Ale, Black Lager, Honey Porter, Irish Red, Blackberry Witbier, Latitude 48 **Seasonals/Special Releases:** Bonfire Rauchbier, Chocolate Bock, Cranberry Lambic, Dunkel-weizen, East West Kolsch, Harvest Pumpkin Ale, Holiday Porter, Noble Pils, Octoberfest, Old Fezziwig Ale, Rustic Saison, Summer Ale, White Ale, Winter Lager, Imperial Series, Barrel Room Collection, Infinium, Utopias **Tours:** Six tours daily, Mon through Sat, between 10 a.m. and 3 p.m. There is also a Friday evening tour and several special events at the brewery.

You can't talk about New England beer without talking about the Boston Beer Company. The story has been told numerous times—how Jim Koch, using a mid-19th-century family recipe, brewed the first Samuel Adams Boston Lager in his kitchen, and the rest is history. They are now the largest American-owned brewery. You can find Samuel Adams Boston Lager everywhere in the country, and it is often the better beer lover's only viable option at bars and restaurants.

But Samuel Adams is about more than the Boston Lager. Nearly every Samuel Adams beer is top-notch. The **Latitude 48** is a solid IPA, and the **Octoberfest** is one of the best of the style brewed in the US, as is the **Noble Pils.** Other seasonals, such as the **Harvest Pumpkin** and **Winter Lager,** and are all worth trying.

Samuel Adams constantly introduces those new to craft beers to styles not often seen from larger breweries. Case in point, the **Bonfire Rauchbier,** or German smoked beer, is a great introduction to the style, as is the **Rustic Saison** and **East West Kolsch.** The brewery also continues to experiment. The **Imperial Series,** all high alcohol beers, features four different ales—the **Imperial Stout, Imperial White,** the **Doppelbock,** and the **Wee Heavy.** They also introduced the **Barrel Room Collection** in 2010, which is a series of barrel-aged beers, all using what Jim Koch describes as Kosmic Mother Funk, a blend of wild yeasts and bacteria that gives the beers a unique quality.

After all the success he's had through the years, Koch has not forgotten his roots as a homebrewer. Samuel Adams sponsors two homebrewing contests every year. The largest is the LongShot contest, which is open nationally. Two homebrewers, as well

Utopias
Style: Strong Ale
ABV: 27 percent or higher
Availability: Released every other year
The Utopias is the strongest beer brewed in the US, and the most unique. It is 27 to 28 percent ABV. It has no carbonation, and maple syrup is used to help jack up the alcohol. It's also fermented for years in different barrels. And, oh yeah, it'll cost about $160 a bottle. But what you get is something akin to a fine liquor, worth savoring and sharing with friends.

as an employee homebrewer, will have their winning beers released in six-packs. The Patriot Homebrew contest is open to New England residents and the winning beer is put on tap at Gillette Stadium, home of the New England Patriots, all football season.

Tours are available at the Jamaica Plain brewery, and they often offer beers not available outside of the brewery for sampling.

CAPE ANN BREWING COMPANY

11 Rogers St., Gloucester, MA; (978) 282-7399; www.capeannbrewing.com
Founded: 2002 **Founders:** Jeremy and Michael Goldberg **Brewer:** Jeremy Goldberg
Flagship Beer: Fisherman's Brew **Year-round Beers:** Fisherman's Ale, Fisherman's IPA
Seasonals/Special Releases: Bavarian Wheat, Pumpkin Stout, Imperial Pumpkin Stout, Fisherman's Navigator **Tours:** Mon through Fri, 11 a.m. to 5 p.m.; free

The Cape Ann Brewing Company has really adopted Gloucester's rich fishing history—all of this small brewery's beers include "Fisherman's" in their title. The beers aren't fishy, though. Cape Ann produces nothing but solid beers, from its year-round rotation to its seasonal releases.

Brothers Jeremy and Michael Goldberg founded the brewery in 2002. Jeremy Goldberg is a homebrewer who took a 40-day cross-country road-trip with a group of friends that included stops at 38 different breweries. That trip, and Goldberg's concern about his weight gain, can be seen in the documentary *American Beer*, directed by Paul Kermizian. That trip inspired Jeremy Goldberg to open the brewery, and thankfully for us, he did.

Cape Ann offers three year-round beers, the Fisherman's Brew, the Fisherman's Ale, and the Fisherman's IPA. The **Fisherman's Ale** is a must-have for German kolsch lovers. Kolsches are light, refreshing, and delicate beers. They are not easy to brew, and tend to come out either flavorless, or ruined by the addition of too much . . . something, that takes them out of the kolsch realm. The Fisherman's Ale strikes a perfect balance of having enough flavor to make it enjoyable, but not crossing the line into another style. The **Fisherman's Brew** is an amber/red lager and is an easy-drinking beer, perfect after a day out on the boats, or, for most people, walking around Gloucester checking out the sights. The **Fisherman's IPA** is just what it says, a straightforward IPA.

Beer Lover's Pick

Pumpkin Stout
Style: Stout
ABV: 7 percent
Availability: Fall Seasonal

Cape Ann's Pumpkin Stout is the cure for those who are sick of the number of regular pumpkin beers that flood the market in the fall. Many are overly spicy and taste like liquid pumpkin pie. The Pumpkin Stout, on the other hand, is a stout first and foremost, with the added flavor of real pumpkin. The pumpkin doesn't overwhelm the roasty-coffee flavors from the stout, providing a balance that is the key to this fantastic beer.

The seasonals are some of the best out there. The **Fisherman's Navigator,** the winter seasonal, is a wonderfully brewed dopplebock—malty and sweet, just like a good doppelbock should be. Spot on. The **Bavarian Wheat** is a German-style hefeweizen. Like the Fisherman's Ale, this is a great summer beer, good on a hot day. Cape Ann also does a twist on the ever popular style of pumpkin beers. They brew two pumpkin stouts, the **Pumpkin Stout** and the **Imperial Pumpkin Stout.** The Imperial Pumpkin Stout is a big beer, 11 percent ABV, but the roastiness and pumpkin flavors do a good job of hiding the booziness usually present in a beer that big. The Pumpkin Stout is an ideal combination of roastiness and pumpkin, a perfect beer for the fall.

Tours are free, and are offered Mon through Fri from 11 a.m. to 5 p.m. Tours are also available on weekends if an employee is free to give the tour. Samples are also available at the bar. When you make a trip to the Cape Ann Brewery, be sure to stop at the on-site restaurant. Not only do they offer a full menu, but they also offer beers available exclusively at the pub, on draft only and not bottled.

CAPE COD BEER

1336 Phinney's Ln., Hyannis, MA; (508) 790-4200; www.capecodbeer.com
Founded: 2004 **Founders:** Beth and Todd Marcus **Brewer:** Todd Marcus **Flagship Beer:** Cape Cod Red **Year-round Beers:** Cape Cod Blonde Ale, Cape Cod IPA **Seasonals/Special Releases:** Berry Merry Holiday Ale, Dunkel Weizen, Harvest Ale, Old Man Winter, Porter, Summer Ale, Stargazer Stout, Cherry Porter, Hot Blonde, Port-O-Vino, Stock Porter, Vanilla Bean Porter **Tours:** Guided tours on Tues at 11 a.m. and Sat at 1 p.m. Self-guided tour during business hours Mon through Fri, noon to 6 p.m., and Sat from 11 a.m. to 2 p.m.

Cape Cod Beer gives vacationing beer lovers on the Cape a fantastic local option to drink while spending time with the family. The brainchild of husband and wife team Todd and Beth Marcus, Cape Cod Beer is a fabulous little brewery. The beers are not that easy to find outside of the Cape Cod and south shore area, but are worth seeking out if you happen to be vacationing nearby.

The year-round offerings are all pleasant beers to drink. They may not be the most exciting styles, but they are done the right way. The **Cape Cod IPA** is on the bitter side, and the **Cape Cod Blonde Ale** is ultra-refreshing. The flagship beer, the **Cape Cod Red,** is an excellent amber ale.

Where Cape Cod really excels is their seasonals and special releases. The **Old Man Winter** is what is called an old ale. This is a malty beast, which is balanced out with a fair amount of hops. The 8 percent alcohol by volume is perfect to warm you up on a blustery winter night. The **Berry Merry Holiday Ale** is brewed with cranberries, cloves, and orange, and the resulting taste is like Christmas morning in a glass. The

Cape Cod Red
Style: Red Ale
ABV: 5.5 percent
Availability: Year-round

Red ales are a dime a dozen, and get overlooked because so many are mediocre. The Cape Cod Red is anything but boring. It's a well-done red ale, has flavors of roasted toffee and caramel, and smells sweeter than it is. There is a bit of a hop presence in the background, but this is a malt forward beer.

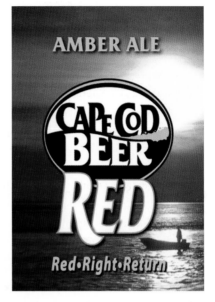

Summer Ale is a German-style hefeweizen, while the **Harvest Ale** is German-style ale and tastes like an ale version of an Oktoberfest. Cape Cod Beer also does several special releases, including different versions of its porter, including the **Cherry Porter** and the **Vanilla Bean Porter.** These beers are not always available, and some are brewery-only releases.

One such brew, the **Port-O-Vino,** is a collaboration with local winery Truro Vineyards. The brewery's porter is aged in fresh Merlot barrels, and the flavors of the chocolate malt and the Merlot work in harmony to create a unique beer. The Port-O-Vino is specially bottled in 750 ml champagne-style bottles and is only available at the brewery.

The brewery tour lasts approximately 45 minutes and includes a description of the brewing process and all of the ingredients, and a history of the brewery is presented. Beer samples are also available. Along with their beer and brewery merchandise, the brewery store also sells other locally made products such as Barnstable Bats, candles, honey, soap, potato chips, ice cream, and other items. Everything sold is made on the Cape.

CISCO BREWERS

5 Bartlett Farm Rd., Nantucket, MA; (508) 325-5929; www.ciscobrewers.com
Founded: 1995 **Founders:** Randy and Wendy Hudson **Brewer:** Jeff Horner **Flagship Beer:** Whale's Tale Pale Ale **Year-round Beers:** Bailey's Blonde Ale, Baggywrinkle Barleywine, Captain Swain's Extra Stout, Grey Lady, Indie Pale Ale, Moor Porter, Sankaty Light **Seasonals/Special Releases:** Celebration Libation, Pumple Drumkin, Summer of Lager, Woods Series, Island Reserve Series **Tours:** Mon through Fri, 4 p.m.; $20

Cisco Brewers has evolved over the years. The Nantucket brewery has always brewed great beers, but a few years ago they started taking advantage of the fact that the Nantucket Vineyard and the Triple Eight Distillery are all on the same grounds. The brewers started to incorporate the barrels used at the vineyard and distillery, and began creating exceptional offerings. At that point, Cisco moved from

Beer Lover's Pick

Pechish Woods
Style: American
Wild Ale
ABV: 4.9 percent
Availability:
Rotating
The Pechish Woods
is a fantastic
beer—I do not
even like peaches,
and I like this
beer. The Pechish
Woods is a wheat
beer that incorpo-
rates real peaches
and is aged in
white wine barrels

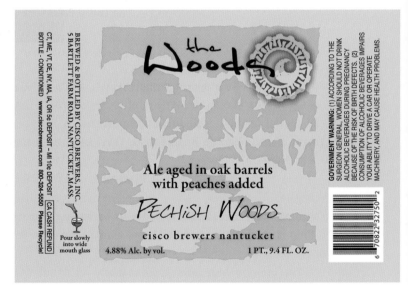

that impart some wine character. Combine that with the use of wild yeast, and the result is a beer that has a nice tartness that makes you want to take one sip after another after another.

a solid brewery with a great track record to one of the best breweries in all of New England.

The **Woods Series** are, without exception, fabulous beers. **Cherry Woods** is one of the best beers brewed in Massachusetts, and definitely the best fruit beer. It is a wheat beer aged in Chardonnay oak barrels, brewed with whole sour cherries. The only fruit beer on Cherry Woods level is also from Cisco, the **Monomoy Kriek,** which is a Flemish sour red ale, is also made with whole sour cherries, fermented in oak barrels. The **Winter Woods** is an ambitious beer. It's a Flemish braggot brewed with wild yeast and aged in French oak barrels with Pinot Noir grapes, mulling spices, and cherry wood smoked malt. If this does not scream "cold winter night beer," nothing does. The **Lady of the Woods** is a white ale aged in oak Chardonnay barrels, and **Full & By Rye** is aged in rye whisky barrels.

If barrel-aged beers are not for you, there are plenty of other choices. The **Whale's Tale Pale Ale,** the flagship beer, is a solid pale ale. The **Sankaty Light Lager** is a good option for those who are not fans of bigger beers with high ABVs. The **Captain Swain's Extra Stout** is a full-flavored stout full of coffee notes, and the **Baggywrinkle Barleywine** is a big beer, meant to be enjoyed slowly. The **Moor Porter** is a good English-style porter. The **Indie Pale Ale** is a hoppy, west coast IPA, while the **Grey Lady** is an excellent Belgian-style witbier (the same beer becomes Lady of the Woods after aging in oak Chardonnay barrels). The **Bailey's Blonde Ale** is an easy-drinking blonde ale.

If you are on vacation on Nantucket, make sure you take the tour at Cisco Brewers because it is much different than the average brewery tour. For $20, brewer Jeff Horner will lead you through a tour of the brewery, the winery, and distillery. There, you will learn about the various processes for all three, and get a chance to try the different products each offers. The tours last about an hour, and are offered daily at 4 p.m. from Memorial Day through Columbus Day. You can also buy beer to go in six-packs of 12-ounce bottles, bombers, and growlers.

CLOWN SHOES BEER
Contract brewed in Ipswich; www.clownshoesbeer.com
Founded: 2010 **Founder:** Gregg Berman **Brewer:** n/a **Flagship Beer:** Hoppy Feet **Year-round Beers:** Blaecorn Unidragon, Brown Angel, Clementine, Eagle Claw Fist, Hoppy Feet 1.5, Lubrication, Muffin Top, Pecan Pie Porter, Tramp Stamp **Seasonals/Special Releases:** None **Tours:** None

Clown Shoes beers draw a lot of attention, and sometimes not for the right reason. Some of their beer labels and names are on the risqué side. For instance, the **Tramp Stamp** features a close-up drawing of a tattoo on the small of a woman's

Eagle Claw Fist
Style: Imperial
          Amber Ale
ABV: 8 percent
Availability: Rotating

The beer with the best label—a Kung Fu warrior striking a pose while wearing, you guessed it, clown shoes—is also the brewery's best beer. This imperial amber ale is splendid and does a wonderful job of melding the flavors of an amber ale

and an IPA into liquid awesomeness. There are plenty of hops in this beer, but the malts do not get overwhelmed, making this incredibly balanced for an 8 percent alcohol by volume beer.

back who is wearing low-riding jeans. And do not forget about the **Lubrication**, which portrays a robot holding a gas nozzle near a certain region of his body. An online debate about these labels became so contentious that it made some local late night newscasts, where owner Gregg Berman explained all of the labels are done in good fun.

Even beer lovers who can be easily offended should not let their scruples overshadow the beer. Clown Shoes is responsible for some really high-quality beer. The brewery, which contract brews its beer at Mercury Brewing Company in Ipswich, started off with just one beer, the **Hoppy Feet.** It was one of the first east coast versions of a black IPA. Clown Shoes later introduced Hoppy Feet's big brother, the **Hoppy Feet 1.5,** which is basically the same beer with one and half times the ingredients. One of Clown Shoes' beers that is often overlooked is the **Pecan Pie Porter.** Big mistake. If you're a pecan pie fan, buy this beer. It is sweet, and it tastes like liquid pecan.

Brown Angel, despite a controversy over its provocative label that shows a woman in clown shoes and angel wings shaking her butt, is a quality brown ale, if not traditional for the style. It is packed with malts and is hoppier than a lot of brown ales. It also comes in at a relatively hefty 7 percent alcohol by volume. The **Clementine Witbier** is another one of the underrated beers from Clown Shoes. This is exactly what a Belgian-style white beer should be and it stands up to any other Belgian wit being brewed today. Like Hoppy Feet and Hoppy Feet 1.5, **Tramp Stamp** is Clown Shoes' version of a newer beer style, this time a Belgian-style IPA. **Muffin Top** is another Belgian IPA, but higher in alcohol (7 percent ABV to 10 percent ABV), and is the better beer. **Lubrication** is an American black ale, not a black IPA. It is a nicely done beer, and there are still enough hops in there to balance the beer out. It is almost like a black pale ale.

CODY BREWING COMPANY

36 Main St., Amesbury, MA; (978) 378-3424; www.codybrewing.com
Founded: 2006 **Founders:** Sean Cody **Brewer:** Sean Cody **Flagship Beer:** Cody's Pub Ale
Year-round Beers: Black Hole Stout, Dog Daze, Cody's Original North Shore Amber Ale, Gee Man's Lemon Honey Hypnotic Tonic, No Name IPA, Powwow Golden Ale, SOS, Wheelers Brown **Seasonal/Special Releases:** Too many to list, dozens of beers make occasional appearances **Tours:** None

The Cody Brewing Company may be one of the best kept secrets when it comes to great New England breweries. They do not distribute far outside of the Amesbury area, but their beers are definitely worth seeking out. Founder Sean Cody originally started Cody Brewing as a brew-on-premises business, but he expanded to distributing his own beer in 2006, and he has not looked back since. Cody Brewing Company's beers are available all over the north shore, and have recently expanded to Boston and central Massachusetts.

Cody brews some phenomenal beers, many with Belgian influences, and others that come straight from the founder and brewer's creative imagination. One of those beers is the **Gee Man's Lemon Honey Hypnotic Tonic,** an 8.8 percent strong ale brewed with "obscene amounts of citrus," as well as 1 pound of honey per 1 gallon of beer, which makes for a sweet, but shockingly drinkable beer. The **SOS** is a Belgian/IPA hybrid. The SOS was first brewed before Belgian IPAs became all the rage. It is brewed with a combination of American, Canadian, and German malts; American hops; and Belgian yeast. The combination works—the SOS tastes like the two styles melded perfectly, unlike most Belgian IPAs that taste like two separate styles working against each other. **Cody's Pub Ale** is an American-style pale ale, nicely hopped with a solid malt body. The **No Name IPA** is a well-hopped IPA. It is

SOS
Style: Belgian IPA
ABV: 5.5 percent
Availability: Year-round

Belgian IPAs are all the rage now, but Cody Brewing Company's SOS was one of the early pioneers of the style. This beer combines the hoppiness of a nice IPA with the sweetness of Belgian yeast and malt. The result is an extremely complex beer. Belgian IPAs can go awry when one side dominates the other, but this one plays it down the middle, and to delicious effect.

not overwhelmingly bitter, but a nicely done beer. It is not quite west coast style, but it is too hoppy to be English style—it's Cody style. The **Black Hole Stout** is an Irish stout with more chocolate undertone than the traditional stout. **Cody's Original North Shore Amber Ale** is Cody's first-ever beer. It is a hoppy amber ale and it remains a solid beer after all these years. Other year-round beers include the **Wheelers Brown,** which is an oatmeal brown ale, and the **Powwow Golden Ale,** a Belgian-style golden ale named for the Powwow River on which the brewery is located. The **Dog Daze** is a light, refreshing hefeweizen.

The Cody Brewing Company brews many other beers throughout the year, but none are regulars and some may not be brewed every year. These occasional releases include some extremely creative beers. The occasional releases include the **Cookie Puss,** which is an oatmeal raisin stout; **Wasabi Lemongrass Lager; Plum Dubbel;** the **Mullet,** a mulled strong ale; **Red Ryder,** a Christmas "fruitcake" ale; and the **Sick Pumpkin,** an imperial pumpkin ale.

ELEMENT BREWING COMPANY

30 Bridges St., Millers Falls, MA; (413) 835-6340; www.elementbeer.com
Founded: 2009 **Founders:** Ben Anhalt, Tom Fields, Dan Kramer **Brewer:** Dan Kramer
Flagship Beer: Extra Special Oak **Year-round Beers:** Red Giant, Dark Element **Seasonals/
Special Releases:** Summer Pilsner Fusion, Altoberfest, Brix, Vernal **Tours:** Thurs through
Sat, noon to 6 p.m.

Element Brewing Company is a tiny brewery that brews big beers—all of their offerings tip the scales at 7.75 percent alcohol by volume or more. Located in the small town of Millers Falls in Western Massachusetts, Element is the brainchild of friends Ben Anhalt, Tom Fields, and Dan Kramer. Both Anhalt and Kramer have had long brewing careers—Anhalt brewed at Maplewood Farms Restaurant & Brewery, Paper City, and Opa-Opa Brewing; and Kramer brewed at the Commonwealth Brewery, River City Brewing (Florida), Owen O'Leary's, and Opa-Opa Brewing. Fields is a jack of all trades, having worked in sales, construction, and business.

Beer Lover's Pick

Extra Special Oak (Cask)
Style: English Strong Ale
ABV: 7.75 percent
Availability: Year-round
Extra Special Oak is an excellent beer, but having it served on cask brings it to another level. It smoothens out and becomes creamy, and the vanilla/oak flavors really come through. The caramel malt sweetness blends with that vanilla to make this a decadent after-dinner dessert beer. If you're lucky enough to find this on cask at a bar, get it—you won't be disappointed.

Element's beers stand out on the shelves—they're packaged in 750 ml caged and corked bottles, wrapped in paper. Currently, this nanobrewery (they only brew 200 barrels of beer a year) only brews three year-round beers. If you're a fan of traditional beers, Element Brewing Company may not be for you since style guidelines really do not exist in their world.

The **Extra Special Oak** is a big, malty beer, coming in at 7.75 percent ABV. Light carbonation allows vanilla from the oak to come through. The **Red Giant** is another malty beer, but this one also has a lot of hop bitterness. It's similar to an imperial red, but sweeter than one of the typical style. Like the Extra Special Oak, this is a sipping beer, weighing in at 8 percent ABV. The **Dark Element** is described as a "New American Black Ale." It tastes like a combination German-style black lager and an American IPA. Flavors of chocolate and toffee mix in well with the hop bitterness. This is their biggest year-round beer at 8.8 percent ABV.

Element also offers four seasonals, called the **Interval Series.** The **Summer Pilsner Fusion,** brewed with pilsner malt and oatmeal, is available during the summer. The **Altoberfest,** a German-style altbier, is available during the fall. **Brix,** Element's winter seasonal, is similar to an English-style barleywine, but brewed with beet sugars and English hops. **Vernal,** the spring beer, is a dark wheat wine.

Tours are available during the day and are run by one of the owners. Samples of the year-round beers are available during the tour, but not of the Interval or other special releases. Their beer is also available to go at the brewery, either in growlers or in the normal 750 ml bottles.

FROSTY KNUCKLE BREWING COMPANY
Commonwealth Avenue, Gloucester; www.frostyknuckle.com
Founded: 2008 **Founders:** Michael and Patrick Beaton **Brewer:** Chris O'Connor **Flagship Beer:** Frosty Knuckle Ale **Year-round Beer:** Seaspray IPA **Seasonals/Special Releases:** None **Tours:** None

The story behind the name of the Frosty Knuckle Brewing Company is one of the best in all of New England. The name comes from Gloucester legend Howard Blackburn. In 1883 Blackburn and his fishing mate got separated from their fishing skiff and were on a small rowboat. Despite the freezing temperatures, Blackburn rowed and rowed all the way to Newfoundland. He lost his fingers to frostbite, and when he returned home, he gave up fishing and opened a saloon.

The brewery chooses to honor Blackburn's memory by featuring him on their **Frosty Knuckle Ale** labels. And what a beer to honor him by—the Frosty Knuckle Ale is a great, if little known, beer. Frosty Knuckle describes their ale as almost a

Frosty Knuckle Ale
Style: Hybrid
ABV: 4.9 percent
Availability: Year-round
Traditional styles are fine and should never be forgotten. But sometimes the truly creative stuff that exists on the outside of the traditional beer style guidelines can be fantastic. Frosty Knuckle Ale is one of those beers. It is not an altbier and it is not a helles bock. It falls somewhere delightfully in between, bringing the best of both styles into one single sip of beer. It is a beer worth seeking out.

hybrid style of beer—a German-style ale that is kind of a blend of an altbier and a helles bock. Whatever style of beer it is, it is a really well-done beer. The color is in between what the two styles would be, copper-colored, with a nice, fruity hop aroma and a creamy, sweet malty body.

Frosty Knuckle does not get a lot of publicity, mainly due to its lack of new beers. They only brewed one beer for most of the first three years of their existence, finally adding a second, the **Seaspray IPA,** after three years in business. The new brew was created by brewer/co-owner Chris O'Connor, who joined Frosty Knuckle in 2011. The beer is an English-style IPA, but brewed with American hops. It's on the malty side, but the hops are still aggressive enough to come through and provide balance.

Frosty Knuckle brews its beers at the Ipswich Ale brewery, and therefore doesn't offer any tours. Luckily, the beer is good enough to stand on its own.

HARPOON BREWERY

306 Northern Ave., Boston, MA; (617) 574-9551; www.harpoonbrewery.com
Founded: 1986   **Founders:** Rich Doyle, Dan Kenary, George Ligeti   **Brewer:** Todd Charbonneau   **Flagship Beer:** Harpoon IPA   **Year-round Beers:** Leviathan Imperial IPA, Munich Dark, UFO Hefeweizen, UFO White, Harpoon Cider   **Seasonals/Special Releases:** Bohemian Pilsner, Celtic Ale, Chocolate Stout, Grateful Harvest Cranberry Ale, Octoberfest, Summer Beer, UFO Pale Ale, UFO Pumpkin Ale, UFO Raspberry Hefeweizen, Winter Warmer, 100 Barrel Series, Leviathan Series   **Tours:** Mon through Fri, 2 to 4 p.m.; free tastings. Tours on Sat from 10:30 a.m. to 5 p.m. and Sun, 11:30 a.m. to 3 p.m., every half hour; $5

The Harpoon Brewery has been around since the beginning of the craft beer revolution in the mid-1980s, and they still continue to evolve even to this day. Founded in 1986 by friends Rich Doyle, Dan Kenary, and George Ligeti, the brewery was inspired by their love of European beer, and their realization that there was nothing up to that standard available locally.

Harpoon's biggest selling beer is the **Harpoon IPA,** which is a perfect example of how the brewing culture has changed over the years. When the IPA was introduced in the late 1980s, it was considered a hoppy, bitter beer. Now, there are pale ales that are hoppier than this beer. That doesn't mean you shouldn't drink it—it's a great, easy-drinking, malty IPA, more along the lines of an English style than an American version.

Nearly as popular as the Harpoon IPA is the **UFO Hefeweizen.** UFO stands for "unfiltered offering." The UFO is based on German-style wheat beers, although it is not the same. It lacks the bubble gum/clove/banana flavors a traditional German hefeweizen typically has. What it does have in common with its German brethren is how refreshing it is. The UFO Hefeweizen's popularity has inspired a whole series

Beer Lover's Pick

Grateful Harvest Cranberry Ale
Style: Fruit Beer
ABV: 5.9 percent
Availability: Fall Seasonal
Cranberries and beer? It really shouldn't work, but it does in this beer. The cranberry does not overwhelm the other flavors, which so often happens in fruit beers. It's also a perfect accompaniment for

Thanksgiving. Much better than that can-shaped pile of cranberry sauce, and with alcohol, which sometimes you need to deal with your family.

of UFO beers—the **UFO Raspberry Hefeweizen,** the **UFO Pale Ale,** the **UFO White,** and the latest series offering, **UFO Pumpkin.** Like the original UFO, these beers are perfect thirst quenchers, with enough flavors to satisfy the discerning palate.

Other year-round beers include the **Munich Dark** (a dunkel weizen), the **Harpoon Cider** (a solid hard cider), and the **Leviathan Imperial IPA.** The Leviathan series was introduced two years ago to give Harpoon brewers a chance to brew "extreme" or high-alcohol beers. The IPA is the only year-round one, but other beers in the series include the **Baltic Porter, Imperial Red,** and the amazing **Triticus.** Harpoon also has another series called the **100 Barrel Series.** The 100 Barrel Series is just that—100 barrels of a beer are brewed just once (although some have been brought back for encores). Typically, one particular brewer, or a guest brewer from another brewery or country develops the beer. There have been 38 installments of the series. Seasonals also include the **Summer Beer, Octoberfest, Winter Warmer, Chocolate Stout,** and the **Grateful Harvest Cranberry Ale.**

Throughout the year, Harpoon hosts several outdoor festivals that include good beer, good food, and good music, right at the brewery, located in the Seaport District. Harpoon also owns a second brewery in Windsor, Vermont. Both breweries host tours and tastings.

HIGH & MIGHTY BEER COMPANY
108 Cabot St., Holyoke, MA; (413) 323-8040; www.highandmightybeer.com
Founded: 2006 **Founder:** Will Shelton **Brewer:** n/a **Flagship Beer:** Beer of the Gods
Year-round Beers: Purity of Essence, Two-Headed Beast, XPA **Seasonal/Specialty Beers:**
Fumata Bianca, Fumata Nera, Home for the Holidays, Pas De Deux, Saint Hubbins Ale
Tours: None

High & Mighty Beer Company has a high opinion of itself. "We're not just brewers, we're beer-evangelists," they say on their website. "We're the clergy of Zymurgy, the Priests of Yeasts, the Joyful Congregation of High Fermentation." With an introduction like that, High & Mighty sets themselves up for a major fail if their beer does not live up to expectations. Luckily, High & Mighty delivers.

The **Beer of the Gods** is High & Mighty's flagship beer. It is a 4.5 percent, easy-drinking blonde ale with a nice hop kick. It holds a special place in my heart. I fondly remember drinking several of these with friends on the deck of a cabin in Cooperstown, New York, in 2007. The **Purity of Essence** is described as an India pale lager. This is a hoppy lager, but different than other hoppy lagers as it is brewed with all German malts and German hops, giving it a much more subtle flavor than American hops. The **Two-Headed Beast** is an excellent, creamy stout, made

Home for the Holidays
Style: American Brown Ale
ABV: 7 percent
Availability: Winter Seasonal
Home for the Holidays is one of the standout brown ales being brewed anywhere, in New England and beyond. This brown ale has a slightly Belgian character, but it has a lot of nutty and caramel flavors. There are also hints of chocolate. There is very little roasted character and it has some flavors of dark fruits. This may be 7 percent ABV, but it so smooth and drinkable, you would never know.

with organic cacao and Belgian yeast. The combination works. The yeast gives it an interesting flavor you do not get with many chocolate stouts. The **XPA** is a pale ale brewed with hops and grains from both the United Kingdom and the Pacific northwest. The middle of the "X" in the XPA is Massachusetts.

Specialty beers include the **Fumata Bianca** and the **Fumata Nera.** Both of these beers are smoked rye beers. However, the Bianca is a smoked white rye beer while the Nera is a smoked black rye beer. Both are excellent, but if you have to pick one, get the Nera. The **Pas De Deux** is a classic Belgian-style saison brewed with French ale yeast. It is a very dry beer, perfect for pairing with foods, particularly chicken and turkey. The **Home for the Holidays** is a superb brown ale, brewed just for the winter. It is smooth, creamy, and wonderfully nutty. The **Saint Hubbins Abbey Ale** is a traditional Belgian-style abbey ale.

Currently, High & Mighty Beer Company brews all of its beers at the Paper City Brewing Company in Holyoke. However, they hope to open their own brewery in the near future. Until then, you can still drink their beers. Praise High & Mighty.

JACK'S ABBY BREWING

81 Morton St., Framingham, MA; (508) 872-0900; http://jacksabbybrewing.com
Founded: 2011 **Founders:** Eric Hendler, Jack Hendler, Sam Hendler **Brewer:** Jack Hendler
Flagship Beer: Jabby Brau **Year-round Beers:** Hoponius Union, Smoke and Dagger
Seasonals/Special Releases: Kiwi's Rising, Copper Legend Octoberfest **Tours:** Fri, 3 p.m.
to 7 p.m. Sat, noon to 4 p.m.; free

Jack's Abby Brewing is a little different than most breweries in New England (or any craft brewery in the US)—they brew only lagers. Lagers take much longer to brew than ales, usually taking up tank space that can be quickly turned around by brewing ales. But Jack's Abby Brewing, one of the newest breweries in Massachusetts, has been inspired by the monastic brewing tradition of Germany, where the best lagers in the world are brewed.

The brewery is a family affair, owned by the Hendler brothers. Jack, the head brewer, is the former brewer of the popular Boston Beer Works brewpub. Sam and

Beer Lover's Pick

Hoponius Union
Style: India Pale Lager
ABV: 6.7 percent
Availability: Year-round
There aren't many hoppy lagers like the Hoponius Union. It hits you with big floral notes and grapefruit flavors from the hops. This is the kind of lager even the most hard-core hop-head will enjoy. The lager yeast really allows the hops to come through. Not the most balanced beer, but it's not supposed to be. Share a growler of this with friends and everyone will be happy.

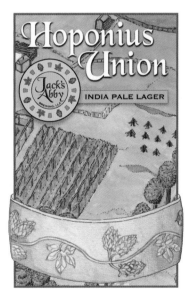

Eric handle all of the other duties (marketing, web, sales). The "Abby" in Jack's Abby Brewing is not a typo—it's named for Jack's wife, Abby.

Although inspired by German brewing, not all of the beers are traditional. They brew four very different beers. The brewery's flagship is the **Jabby Brau,** which is described as a "session lager." It is only 4.5 percent alcohol by volume. The beer has some qualities of a pilsner, but is darker than the golden yellow that most pilsners are. The **Smoke and Dagger** is a smoky, black lager. The smokiness goes well with the roastiness. Neither flavor dominates, and neither is so overwhelming that you can't have more than a glass. An overly smoky beer can be a chore to drink, but the Smoke and Dagger strikes the perfect balance of smokiness and drinkability. The **Hoponius Union** is Jack's Abby Brewing's attempt at an India pale lager. It's hopped like a west coast IPA, but it still has the clean lager taste.

The **Copper Legend Octoberfest** is Jack's first seasonal beer. They also have plans to brew a still-unnamed wet hop lager. The beer will be brewed with fresh hops picked from their family farm in Vermont. They also have an on-site garden where they grow hops, as well as several herbs they plan on using in future brews. The **Kiwi's Rising** is a double India pale lager. There are no kiwis in this beer. The name comes from the use of New Zealand hops. This may not be a true double IPA, but it is a great beer for hopheads.

Jack typically leads the brewery tours, although Eric or Sam may fill in. It's not an uncommon occurrence to see the brothers wearing lederhosen when you come in for a tour of their 4,500-square-foot brewery. There is also a tasting room and store. Two-ounce samples of all the beers are available. Growlers are available at the brewery.

JUST BEER BREWING COMPANY

98 Horseneck Rd., Westport, MA; (508) 636-2288; www.justbeer.us
Founded: 1997 **Founder:** Bill Russell **Brewer:** Bill Russell **Flagship Beer:** None **Year-round Beers:** None brewed fully year-round. Mostly year-rounds are Cranberry Saison, Golden Flounder, Horseneck Golden IPA, Moby D, 1602 Colonial Porter **Seasonals/Special Releases:** "Not-So-Great" Punkin Ale, Hot Cocoa Winter Ale, Summer Ale, several one-offs **Tours:** Tours are offered occasionally on Sat at 2 p.m. Call ahead to see if they are available.

When the Buzzards Bay Brewing Company stopped brewing beer a few years ago, it was a sad time for lager lovers. They brewed a great pilsner and a fantastic black lager. But, just because Buzzards Bay is gone, does not mean beer isn't being brewed at the Westport brewery. Just Beer Brewing Company has taken its place.

Golden Flounder
Style: Pale Wheat Ale
ABV: 4.6 percent
Style: Year-round

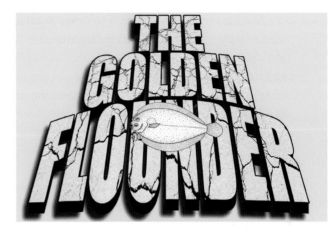

Sure, a great name will catch your attention, but it's what's in the bottle that will make you buy more than one. American wheat ales tend to be boring compared to their German and Belgian counterparts, but this is a really well-done one. It is a refreshing, easy drinking beer, a perfect refreshment for a hot day by the pool.

Owner Bill Russell, a former award-winning homebrewer, originally founded the brewery in 1997 on the site of the Russell Family Farm. Since then the brewery has grown and expanded, and contract-brews beers for several other breweries. Just Beer brews a wide variety of beers. The **1602 Colonial-style Porter** is a really solid porter, spot on for the style, reminiscent of a true English porter. The **Cranberry Saison** adds an interesting twist to the Belgian-style ale. Saisons are great food beers, particularly with chicken and turkey, so add the cranberry flavor with the saison, and you have yourself a perfect Thanksgiving accompaniment. The **Horseneck Golden IPA** is kind of old school. It does not seek to smack you in the face and burn your taste buds with abundant hops. Just Beer's version of the IPA is more mellow, balanced, and easy to drink, without ruining your palate for a second beer. The **Hot Cocoa Winter Ale** is a stout and a perfect wintertime beer. After spending an hour outside shoveling a foot of snow, come inside and pour one of these into your mug, instead of taking time to make a hot cocoa from scratch. The **Summer Ale** and **Moby D** are two very different pale ales. Taste them side by side to see how different the same style of beer can taste, even when brewed by the same brewery. The **Golden Flounder** has more than an awesome name, it is a refreshing wheat beer, perfect for the summer.

Massachusetts

Russell, who also runs his family's Westport River's Vineyard, has a creative streak to him. In the past, he released what was called "The Mystery IPA." Each bottle in the case told a portion of a story. To read the whole story, you had to buy the case.

The brewery runs occasional tours on Saturday at 2 p.m. A brewery employee usually leads the free tour. Tastings are available. There is also a brewery store, where you can buy beers in six-packs, growlers, bombers, 750 ml bottles, half-barrel kegs, and sixth-barrel kegs. Just make sure to call ahead. Just Beer is a small brewery, and often runs out of beer. So if there's something you're looking for specifically, give them a ring to see if they have it. But, don't worry if they don't, Just Beer Brewing Co. has just the right mix of beers to make anyone happy.

LEFTY'S BREWING COMPANY

301 Wells St., Greenfield, MA; (413) 648-6111; www.leftsbrew.com
Founded: 2010 **Founder:** Bill Goldfarb **Brewer:** Bill Goldfarb **Flagship Beer:** IPA
Year-round Beers: Chocolate Oatmeal Stout, Coffee Porter, English-style Porter, Irish-style Stout, Pale Ale **Seasonals/Special Releases:** None **Tours:** None

Like Greenfield, the town that hosts it, Lefty's Brewing Company is not well known outside of the general geographic area. People in Boston have probably never heard of either the town or the brewery. That's okay. The brewery, founded in 2010 by Bill "Lefty" Goldfarb, is a hidden jewel in western Massachusetts.

Goldfarb was a longtime homebrewer who left his roofing job to pursue his dream of brewing professionally. His brewery is tiny: a small two-barrel brew house that includes retrofitted milk tanks. He hand bottles all of the beer. He only brews 320 barrels of beer a year, not a lot, but for a one-man operation, it's impressive.

Currently, Lefty's Brewing Company brews six different beers, Pale Ale, IPA, English-style Porter, Coffee Porter, Irish-style Stout, and a Chocolate Oatmeal Stout. The **Pale Ale** is on the hoppier side of the style, which gives it a nice bitter zing when you take that first sip. The **IPA** is well balanced, leaning toward west-coast style with enough hops that a hophead won't be bored by it, but not too overwhelming to those who aren't hop lovers. The two porters are fantastic. The **English-style Porter** is spot on for the style. No hop presence, rich and creamy, just like a real porter should be. The **Coffee Porter** is similar to the English-style Porter, except for the addition of Sumatra coffee beans, hand-roasted by Lefty himself. The two stouts may be Lefty's best beers. The **Irish-style Stout** is a little stronger than the average Irish stout (6.6 percent alcohol by volume to about 4.5 percent ABV), but don't let that scare you. It still has the requisite creaminess. A great after-dinner beer, or

Chocolate Oatmeal Stout
Style: Oatmeal Stout
ABV: 7.2 percent
Availability: Year-round

The problem with many chocolate stouts is they often overload the beer with chocolate, ignoring the rest of the ingredients. Lefty's Chocolate Oatmeal Stout does not do that. This is a lusciously creamy stout, and the chocolate adds to this beer rather than overwhelms it. It is not a huge imperial stout, either, but you do get hints of alcohol, particularly in the finish.

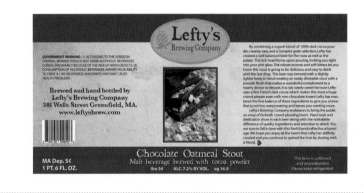

maybe to enjoy with some meat loaf or pot roast. The **Chocolate Oatmeal Stout** is a decadent dessert beer. Not as chocolaty as some imperial stouts that incorporate chocolate, this still provides enough chocolate to be like a liquid dessert, while still retaining its beeriness. The Valrhona cocoa powder adds a bitterness to the beer. The Chocolate Oatmeal Stout is also Lefty's strongest beer, coming in at 7.2 percent ABV.

Tours are not currently available at Lefty's Brewing Company, although Lefty said he hopes to begin offering them when he is finished with some renovations. Lefty's Brewing Company's beers are available in 12-ounce bottles, bombers, and growlers at 21 stores, all within driving distance of Greenfield (and a minimum of an 1.5 hours from Boston). They are also available at 10 different restaurants and bars, also in the same general area. Basically, if you're not in Franklin County, don't expect to be able to find Lefty's beers. Lefty does hope to expand to other areas in the future.

MAYFLOWER BREWING COMPANY

12 Resnik Rd., Plymouth, MA; (508) 746-2674; http://mayflowerbrewing.com
Founded: 2007 **Founder:** Drew Brosseau **Brewers:** Ryan Gwodz and Michael Smith
Flagship Beer: Mayflower Pale Ale **Year-round Beers:** Golden Ale, IPA, Porter **Seasonal/
Special Releases:** Autumn Wheat Ale, Spring Hop Ale, Summer Rye Ale, Thanksgiving Ale,
Winter Oatmeal Stout **Tours:** 11 a.m. to 3 p.m.

Some say the *Mayflower* landed at Plymouth Rock because the Pilgrims got lost on their way to Virginia. But, according to several of the passengers' diaries, they landed because they ran out of ale. Mayflower Brewing Company's founder Drew Brosseau is the tenth great-grandson of John Alden, beer barrel cooper on the *Mayflower,* and you could say he was destined to open his own brewery in 2007.

Mayflower Brewing Company quickly built up a reputation for brewing good beers that don't cross into the extreme category. They all have moderate alcohol levels, but are full-flavored. The **Mayflower Pale Ale** is a solid pale ale—hoppy and balanced, a real treat to drink. The **Golden Ale** is a lighter-tasting ale, easy to drink

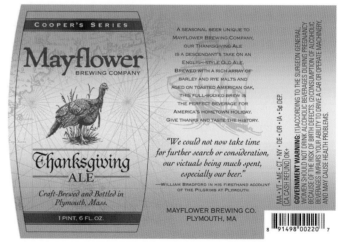

Beer Lover's Pick

Thanksgiving Ale
Style: Strong Ale
ABV: 8 percent
Availability: Fall Seasonal
Mayflower's Thanksgiving
Ale is a fabulous beer. This
is a dark red beer, full of
malty sweetness with an
herbal hop presence. This
is a toasty beer, but not
overwhelmingly so, with
some notes of toffee and
caramel. The beer is aged
on white oak, and you
get the flavor of oaky vanilla in the beer. A perfect beer to pair with—what
else?—a turkey. Gobble, gobble.

with enough flavor to make it worth seeking out. Mayflower's **IPA** is one of the better India pale ales brewed in Massachusetts. It is well-bittered from the hops, and the malt backbone makes this a fantastic beer. It is the biggest of the year-round beers, coming in at 7 percent alcohol by volume. The **Porter** is a straightforward English-style porter. It is creamy, slightly roasty, and just plain tasty.

Mayflower also does a really good job with its seasonals. The **Autumn Wheat Ale** is a dark wheat beer, with bready malt character and fruity aromas. The **Spring Hop Ale** is a welcome change from most spring beers. Many spring beers are light and bordering on flavorless. This is a full-flavored, hoppy red ale. The caramel malts play off nicely with the hops. It's definitely worth seeking out. The **Summer Rye Ale** is a perfect light beer for summer at only 3.8 percent ABV. It is light-bodied, but has a nice hop zing. The rye adds a pleasant spiciness, so even though this beer is low on alcohol it is not low on flavor. The **Winter Oatmeal Stout** is a full-flavored oatmeal stout, with hints of chocolate and coffee. It is creamy and is sweeter than many oatmeal stouts, a wonderfully done beer. The **Thanksgiving Ale** is a treat. It is a blend of an American strong ale and English old ale, aged in oak barrels. Obviously, a perfect beer to share on Thanksgiving.

The Mayflower Brewing Company offers tours of its brewery and also has a tasting room where beer fans can try the various beers they have on draft. You can buy growlers, or the freshest six-packs, 12-packs, and cases of beer to go.

MERCURY BREWING COMPANY

23 Hayward St., Ipswich, MA; (978) 356-3329; www.ipswichalebrewery.com
Founded: 1991 **Founders:** Jim Beauvais and Paul Sylva **Brewer:** Dan Lipke **Flagship Beer:** Ipswich Ale **Year-round Beers:** Ipswich Dark, Ipswich IPA, Ipswich Oatmeal Stout; Stone Cat line: Blonde, Blueberry, ESB, IPA **Seasonal/Special Releases:** Ipswich Harvest, Ipswich Summer, Ipswich Winter, 5-Mile Stock Ale, Castle Hill Summer Barley Wine, Choate Bridge Imperial Stout, Hosiery Mill Double IPA; Stone Cat line: Hefeweizen, Octoberfest, Pumpkin, Scotch Ale, Winter Lager **Tours:** None

The Ipswich Ale Brewery, technically the Mercury Brewing Company, is one of the most important breweries in Massachusetts. Not only do they brew their own Ipswich beers, they also brew the Stone Cat line of beer that owner Rob Martin purchased in the late 1990s, in addition to brewing Notch Session Ales, Sherwood Forest, Clown Shoes Beers, and others.

Despite brewing all of those other beers, the Ipswich line certainly doesn't suffer. The **Ipswich Ale** (once named one of the top 10 beers in the world by *Wine Spectator* magazine) is a classic English-style pale ale. It is not too light and not too

Ipswich Dark Ale
Style: Brown Ale
ABV: 6.3 percent
Availability: Year-round

A lot of New England breweries make brown ales, and many of them are kind of boring. The Ipswich Dark Ale is not one of those beers. This is a full-flavored brown ale, with hints of chocolate, molasses, and a little almond nuttiness. There are more hops present than typically seen in the style, and that provides a pleasant fruity flavor. A nicely done beer worth getting your hands on.

heavy, malty, and almost creamy, with just a touch of hops. The **Ipswich IPA** is a blend of American hops and English malts. The dry bitter hops and the sweet English malts work well together. The **Ipswich Oatmeal Stout** is a bigger than usual oatmeal stout at 7 percent alcohol by volume. It still retains the creaminess you want in an oatmeal stout, and it has a stronger espresso-like flavor from the roasted malts. The **Ipswich Dark** is an exceptional brown ale with more hops than the usual brown ale.

Ipswich seasonals include the **Summer,** which is a light and refreshing blonde ale; the **Harvest,** which is almost like a lighter-colored black IPA; and the **Winter,** an English-style old ale. Ipswich also brews a series of beers called the **5-Mile Stock Ale.** The beer is made with at least one ingredient, and as many as possible, from within 5 miles of the brewery. This beer changes each time it's brewed, and the style varies. In addition, Ipswich brews a series of bigger beers as limited releases, all inspired by local Ipswich landmarks. Those beers include the wonderful **Choate Bridge Imperial Stout.** Ipswich also brews the **Stone Cat** line of beers. The beers are all pretty straightforward—the **Blonde** is light and refreshing, the **Blueberry** is a solid blueberry beer, and the **IPA** is a malty English-style IPA.

The seasonals include a really well-done **Octoberfest** lager and a big and malty **Scotch Ale.** Ipswich also makes a series of sodas under the Mercury label, as well as mustards, both of which can be bought at various stores. At the time of this writing, Ipswich does not offer tours at their breweries, but they were working to open a new brewery where they would offer tours. Check their website for more information.

NASHOBA VALLEY WINERY
100 Wattaquadock Hill Rd., Bolton, MA; (978) 779-5521; www.nashobawinery.com
Founded: Winery, 1978; brewery, 2004 **Founder:** Jack Partridge **Brewer:** Tom Knight
Flagship Beer: Heron Ale **Year-round Beers:** Bolt 117 Lager, IPA, Wattaquadock
Wheat **Seasonals/Special Releases:** Belgian Pale Ale, Dunkelweizen, Imperial Stout,
Oaktoberfest, Robust Porter, Summer Stout, Watermelon Wheat, Nashoba Special Reserve
Series **Tours:** Sat, 11 a.m. to 4 p.m.; $7

The Nashoba Valley Winery is a one-stop bonanza for those who like adult beverages. They produce many phenomenal fruit wines (the Blueberry Merlot is to die for), as well as spirits, such as whiskey, brandy, and vodka. They are also home to a small craft brewery that brews great beers, only available at the winery. The brewery was added to the winery and distillery in 2004, and has been steadily improving its quality of beers throughout the years, adding several interesting seasonals and special releases to the solid lineup of year-round beers.

The **Heron Ale,** the flagship beer, is a traditionally English-style bitter. It uses British hops to give it the traditional earthy flavors. Actually slightly stronger than some versions at 5.3 percent alcohol by volume, it is still an easy-drinking beer. The **Bolt 117 Lager** is a German-influenced Dortmunder lager. It is slightly dark, and it has a strange, but not unpleasant, aftertaste that comes from the use of German noble hop varieties. The **IPA** is a solid New England IPA, meaning it is not full of grapefruit or piney aromas and flavors, but rather more malt-forward. It's definitely worth drinking. The final year-round beer is the **Wattaquadock Wheat,** a German-style hefeweizen with hints of clove and banana, thanks to the use of traditional hefeweizen yeast.

Nashoba's seasonals and special releases are even better than their year-round beers. Nashoba's summer seasonal is an unusual pick for a summer beer, a stout. But the **Summer Stout** is easy drinking and quite light, so it kind of fits. The **Oaktoberfest** is also different than most, if not all, American and German Oktoberfest-style beers. It is aged on oak, giving it some flavors, such as a little

Oaktoberfest
Style: Oktoberfest
ABV: 5.3 percent
Availability: Fall Seasonal

The Oaktoberfest is not the best Oktoberfest you may try, but it may be the most unusual. This is a traditionally brewed Oktoberfest/Marzen lager, but aged on oak chips. The combination of caramel flavors typically found in an American Oktoberfest blend well with the vanilla oak characters to create a unique beer. Try this side-by-side with a beer like Samuel Adams Octoberfest to see the difference.

vanilla, not found in traditional Oktoberfests. The winter seasonal, the **Imperial Stout,** is a big beer, at 8.5 percent alcohol by volume. This beer has strong flavors and aroma of dark, bitter chocolate, and it is aged on oak, giving it more depth of flavor. Other special releases include the **Belgian Pale Ale,** the **Dunkelweizen,** and the **Watermelon Wheat.**

Nashoba Valley also brews what is called the **Special Reserve Series.** These are extra-small batches of beer, and available while supplies last. Some of the Special Reserve beers have been the **Chai Brown,** the **Special Reserve Porter,** and the bourbon-barrel-aged **Vanilla Porter.**

The Nashoba Valley Winery is also family friendly, with apple picking in the huge apple orchards, as well as having a sit-down fine-dining restaurant, J's, that also sells picnic lunches to those who want to take advantage of the beautiful scenery and sit outside.

Tours and tastings are available on Saturday, and the winery store has all the wines, spirits, and beers, as well as glassware and other goods, available for sale. Along with 12-ounce bottles of beer, they also sell growlers of the various beers to go.

NOTCH BREWING

Contract brewed at Ipswich Ale Brewery in Ipswich, MA, and Kennebunkport Brewery in Kennebunkport, ME; (978) 853-9138; www.notchsession.com
Founded: 2010 **Founder:** Chris Lohring **Flagship Beer:** Notch Session Ale **Year-round Beers:** Notch Session Pils, Notch Saison **Seasonals/Special Releases:** Notch BSA Harvest, Notch Cerne, Notch Table Beer, Notch Berliner Weisse; a series of cask-conditioned beers, not bottled **Tours:** Not available

Most breweries try to enter the market with a big, high-alcohol beer, something that will catch beer geeks' attention right away. Notch Brewing is not like most breweries. They brew nothing but low-alcohol beers, or session beers. A session beer is a low alcohol ale or lager, 4.5 percent alcohol by volume or less. The idea behind session beers is that you can sit at a bar for a few hours and have a few beers without becoming intoxicated.

The key for session beers is to somehow have enough flavor without increasing the alcohol. Notch does this perfectly and dispels the myth that good beers have to have loads of alcohol. All three of Notch's year-round beers are full-flavored. The **Notch Session Ale** is an American pale ale with a big hop presence, and just enough sweet

Beer Lover's Pick

Notch Session Pils
Style: Pilsner
ABV: 4 percent
Availability: Year-round
Pilsners get a bad rap in the US because nearly all mass-produced beers are based on pilsner. But, those beers have strayed, and the Notch Pils is the real deal. It's light, unfiltered, dry, and crisp and it has enough hops, resulting in a delightful taste. It's a refreshing beer, perfect for a hot summer day, or to sit at a bar and have a few while sharing stories with good friends. It is a joy to drink. The best thing about it is the low alcohol percentage, making this an all-day type of beer.

malt to balance the beer out. It drinks dry and comes in at a low 4.5 percent ABV. The **Notch Session Pils** is a Czech-style pilsner. A pilsner should be light colored, moderately hopped, and delicate on the tongue, but with enough flavor that you want to take another sip. This fits the bill. At 4 percent ABV, this is a perfect beer for a party. You can have a few and not get stupid. The **Notch Saison** is a traditional Belgian-style saison. While American versions have strayed from the original style of low-alcohol beers, Notch Saison strives to be true to the classic style, a low-alcohol beer that is refreshing and goes well with food, such as a roasted chicken or grilled salmon.

The seasonals include some hard-to-find styles. The **Notch Cerne** (winter) is a Czech black lager, while the **Notch Table Beer** (spring) is a Belgian-style table beer, meant to be an everyday beer. The **Notch Berliner Weisse** (summer) is a German-style wheat beer that is known for being tart. The **Notch BSA Harvest** (fall) is an American-style farmhouse ale, which is similar to a saison.

Notch Brewing also does a series of one-off cask-conditioned beers, so if you're lucky enough to find one on draft, try it as soon as possible because it will never be available again. Notch has done two cask-conditioned beers, the **Notch Mild** and the **Notch Bitter.**

All of Notch Brewing's beers are available in 12-ounce bottles, except for the cask-conditioned beers.

PAPER CITY BREWING COMPANY

108 Cabot St., Holyoke, MA; (413) 535-1588; www.papercity.com
Founded: 1995 **Founder:** Jay Hebert **Brewer:** Ben Anhalt **Flagship Beer:** Holyoke Dam Ale **Year-round Beers:** PC Blueberry Brew, Fogbuster Coffee House Ale, Hop Monster, India'n IPA, One Eared Monkey, Riley Stout **Seasonal/Special Releases:** Summit House Oktoberfest, Nut Brown Ale, Radler Brau, Paper City Spring Beer, Paper City Summer Brew, Winter Palace Wee Heavy **Tours:** Tastings Thur and Fri nights, 6 to 8 p.m.; $6

The Paper City Brewery is one of the best breweries where you can just kick back and hang out. On Friday nights, head to the Paper City Brewery for the weekly 6 p.m. tasting/open house, and you are in for a good time. The brewery is located in an old warehouse, so make your way to the fifth floor and pay the $6. For that money, you get to drink plenty of good Paper City beers, but you also get to listen to live music from a band that typically plays every Friday night. Food is not served, but feel free to bring in some snacks (as long as you clean up after yourself). Not into live music? The tasting/open house also takes place on Thursday without a band for the same $6.

Besides being a great hangout spot, the Paper City Brewery is one of the oldest breweries in Massachusetts, and they brew many good beers. The **Holyoke Dam Ale** was Paper City's first beer, and it is still the flagship after all these years. It is

Hop Monster
Style: Double IPA
ABV: 9.5 percent
Availability: Year-round
Hop Monster combines a mix of piney and citrusy hop aromas, which continue into the taste. The hops almost taste oily, with a lot of bitterness. The malt is sweet, almost to the point of crossing over to cloying, but not quite. That works to keep this beer relatively balanced, despite the amount of hops used. This is one of the better New England double IPAs.

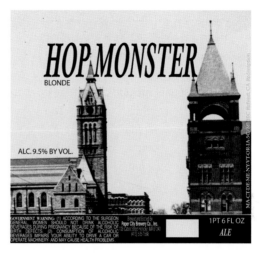

an English-style pale ale, with sweet malty flavors and just a touch of hops. Other year-round beers include three beers with some of the best names in New England— **Fogbuster Coffee House Ale, Hop Monster,** and **One Eared Monkey.** But, names on the labels do not matter—it's what's inside that counts. All three are superb beers. The Fogbuster Coffee House Porter is strong on big roasted coffee flavors. It is almost like Paper City brewed a porter, brewed coffee, and blended them together. The Hop Monster is a big, 9.5 percent alcohol by volume beer. The One Eared Monkey is a light golden ale with peach flavoring added. The **India'n IPA** (named for Indian motorcycles) is a solid IPA. It may not be a hop bomb, but it is well-balanced and pleasant to drink. The **PC Blueberry Brew** is a typical New England blueberry beer. The **Riley Stout,** meanwhile, is an excellent dry Irish stout, better than any of the stouts brewed in Ireland and available in the US.

The seasonal beers include the **Radler Brau,** one of the most refreshing summer beers available. A radler is basically a beer and lemonade blended together to create an ultra-refreshing brew. This is no different. The **Summit House Oktoberfest** is also a well-done beer, as is the extremely malty **Winter Palace Wee Heavy Ale.** The **Paper City Spring Beer** is a really nice German-style bock, while the **Summer Brew** is a lighter helles bock.

Massachusetts

PIONEER BREWING COMPANY

195 Arnold Rd., Fiskdale, MA; (508) 347-7500; www.pioneerbrewingcompany.com
Founded: 2004 **Founder:** Todd Sullivan **Brewer:** Chris Courtney **Flagship Beer:** Pale Ale
Year-round Beers: Blueberry Ale, Kolsch, IPA, Nitro Stout, Red Ale **Seasonals/Special Releases:** Dark Harvest, Doppelbock, Belgian Wit, Oktoberfest, Hop Whammy, American Lager, Path of the Unknown **Tours:** Sun, 2 p.m.

The Pioneer Brewing Company is the kind of brewery that you would want down the street from your house—and who wouldn't want a brewery within walking distance? Starting at 5 p.m. every Friday, the brewery hosts a party where people can come in to their Stein Hall, drink some of the fine Pioneer beers, and eat free food—chili, pizza—and hang out with the brewers, listen to music, and generally have a good time. Tours are on Sunday at 2 p.m., and there is always live music during the tour. If there's a game on, you can be sure it will be on the large-screen television in the Stein Hall. And their location, on the grounds of 200-acre Hyland's Orchards, is awesome. It is also the home of an 18-hole disc golf course.

More important, of course, is that Pioneer brews some really good beer. Just do not expect to find it outside of the general Fiskdale area; they only distribute locally, but the beers are worth the trip. The year-round beers are all really well done. The flagship **Pale Ale** is extremely drinkable, with a nice touch of hops. The **Red Ale** is suitably malty, while the **IPA** is suitably hoppy and balanced. The **Blueberry Ale**

Beer Lover's Pick

Doppelbock
Style: Doppelbock
ABV: 8 percent
Availability: Spring Seasonal
Pioneer Brewing Company's Doppelbock is an exceptional example of the German dark, strong lager. It is a hefty beer at 8 percent alcohol, and you can feel just a hint of the booze burn in the back of your throat. This is a big malty beer, with biscuity, chocolaty goodness, and a little vanilla flavor from the oak on which it is aged. The hops are there just for balance. A truly great beer.

dials down the blueberry flavor a little, making it less sweet than many blueberry beers, and the **Nitro Stout** and the **Kolsch** are both very good.

The seasonals are just as good. The **Dark Harvest** is a big, double robust porter, coming in at 10 percent alcohol by volume, Pioneer's biggest beer. The **Doppelbock** is an excellent beer, as is **Oktoberfest** and **Belgian Wit.** Pioneer's most sought after beer may be the **Hop Whammy,** a wet hop pale ale that is part of the **Sessionals Series.** The Hop Whammy is released on the last day of summer at exactly 4:20 p.m. The other Sessional beers are the **Pioneer American Lager** and the **Path of the Unknown,** a 9 percent alcohol by volume double brown ale.

PRETTY THINGS BEER & ALE PROJECT

Offices located in Cambridge, beer brewed in Westport; (617) 682-6419; www.prettythings beertoday.com

Founded: 2008 **Founders:** Dann Paquette, Martha Holly-Paquette **Brewer:** Dann Paquette **Flagship Beer:** Jack D'Or **Year-round Beers:** Baby Tree, Saint Botolph's Town **Seasonals/ Special Releases:** American Darling, Babayaga, Field Mouse's Farewell, Fluffy White Rabbits, Magnifico!, Our Finest Regards, Through the Looking Glass Series **Tours:** None

Pretty Things Beer & Ale Project is what you would call a gypsy brewery. They don't have a home of their own. Instead, Dann Paquette rents space at existing breweries and brews the beer himself. That's why it's called a "project" instead of a "brewery." Whatever the Paquettes want to call it, Pretty Things beers are amazing. Not good, not great, but amazing. Almost without exception, you'd be hard-pressed to find better beers for the styles they're doing.

The styles are American takes on classics. The flagship beer, **Jack D'Or,** is called a "Saison Americain." Again, the styles don't really matter here. What does matter is how good this beer is. There's a lot of spiciness in this beer—pretty amazing for a beer that has no spices added to it. Just oats, barley, yeast, hops, and water. The **Baby Tree,** a Belgian-style quad brewed with dried plums, is one of the best beers ever brewed in Massachusetts. The plum adds interesting notes to this big, sweet beer. It almost tastes like you could pour it on ice cream and use it as a syrup. But, it's not so sweet that you couldn't drink a full glass of it. Like all Pretty Things beers, it comes in a bomber. It's a big beer at 9 percent ABV, so you may want to share it with a friend or special someone, or be selfish like me and drink the whole thing. The third year-round beer from Pretty Things is **Saint Botolph's Town,** described as "a malty northern brown ale." A great beer to drink alone, or pair it with some grilled beef and you have a perfect night.

Baby Tree
Style: Belgian Quad
ABV: 9 percent
Availability: Rotating

Not an easy choice—pretty much every beer from Pretty Things is a "must have," but this is the standout. A big beer, meant to be sipped, savored, and enjoyed, rather than pounded back like you're still a frat boy. All the sweet malt-iness and Belgian-yeast flavors you want from a quad, with plums added. You can taste the 9 percent alcohol by volume, but many quads have some alcohol burn, and it does not detract from a beer. This is a perfect nightcap.

Pretty Things' seasonal beers are also worth seeking out. **American Darling** is Paquette's take on an American lager. Although it looks like your typical mass-produced lager, there are no other similarities. The use of all malt, quality pilsner malt, and hand-crafted brewing create a perfect summer beer. The result is a fla-vorful, refreshing, 7 percent ABV lager. Other seasonals include the **Fluffy White Rabbits** (Belgian-style tripel), **Field Mouse's Farewell** (saison), **Babayaga** ("rustic" stout), **Our Finest Regards** (barleywine) and **Magnifico!** ("robust minimal ale").

The Paquettes also have started an interesting project called "Once Upon a Time." They partner with British beer historian Ron Pattinson to find classic beer recipes. The series features offerings based on historical recipes from the 1800s and early 1900s. Each one is named for the date the recipe was written—**February 27, 1832** (mild ale), **November 15, 1901** (Burton ale), and **December 6, 1855** (India porter) are the three beers so far.

RAPSCALLION

200 Hanscom Dr., Bedford, MA (corporate office); (617) 869-5702; www.drinkrapscallion.com
Founded: 1993 **Founder:** Brett Pacheco (as Concord Junction Brewery) Cedric and Peter
Daniel (as Rapscallion Brewry) **Brewer:** No brewer, contract brewed **Flagship Beer:**
Honey Ale **Year-round Beers:** Blessing, Lager, Premier **Seasonals/Special Releases:**
None **Tours:** None

The history of the Rapscallion Brewery is like a roller coaster ride. Brett
Pacheco founded the small brewery, originally called the Concord Junction
Brewery, in 1993. In 2000, then brewer Dann Paquette (now of Pretty Things Beer
& Ale Project) created the Rapscallion line of artisan beers. In 2002, new owner
Mike Labbe moved the brewery from Concord to Shirley, renaming it the Concord
Brewery. The following year, he sold the brewery and remained on as the head
brewer. Finally, in 2007, brothers Cedric and Peter Daniel bought the brewery with
an idea in their minds. They renamed the brewery the Rapscallion Brewery, naming
it after the popular line of beers. They also decided to go draft only, originally just
brewing the Honey Ale.

Beer Lover's Pick

Lager
Style: American Pale Lager
ABV: 4.5 percent
Availability: Year-round
Based on the name alone, this might sound
like the most boring of Rapscallion's beers,
but it is not. If you want to see what our
grandfather's grandfathers were drinking,
and to see how far American brewers fell,
try this beer to see what a real American
lager can taste like. This is a flavorful lager
that uses all malts, no corn or rice extracts.
There is also a touch of hops that you will
not find in mass-produced lagers, even
those that claim to be "triple hopped."

Since then, things have settled down for Rapscallion. They contract brew their beer at the Paper City Brewing Company in Holyoke and the Pioneer Brewing Company in Sturbridge, and now have increased the number of beers they release. Along with the flagship Honey Ale, they have reintroduced the Premier and Blessing, and added the Lager. The **Honey Ale** is an extra pale ale, brewed with real local honey. Some honey beers tend to be overly sweet. Rapscallion's version is certainly sweet, but it keeps the balance, avoiding becoming cloying. And, at 4.5 percent alcohol by volume, it is low enough in alcohol that you can have a couple of them without worrying about falling over. The **Lager** is a classic American lager. No, not like the mass-produced beer you see commercials for; it's based on a recipe dating back to the late 1800s, so this is what a lager tasted like before Prohibition. The **Premier** is a Belgian-style blonde ale, along the lines of the popular Belgian-style golden ale Duvel. Although it is 7 percent ABV, it still drinks like a lighter beer. It has fruity notes to it, a little bitterness at the end, and a delicate carbonation that tickles the roof of your mouth.

The **Blessing** is an unusual beer. It has Belgian-beer tendencies, but it is not quite Belgian. It has a nice hop character, but it is not an IPA, or even a pale ale. I guess the best description would to be call it a hoppy Belgian amber ale. Whatever style it is, this is an excellent beer. It is 8 percent alcohol by volume, and although you will not taste the booze, you will feel a warmth as it slides down the back of your throat.

SHERWOOD FOREST BREWERS

655 Farm Rd., Marlborough, MA (corporate office); (508) 466-8082; www.sherwood brewers.com
Founded: 1997 **Founder:** Dave Lambert **Brewer:** John Carlman **Flagship Beer:** Archer's Ale **Year-round Beers:** Friar's Ale, Maiden's Blueberry Ale, Sheriff's IPA **Seasonals/ Special Releases:** None **Tours:** None

Sherwood Forest, started in 1997 by Dave Lambert, does not have the name recognition of many breweries throughout the state, but they have nonetheless carved a niche for themselves by brewing good, solid, easily accessible beers.

The brewery is ever-evolving. When Sherwood Forest first started, they were a contract brewery. They then opened up their own brewery, but soon outgrew their own Marlborough facility, and have once again started contract brewing. They have kept their old facility so brewer John Carlman can develop the new beers before they start brewing them on the larger scale.

The beers are simple, easy-drinking beers. None are overly complex, but that's all right when you have beer that's this good. The **Archer's Ale,** the brewery's first beer, is still the best. It is a good, solid, English-style pale ale. Flavorful and extremely

Archer's Ale

Style: English Pale Ale

ABV: 5.3 percent

Availability: Year-round

This is a classic English-style pale ale. It is ultra-creamy, with just a touch of hops. You will never confuse Archer's Ale with an American pale ale. The hops are more earthy than piney or citrusy, and the malt is in the forefront.

Perfect for a night at a pub and chatting with friends, or to enjoy at home while cooking out. A fantastic beer.

easy to drink, it is full-bodied and tasty. The label features the image of Robin Hood of the original Sherwood Forest fame, pointing his arrow straight at you, suggesting you better drink, or else. The beer is based on an original homebrew recipe by Lambert. The **Sheriff's IPA** is somewhere between an English-style IPA and a west coast–style IPA. It has the citrusy hop aroma that you expect from the west coast, but the malt flavor seems more reminiscent of an English-style IPA. It is different than most IPAs, so try it to see what you think. The **Friar's Ale** is a Belgian-style white ale. It has the classic flavors of coriander and bitter orange peel, but it is much creamier than the average Belgian-style white. Belgian white beers, or witbiers, are fantastically refreshing summer beers, but with the Sherwood Forest version being so creamy, it almost comes off as a white beer for all seasons. It is definitely not too light for a winter night.

The **Maiden's Blueberry Ale** may be the most aromatic blueberry beer being brewed today. Pour it in a glass and leave the room for a minute. When you come back, the entire room will smell of blueberries. This beer is sweet, smells of blueberry pie, and the blueberry flavor is overwhelming. This is not a beer that strives to balance its fruitiness while keeping its beeriness. This is straight up blueberry.

Massachusetts

Besides offering great beers, Sherwood Forest likes to get involved in local events. Recently, they were the official beer sponsor of an international squash tournament held in Natick, Massachusetts, and were one of the main sponsors of the first downtown Marlborough beer festival.

WACHUSETT BREWING COMPANY

175 State Rd., Westminster, MA; (978) 874-0065; www.wachusettbrew.com
Founded: 1993 **Founders:** Kevin Buckler, Ned LaFortune, Peter Quinn **Brewer:** Dave Howard **Flagship Beer:** Country Pale Ale **Year-round Beers:** Black Shack Porter, Blueberry Ale, Green Monsta, IPA, Nut Brown Ale, Ryde Beer **Seasonals/Special Releases:** Larry, Milk Stout, Octoberfest Ale, Quinn's Amber Ale, Summer Ale, White Ale, Winter Ale **Tours:** Wed and Thurs, noon to 4 p.m., Fri and Sat, noon to 5 p.m.

For years, the Wachusett Brewing Company was the only central Massachusetts option for good, locally brewed, fresh beers. Although things have changed over the years, Wachusett Brewing Company has continued brewing quality ales, while remaining the local's first choice for craft beer.

Wachusett's most famous beer is the **Blueberry Ale.** Pretty much every bar in the Leominster/Fitchburg area will have this on tap. It is a light, refreshing ale, strong on blueberry flavors. Some bars will actually put a spoonful of fresh blueberries in the beer to give it that added flavor. The **Country Pale Ale,** formerly known as the Country Ale, is a popular beer. For some reason a Country Pale Ale on draft tastes so much better than a bottle. It is a treat to find this on draft at a local watering hole. Wachusett's **IPA** is a solid, English-style IPA. It does not get the respect that it deserves because it is not a hop monster like a lot of the IPAs being brewed today. Rather, this is a good, balanced beer.

If you like your IPAs a little bit hoppier, Wachusett does offer other options. The Wachusett **Green Monsta,** named for the iconic left-field wall at Fenway Park, is a more straightforward American-style IPA. If you want even more hops, grab a **Larry,** the wildly popular double IPA brewed with David Ciccolo, owner of the Publick House in Brookline. Rye adds a lot of interesting spice notes to beers, but the final result often leans toward being high in alcohol. Wachusett's **Ryde Beer** is a great low-alcohol option.

Wachusett also brews several seasonals. **Quinn's Amber Ale** is an easy-drinking, reddish-hued beer, that is available from mid-winter through April. The **Summer Ale** is a light wheat beer, low in alcohol and easy to drink. The **Octoberfest** is available in the fall. It is not a traditional German-style Oktoberfest. Traditionally, Oktoberfests are lagers, while Wachusett's Octoberfest is an ale. That does not take away from the fact that it is a solid beer. The **Winter Ale** is one of the better winter seasonals. It is a Scotch ale, which is a heavier, malty beer perfect for the cold months.

Milk Stout
Style: Milk Stout
ABV: 5.8 percent
Availability: Winter

A well-done milk stout can be incredible. Brewers add lactose, or milk sugar, to the beer. The lactose is not fermentable, so it does not raise the alcohol percentage, but it does result in a fuller beer. Wachusett's Milk Stout is one of the best milk stouts available. Smooth, creamy, and full-bodied, it is appropriately sweet, yet not cloying. There is some roasted character, with hints of chocolate. Overall, just a wonderful beer.

In the past few years, Wachusett has introduced a few beers in bombers for the first time. To go along with Larry, they have the **White Ale,** which is available for half the year, and the **Milk Stout,** which is available the rest of the year.

The Wachusett Brewery also hosts tours led by a brewery employee and they include tastings. Growlers are also available to go.

WANDERING STAR BREWING COMPANY

11 Gifford St., Pittsfield, MA; (917) 573-3942; www.wanderingstarbrewing.com
Founded: 2011 **Founders:** Chris Cuzme, Alex Hall, Chris Post **Brewer:** Chris Post
Flagship Beer: Raindrop Pale Ale **Year-round Beer:** Bash-Bish-Bock **Seasonal/Special Releases:** Alpha Pale, Berkshire Hills 01201, Bert's Disqualified Imperial Stout, Mild at Heart, Zingari **Tours:** Tasting room, no tours

The Wandering Star Brewing Company is the brainchild of three beer loving friends who realized their dream by opening a brewery. The shared dream by founders Chris Cuzme, Alex Hall, and Chris Post must have included a lot of excellent beers, because the beers Wandering Star Brewing releases are nothing short of excellent.

Massachusetts

Mild at Heart
Style: English Dark Mild
ABV: 4.3 percent
Availability: Occasional
The Mild at Heart is the perfect beer for a pub. When you go to a bar, you can buy one or two high-alcohol beers, but you will have to stop at a couple if you plan on staying for a while. But with the Mild at Heart, you can have a few of these low-alcohol beers without sacrificing flavor. It is a dark, creamy beer, with hints of chocolate and dark fruits with a nice hop presence.

The brewery only brews two year-round beers, its flagship Raindrop Pale Ale and the Bash-Bish-Bock. The **Raindrop Pale Ale** is an American pale ale brewed with west coast hops, as well as hops from New Zealand and England, giving it a more unique taste than many pale ales. The **Bash-Bish-Bock** is a German-style bock brewed with authentic German hops and yeast. Even at 6.8 percent alcohol by volume, this is a smooth drinking beer that goes down incredibly easy. It is a tad on the sweet side, but not overly so, so it is easy to enjoy.

Bert's Disqualified Imperial Stout is a beer based on a recipe by western Massachusetts homebrewer Bert Holdredge, whose imperial stout was named the winner of a large homebrewing competition in New York, only to be disqualified because he forgot to remove the label from the beer. The **Alpha Pale** is an English style pale ale—smooth, creamy, and malty, with a nice little hop kick. The **Berkshire Hills 01201** is a Belgian-style saison using the same yeast as Saison Dupont (one of the best saisons). It also uses locally malted wheat, with almost all of the ingredients for this beer bought in Massachusetts. The **Zingari** is Wandering Star's interpretation of a Belgian witbier. While most witbiers are brewed with coriander and bitter orange peel, this one is brewed with coriander, lemongrass, cardamom, and fenugreek. These added herbs give it a unique, yet refreshing, flavor. The **Mild at Heart** is an English-style dark mild. It is a dark, but light-drinking beer, and it is only 4.3 percent alcohol by volume, so it is easily a beer you can drink a few of in one sitting.

Wandering Star does not offer brewery tours, but does have a tasting room where people can come and try the various beers available. They also sell growlers of their beer to go. Growlers are the only way Wandering Star's beers can be enjoyed at home because they are a draft-only brewery.

WORMTOWN BREWING COMPANY

455 Park Ave., Worcester, MA; (774) 239-1555; www.wormtownbrewery.com
Founded: 2010 **Founders:** Ben Roesch and Tom Oliveri **Brewer:** Ben Roesch **Flagship Beer:** Seven Hills Pale Ale **Year-round Beers:** Be Hoppy IPA, Elm Park Amber, Turtle Boy Blueberry **Seasonals/Special Releases:** O'Connor's Irish Red, Blonde Cougar Summer Ale, Pumpkin, Wintah Brown; 20 to 30 special releases a year **Tours:** Daily, no specific hours. If a brewer is there, tours are available.

"Prolific" is a word that can be used to describe the Wormtown Brewery. In their first year of brewing, they produced more than 25 beers. And the amazing thing is, almost all of them were top-notch beers. The year-round beers are all good, solid beers, better than the average of the various styles. The seasonals range from good (Blonde Cougar) to fantastic (Wintah Brown).

But it is really the special releases that set Wormtown apart. The **Sweet Tat's Imperial Breakfast Stout** is one of the best beers brewed in New England. The **Red Headed Bitch,** which is Wormtown's Elm Park Amber fermented in red wine barrels and aged with fresh raspberries, is amazing. Wormtown has also released three different double IPAs—the **FU IPA, Birthday Brew #1,** and **Be Hoppier**—that are all excellent beers for hopheads.

Roesch also brews a rare coconut beer, **Joe Z's Coconut Porter,** along with an excellent barleywine, **Beer Goggles.** Wormtown also jumped on the black IPA bandwagon with the **Dark Days IPA,** which is one of the better black IPAs currently being brewed. Other special releases include the **O'Fest** (an Oktoberfest-style lager), the **Buk** (a rye pale ale), **Foxy Brown Maple Brown Ale, Bennie's Brew** (cream ale), **Tennessee Tat's** (Sweet Tat's aged in Jack Daniel's barrels), and **Charles the II Scotch Ale.**

Wormtown Brewery also likes to support other local businesses. Every single beer has at least one ingredient from Massachusetts, and two different beers, **Mass Whole** and **Local First,** are brewed with every single ingredient produced in the Bay State. The brewery is connected to Peppercorn's Grille & Tavern, a popular Worcester restaurant that features American and Italian cuisine. All of the Wormtown beers that are being brewed are always on tap there.

Sweet Tat's Imperial Breakfast Stout
Style: Imperial Stout
ABV: 8 percent
Availability: Rotating

This beer has everything you want from a breakfast stout. It's brewed with oatmeal, chocolate, coffee, and vanilla. It starts with strong flavors of chocolate and coffee, and as the beer warms, the vanilla begins to come out. If you have a chance, try the other version of this beer, the Tennessee Tats, which is the same beer, but aged in Jack Daniel's whiskey barrels. It picks up a lot of the whiskey notes, making it a completely different drinking experience.

The brewer, Roesch, typically leads the tours that usually end at the bar where you can try any number of the current Wormtown brews. Growlers of Wormtown beers are also available for sale, and cost between $8 and $11 (plus a $5 deposit for the growler). Wormtown recently started bottling its beers. The first bottled beer was the **Pro-Am Porter,** a porter brewed with local homebrewer Keith Antul that won third place in the Pro-Am competition at the Great American Beer Festival in Denver, Colorado, in 2010.

Brewpubs

AMHERST BREWING COMPANY

10 University Dr., Amherst, MA; (413) 253-4400; www.amherstbrewing.com
Draft Beers: 22 (mix of house and guest taps) and 4 casks

The Amherst Brewing Company is in the midst of the college town of Amherst. Many brewpubs in an area heavy with colleges will often dumb down their beer to cater to college students, but the Amherst Brewing Company is not one of those establishments. They have a full range of house beers, cask beers, and guest beers on tap that will satisfy the most discerning palates.

The standard beers are all good beers. The **Ace in the Hole Pilsner** is a very good pilsner, while the **Honey Pilsner** adds a nice twist on the style. The **Cascade IPA** gets its name from the use of Cascade hops and it is excellent. The **Puffers Smoked Porter** is a tasty porter with smoky flavors. The **North Pleasant Pale Ale** is nicely hopped, and the **Two Sisters Imperial Stout** is absolutely phenomenal.

Amherst Brewing Company also brews a number of seasonal and specialty beers. They include the **Belgian Tripel, Captain Code's Baltic Porter,** the **Chocolate Porter,** the **Heather Ale, Lewmeister Oktoberfest, Pumpkin Ale, Ryeteous Red, Super Stout,** and the **Muddy Brook Maibock.** Along with the house-brewed beers, the Amherst Brewing Company also has a number of guest beers, featuring such breweries as Ballast Point from California, Berkshire Brewing Company in Massachusetts, and Schlenkerla from Germany.

The brewpub also hosts several beer dinners a year, as well as monthly beer tastings. On the first and third Monday of every month, they host the Amherst Jazz Orchestra.

Hungry? Start with the Beer-Battered Fried Pickles or the ABC Beer Bread, which is made with light lager, smoked cheddar, scallions, and a sharp beer and cheese dipping sauce. Next, consider ordering from a variety of ABC Hot Dog Sliders. The options include bratwurst, Chicago-style wieners, cheese-filled hot dogs, and jalapeño hot dogs. Entrees include several sirloin steaks, the Tequila Lime Grilled Chicken and Shrimp, the German Sausage Platter, bangers and mash, Brewers Meatloaf, and shepherd's pie.

Tours are available by appointment. Do not leave empty-handed. You can buy a growler of beer to go, as well as several different T-shirts and an awesome ceramic Amherst Brewing Company mug.

BARRINGTON BREWERY & RESTAURANT

420 Stockbridge Rd., Great Barrington, MA; (413) 528-8282; www.barringtonbrew.net
Draft Beers: 9

Take a look at the sky and thank the sun for the beers at the Barrington Brewery & Restaurant. This western Massachusetts brewpub became the first on the east coast to brew their beer using solar panels in 2007. The solar panels heat up the water used in both the brewery and the restaurant.

Maybe it's the sun, or maybe it's just talented brewing (we're going to guess the latter), but the beers at the Barrington Brewery and Restaurant are very good. Barrington always has 9 of its house-brewed beers on tap, and they brew between 20 and 25 beers every year. Beers that are always on tap include the **Hopland Pale Ale, Barrington Brown Ale,** the **Black Bear Stout,** the **Raspberry Ale,** and the **Ice Glenn IPA.**

Like many brewpubs, Barrington really shines with its occasional releases. The **Vienna** is a lighter German-style lager, while the **Wedded Bliss** is a darker, Dortmunder-style lager. Other German-style beers available include **Alt** and the **Bavarian Wheat.**

Barrington's biggest beer is the **Firecracker Imperial IPA,** which is an 8.5 percent alcohol by volume, west coast–style hoppy beer. The **"R" Hop** is an IPA brewed every year with hops Barrington grows themselves, while the **Yule Fuel** is a popular winter brew and tastes like what Christmas would taste like if you could fit it in a pint glass.

If you're grabbing a beer, why not grab some food? For a starter, the cheddar ale soup is a good choice (see recipe, page 235), as is the mixed sausage sampler, which includes slices of bratwurst, bauernwurst, and kielbasa, all steamed in beer. The Plowman's Lunch is large enough for two, and includes ale bread, dried sausage, brie cheese, chutney, and apples. All hamburgers are made of grass-fed beef, and include a choice of toppings. Where Barrington really excels is their sandwiches. The Chicken Philly Cheese Steak is a traditional Philly cheese steak with one twist—no beef, all grilled chicken. The Mixed N.Y. Grille is a large sandwich that includes corned beef, pastrami, and cheese, served Reuben-style, except with cole slaw instead of sauerkraut. The Steak & Stout Sandwich features sliced sirloin steak that is marinated in Barrington's stout. Don't forget to leave room for dessert; Barrington's offers coconut custard pie and chocolate stout cake, among other dishes.

If you fall in love with a beer at Barrington, buy it to go. You can buy beer in 22-ounce bottles and half-gallon kegs. Of, if you're lucky enough to have a kegerator at home, grab a keg and host a party, sharing your favorite Barrington Brewery & Restaurant beer with all of your friends.

BEER WORKS

Two locations in Boston. Locations in Hingham, Lowell, Salem, and inside Logan Airport; www.beerworks.net
Draft Beers: 12 to 16

If you have ever been to a Boston Red Sox game, there is a good chance you saw a long line outside of the Boston Beer Works. The Beer Works is a Massachusetts chain of brewpubs. Along with the location outside Fenway Park, there is a second Beer Works outside TD Banknorth Garden, home of both the Bruins and Celtics.

All of the beers are solid. They may not be the most complex styles, but they serve their purpose of satisfying large, quick-moving crowds who are coming in for a beer or two before or after a game. The **Back Bay IPA,** named for the Back Bay section of Boston, is a solid IPA worth grabbing. The **Beantown Nut Brown Ale** is a tasty, easy-drinking brown ale, and the **Boston Garden Golden** (say that three times fast) is a light golden ale. The **Boston Victory Bock,** brewed in honor of the Boston sports world's many championship wins, is a good bock beer, and the **Brookline Weizen Bock** is one of the Beer Works' best beers.

Other beers include the **Bunker Hill Blueberry Ale,** served with real blueberries in the beer, the **Curley's Irish Stout,** and the **Kenmore Kolsch.** If you happen to be there in the summer, you may see a lot of people drinking the watermelon beer with a slice of watermelon wedged on the side of the glass. There are more complex options, particularly during the off-season. The imperial stout, barleywine, and Belgian-style quads are all standouts.

Beer Works also bottles and distributes three of their more popular beers: the Bunker Hill Blueberry, the Fenway Pale Ale, and the Boston Red Ale. They actually taste better bottled.

At the pubs, there is always a large selection of pub grub. Chicken fingers, wings, and fried mozzarella are all available as appetizers. The menu is also heavy on burgers, sandwiches, and other easy to eat food, such as pizza. Growlers of beer are always available, as are six-packs of the bottled beers. If you're going to a sporting event, there are worse options than getting a well-crafted beer at one of the Beer Works.

CAMBRIDGE BREWING COMPANY

1 Kendall Sq., Building 100, Cambridge, MA; (617) 494-1994; www.cambrew.com
Draft Beers: 10 to 14

Cambridge Brewing Company is the premier brewpub in Massachusetts, and it just happens to be a pretty good place to grab a meal. Phil Bannatyne founded Cambridge Brewing Company in 1989, when good beer was hard to find at any

Barleywine Festival

Usually in January, the Cambridge Brewing Company hosts its annual Barley-wine Festival, a celebration of its two fantastic barleywines, the Arquebus and the Blunderbuss. There will be several vintages of each of the two barleywines available, as well as versions of each beer aged in different types of barrels. For a barleywine fan, this is the mecca of all events. The beer is world-class, and the Cambridge Brewing Company also offers up a special tapas menu during the event.

restaurant, and brewpubs in Massachusetts were scarce. Brewmaster Will Meyers came to the restaurant in 1993.

Cambridge Brewing maintains 10 to 14 beers on draft at all times—all brewed in house, except for special events. The year-round beers are the **Regatta Golden** (cream ale), **Cambridge Amber, Tall Tale Pale Ale,** and the **Charles River Porter.** Meyers also brews several seasonal beers: **Big Man Ale,** an old stock ale brewed for winter; **Spring Training IPA,** for the spring; the **CBC HefeWeizen** for the summer; and the insanely popular **Great Pumpkin Ale** for the fall.

The Great Pumpkin Ale is so popular that the CBC, as it is often called, hosts a pumpkin beer festival every October, featuring several different house-brewed pumpkin beers, and guest pumpkin beers from around the country. A highlight a few years ago was a cask-conditioned pumpkin beer served out of a giant pumpkin.

The brewery also brews 22 other beers at least once a year, and introduces 10 to 12 totally new beers every year. Some of those beers brewed every year include the **Blunderbuss Barleywine** and the **Arquebus Summer Barleywine.** They are two of the best barleywines brewed in the world. Other standout beers include the **CBC Heather Ale,** one of the rare beers brewed without hops; **Cerise Cassee,** an American sour ale aged in oak barrels and **Om,** an American wild ale aged in chardonnay barrels.

Although beer is the star at the Cambridge Brewing Company, don't forget the food. The menu is a mix of traditional pub foods like burgers and chicken tenders, and more adventurous foods like grilled swordfish and beer-brined half chicken. The menu features several appealing appetizers, including the native corn and clam hushpuppies and the organic pork pate. The burgers are cooked well and to order, but the best sandwich on the menu is the slow-cooked pulled pork served with onions, Vermont cheddar, and pale ale–infused barbecue sauce. There is also a brunch, or beerunch, served on Sunday. Locavores and foodies rejoice: Many of the ingredients that CBC uses for its dishes come from local farms and the chefs head out to local farmers' markets looking for fresh ingredients daily.

THE GARDNER ALE HOUSE

74 Parker St., Gardner, MA; (978) 669-0122; www.gardnerale.com
Draft Beers: 12

North Central Worcester County is not known as a beer haven. But, thanks to the Gardner Ale House, there is a sanctuary for better beer lovers. The Gardner Ale House opened its doors in 2006 with owner Rick Walton, a homebrewer who also liked to cook. Along with head brewer Dave Richardson, Walton has created a brewpub that appeals to anyone and everyone. A craft beer lover? Richardson's beers are excellent. Don't care about craft beer? Go there for a good meal and to listen to the frequent live musical acts playing in the pub.

The bar has a townie feel, but that's not a bad thing. There are always regulars at the bar and the bartenders seem to know everyone. The highlight is the beer. There are always at least five Gardner Ale House beers on tap, a few popular American domestics and a few other guest brews.

Richardson's beers are top-notch. The year-round beers include the **Summer's End Kolsch, Chair City Pale Ale, American Pale Ale, Facelift IPA, Naked Stout,** and the **XSB.** The Gardner Ale House also has a number of special beers and seasonals that seem to be inspired by every major brewing country—Belgium, England, Germany, and, of course, the US. **Belgian Chair** is the Chair City Pale Ale brewed with Belgian yeast, the **Old School Pilsner** is exactly what the name describes, and the **Rocker Red** is a traditional red ale. The **Dunkelweizen** is a German-style dark wheat bear, the **Chocolate Porter** is a wonderful dessert beer, and the **Face-Off Double IPA** is a big, hit-you-in-the-mouth, west coast–inspired double IPA. **Oma's Altbier,** the brewpub's best beer, is spot on for the style, with biscuity flavors and just a hint of grassy hops.

The Gardner Ale House has a full menu of appetizers, sandwiches, salads, pizzas, fish & chips (see recipe, page 238), and entrees. Appetizers include warm crap dip, crap cakes, coconut shrimp, and the best sweet potato fries in central Massachusetts. If you are lucky enough to be at the Gardner Ale House during the summer, do yourself a favor and get the lobster roll—it's as good as any beachside clam shack's.

Massachusetts

JOHN HARVARD'S BREW HOUSE

33 Dunster St., Cambridge, MA; (617) 868-3585; www.johnharvards.com
Draft Beers: Around 8

John Harvard's Brew House might be a chain, but the beers they brew are better than most chain brewpubs. Though most of the beers are on tap at the three locations, each of the brewers has autonomy to brew beers of their own creations. Most of the time there are also several interesting beers available.

The John Harvard's Brew House in Cambridge is the original pub. It is in the lower level of a building right off of Harvard Square, and it is a slightly dark, older-feeling bar. The John Harvard's in Framingham is located in the Shoppers World mall at 1 Worcester Rd. (508-875-2337). It is a much larger location and is set up more like a family restaurant. The third John Harvard's is located in Hancock at the Jiminy Peak ski area at 37 Corey Rd. (413-738-5500, ext. 3780) and is only open during the winter.

Year-round beers include the **All American Light Lager, Dry Irish Stout, John Harvard's Pale Ale, Nut Brown Ale,** and the **Old Willy IPA.** Their extensive roster of seasonals includes the **Mid-Winter Strong Ale** (Jan), **Celtic Red** (Feb through Mar), **Queen Bee Honey Beer** (Apr through May), **Wheat Beer** (June), **Summer Blonde** (July through Aug), **Oktoberfest** (Sept through Oct), and the **Holiday Red** (Nov through Dec).

If you do go to John Harvard's, expect a few surprises on tap. There are always some goodies available. The **Fade to Black Porter** is an excellent porter, while the **Bavarian Hefeweizen** is a nice, refreshing beer. The **Belgian Quad** is a big sipper of a beer, and the **Blackout IPA** is a solid black IPA. The **Espresso Stout,** brewed using real espresso beans, is top notch. The **Pumpkin Spice Ale** is very popular—get it with or without the rim of the glass dipped in cinnamon—and the **West Coast IPA** is a nicely hopped beer. If you like a particular beer on tap, grab a growler and bring it home.

The appetizer menu includes a huge hummus platter and a plate of nachos, perfect for sharing. The Asian Crispadillas features tortilla triangles with chicken and ginger drizzled with apricot ginger and Asian barbecue sauces, and the fried chicken wings are a step above the average pub wings. Instead of throwing away the grains after the brewers are done, John Harvard's actually uses the spent grain to make the dough for their pizzas. Entrees include the Maple Dijon Salmon, the Ale and Mustard Chicken, meat loaf, ribs, chicken pot pies, and fish and chips with a huge slab of fried cod.

NORTHAMPTON BREWERY

11 Brewster Court, Northampton, MA; (413) 584-9903; www.northamptonbrewery.com
Draft Beers: 10

The Northampton Brewery is part of New England brewing history. It is the oldest existing brewpub in all of New England. The brewery was founded in 1987 by brother and sister team of Peter and Janet Egleston, who later went on to open the Portsmouth Brewery in New Hampshire.

For a brewpub to last this long, they have to brew good beers, and Northampton certainly does just that. The standard beers that can be found at most times include the **(Snow) (Sand) (No) Shovel ESB,** the **Altbier,** the **Byzantine Blonde,** the **Golden Lager,** the **Nontuck IPA,** and the **Red-Headed Stepchild.** If you have ever visited the Portsmouth Brewery, you will notice some of the same beers, such as **Old Brown Dog** and the **Black Cat Stout,** are available at both locations, even though they are not technically connected anymore.

The Northampton Brewery also offers a number of specialty beers. The **88' Tor** is a doppelbock, while the **Black Boots** is a black IPA. The **Conundrum,** a German-style schwarz beer, is an excellent black lager. The **Hoppily Ever After** and the **Hopzilla** are both hoppy IPAs, and the **Wild Blue Funk** is a beer brewed with fresh Maine blueberries and then fermented with wild yeast, making this a wonderfully tart/sour beer. The brewpub also offers several seasonals, such as the **Graduation Ale,** a wheat ale brewed with raspberries, the **Octoberfest,** and the **Pumpkin Ale.** Along with its own beer, the Northampton Brewery almost always features several guest beers from other breweries.

The inside bar area is larger than many brewpubs and Northampton also has a rooftop beer garden with a bar so you do not have to worry about going in and out every time you want a drink. There is also a sun room that is open if there are no special events taking place.

Grub-wise, the Northampton Brewery has a large and varied menu. Appetizers include Cajun Catfish Bites, which are fried and dusted with Cajun spices, and Arancini, which is mozzarella encased in Parmesan risotto, panko battered, and deep-fried. The Northampton Brewery has numerous interesting sandwiches, including the Hot Poblano, which features bacon-wrapped poblano-stuffed meat loaf, topped with chipotle mayo, black beans, and grilled corn salsa. Another option is Basil's Rathbone, which is a sandwich filled with sliced tomatoes, roasted red pepper, red onions, fresh basil, provolone cheese, and garlic mayonnaise. If you're part of a large group, try one of the brewpub's platters, such as the New England Cheese Platter and the Ploughman's Platter.

Massachusetts

OFFSHORE ALE COMPANY

30 Kennebec Ave., Oak Bluffs, MA; (508) 693-2626; www.offshoreale.com
Draft Beers: 8

Martha's Vineyard is a picturesque summer destination, and the Offshore Ale Company in Oak Bluffs is the best place to grab a beer on the small island. Offshore Ale is a brewpub that serves good beer all year-round.

There are always 8 beers on draft, and cask offerings are sometimes available. The standard beers include the **Offshore Amber Ale,** the **Offshore IPA,** and the **East Chop Light House Ale.** The best of the standard-line beers is the **Menemsha Creek Pale Ale,** which is one of the top pale ales being brewed in New England. It is hoppy, but balanced. Each sip makes you want to take another sip. Get this if it is the only beer you get at Offshore.

Offshore also has a number of occasionally brewed beers. The **Argus** is a nice Belgian ale, while the **Helles Bock** is a great interpretation of the German style. The **Island Double IPA** is a big, hoppy beer, and the **Hop Goddess** is a hoppy Belgian pale ale, almost an IPA. The **Inkwell Stout** is a beer worth seeking out. The alcohol changes each year, and each version of the beer tastes slightly different than past years.

The restaurant has a good mix of food—from simple, down-home cooking to more sophisticated dishes. Starters include some items you might not see on a typical brewpub menu, such as the turkey wings, which includes four wings with honey

Beer Event

Oktoberfest

Although Martha's Vineyard is thought of as more of a summer playland, Offshore does host Oktoberfest, which will give you a reason to venture out onto the island during the fall. The event features great beer, German-style food and oompah music, and, of course, tons of Offshore's fresh and fantastic beers. It becomes a big party, and you should go if you get a chance.

barbecue sauce. The grilled brie, Parmesan truffle fries, and the Bavarian pretzel spears are other delicious options. Offshore also offers several brick-oven pizzas. Options include the white clam pizza that has a garlic oil base with bacon, onions, mozzarella cheese, and chopped littleneck clams. The portobello pizza and roasted duck pizza are also worth getting. There is also a raw bar that includes littleneck clams and oysters on the half-shell.

Offshore typically has live music every Tuesday and every Wednesday. They offer tours during business hours, and have plenty of items for sale, such as golf balls, shirts, hats, glasses, and Frisbees. Can't get to the island? Several of Offshore's beers, including the Offshore Amber Ale, the Menemsha Creek Pale Ale, and the East Chop Light House Ale are available in 12-ounce bottles throughout Massachusetts.

OPA OPA STEAKHOUSE & BREWERY
169 College Hwy., Southampton, MA; (413) 527-0808; www.opaopasteakhousebrewery.com
Draft Beers: 20

Put on your 10-gallon hat and grab your cowboy boots—it's time to head to the Opa Opa Steakhouse. Opa Opa is a western-style steakhouse that also happens to brew some pretty good beer.

Opa Opa has a large selection of beers, including the **Opa Opa Light,** the **Kix Beer, Honesty 47 Pale Ale, Buckwheat IPA,** the **Brown Ale,** the **Southampton Porter,** the **King Oak Milk Stout,** and the **Red Rock Ale.** The **A-10 Warthog Double IPA,** a big, hoppy monster of a beer, is also routinely available. Opa Opa also brews several seasonals and fruit beers, including the **Belgian White,** the **Blueberry Lager,** an **Oktoberfest,** and the **Raspberry Wheat.**

Although the beers are quite good, Opa Opa is one of the few brewpubs where the food is the star. Opa Opa is a carnivore's dream. Sure, there are a few veggie options, several salads, as well as a vegetarian pie called the Hey Grazers, which is stuffed with spinach, garlic, carrots, ginger, grilled eggplant, zucchini, squash, tomatoes, mushrooms, fennel, and onions, but it's really all about the meat. Not too hungry? Get the Tenderfoot, which is an 8-ounce filet. Have a bigger appetite? Go for the Trail Hand, a 16-ounce T-bone steak. Or if you're *really* hungry, the Trail Boss, a 20-ounce porterhouse, is for you. The prime rib is one of the best you'll ever have, and available in three sizes: the Deputy is 8 ounces, the Sheriff is 12 ounces, and the Marshall is 16 ounces.

Several of Opa Opa's beers are available in stores in six-packs or in growlers. They also have brewed several exclusive beers for Julio's Liquors in Westborough, Massachusetts, which are definitely worth seeking out.

THE PEOPLE'S PINT

24 Federal St., Greenfield, MA; (413) 773-0333; www.thepeoplespint.com
Draft Beers: 8

Downtown Greenfield is a place that appears to be about 10 years behind the times, but in a good way. They have neighborhood video stores, family-run pizza places, and a bunch of corner stores. It is also the home of the People's Pint, a popular brewpub that is known just as much for their use of local ingredients in almost all their food as they are for their lineup of freshly brewed beers.

The beers are actually not brewed on-site, but at the People's Pint's nearby brewing facility on Hope Street. There are always 8 house beers on draft (and sometimes a guest draft or two). Most of the beers are typically New England styles, but all done really well. The **Natural Blonde Ale** is a light, refreshing, blonde ale that goes down easy. The **Provider Pale Ale,** a nice, hoppy pale ale, is the People's Pint's most popular beer. The **Pied Piper IPA** tastes like a hoppier version of an English-style IPA. The **Oatmeal Stout,** meanwhile, is the People's Pint's best beer. It is a work of art in a glass; utterly and completely fantastic. Other beers include a few lagers, such as the **Doppelbock, Dark Helmut** (German-style black lager), and the **Oktoberfest.**

The People's Pint also brews some adventurous styles you might not see at any other brewpub. The **Slippery Slope** is a braggot-style ale, extremely heavy on ginger. The **Tap & Die Malt Liquor** is a craft interpretation of those old 40-ounce bottles of cheap, high-alcohol malt liquor like Cobra. Suitably, if you buy a bottle of this beer in a store, it actually comes in a 40-ounce bottle. Also available is the **Midnight Special,** which is an imperial black IPA. The People's Pint also offers locally made meads and hard ciders.

The menu is an interesting mix of traditional pub food and more ambitious fare. Starters include the incredible smoked wings, as well as the house-made pickled eggs. The People's Pint has several sandwiches on the menu, but the one you can't miss is the Squealer; it's made with local, grass-fed beef and house-made bacon ground together into one patty. Their entrees are especially interesting. Case in point, the Green Thai Curry Bowl is made with chicken or tofu in a Thai curry, with local seasonal vegetables and a spicy green Thai curry sauce served over basmati rice. Consider ordering the El Salvadorian Pupusa, which consists of two house-made corn tortillas stuffed with organic beans and cheese, served with black beans, Spanish rice, and salad greens tossed with lemon tahini and salsa.

Beer is also available to go in the form of 22-ounce bombers and growlers. But make sure to bring cash—the People's Pint does not accept credit or debit cards.

THE TAP BREWPUB

100 Washington St., Haverhill, MA; (978) 374-1117; www.tapbrewpub.com
Draft Beers: 8

The Tap at the Haverhill Brewing Company is one of those underrated brewpubs that is overlooked because of its location; Haverhill is not near anywhere else that is considered a beer destination. But the beers brewer Jon Curtis produces are good enough to make any beer lover make the trek out to Haverhill.

The Tap has a great rotating lineup, heavy on German-style beers, which is not common for brewpubs. Among the German-style beers brewed at the Tap are the **Annie Schwartz Black Lager,** the **Beerstand Berliner Weiss, Dunkel Weizen, GestAlt, Hefe Dampfbier, Helles Belles, Kolsch, Munich Dunkel,** and the **Scapegoat Bock.** The best are the Beerstand Berliner Weiss, a tart German-style wheat bear that has become more popular in New England brewpubs in the past couple of years, and the GestAlt, an excellent altbier. The Tap does not ignore Belgian ales. They have several on tap, including the popular **Whittier White,** as well as the **Ascension Belgian IPA,** the **La Dame De Peronne, Ruby Bruin,** and **Three Graces.** The Ruby Bruin is a solid Flemish Belgian sour ale, and the Ascension Belgian IPA is one of the best of the style.

Then there are the American beers—the **Breakout India Dark Ale,** the **Chocolate Porter,** the **Haver Ale, Homerun APA, Leatherlips IPA,** and **Pumpkin Eater Ale.** The Leatherlips was one of the earliest New England IPAs that abandoned the British tradition and became more hop forward. It may not be as extreme as it used to be, but it is still a very good IPA.

They also bottle several of their beers in six-packs under the Haverhill Brewing Company name. These include their flagship beers—the Leatherlips, the Homerun APA, Whittier White, and the Haver Ale. Haverhill also bottles some of the Tap's other beers, mostly the special releases, in 22-ounce bottles. They are Ascension, GestAlt, Joshua Norton Imperial Stout, La Dame De Peronne, Snowbound, Three Graces, and Triskelion. Beer in growlers, six-packs, and bombers are all for sale to go from the Tap.

If you are at the Tap, you have to order the Portabella Pub Fries. They are thin strips of portabella mushrooms, fried and served like french fries. Other appetizers worth trying include the Witbier Mussels and the Artisan Cheese Plate. Or, grab a potato, leek, and ale soup to whet your appetite for the main meal. The menu features several flatbread pizzas and hamburgers. The Back Deck Burger features an 8-ounce burger rubbed with Jamaican jerk seasoning, topped with lettuce, tomatoes, onions, and banana-mango ketchup. The top entree is the Sea Captain's Platter, which consists of a 4-ounce piece of haddock served with mussels and shrimp.

The Tap is proof that good beer can be found almost anywhere you look, as long as you search it out.

WATCH CITY BREWING COMPANY

256 Moody St., Waltham, MA; (781) 647-4000; http://watchcitybrew.com
Draft Beers: 8 plus 2 casks

People say bacon makes everything better, but did they mean beer, too? Watch City Brewing Company's head brewer, Aaron Mateychuck, thinks so. He brews bacon beer. Let that sink in—beer made with real bacon. Salivating yet?

If not, give this even more thought: In 2011 Watch City held the "14 Degrees of Making Bacon Cask Extravaganza" at the Moody Street brewpub. The event featured 14 different versions of the bacon beer, all cask-conditioned. Every single one of them had bacon essence in the flavor, smokiness, and then some wild and crazy spices. Thai coconut curry and bacon? Hot peppers and bacon? Chocolate and bacon? Yeah, they were all there. Some were great, some not so much, but it was a worthy effort, and sure to make a return to the pub.

But don't get the wrong idea. Watch City is not all about gimmicks. The year-rounds—**Hops Explosion IPA, Moody Street Stout, Shillelagh Irish Red Ale,** and **Titan Ale**—are all great beers. There are also always tons of special beers and seasonals on tap. The **'FNA Imperial IPA** is an excellent beer. The **Monkey Monk Saison** is another winner. The phenomenal Toasted **Ah Ah Pale Ale** is brewed with coconut and hibiscus flowers. If you want a big beer, try **Lunarshine Burleywine,** a 9.8 percent alcohol by volume barleywine. The **Chocolate Thunder Porter,** brewed with local chocolate, is perfect as a nightcap, while the **BitchLoden Wheat Lager** offers a different twist on wheat beers. The **Beejeszus Botanical Ale** is a hopless beer and uses ingredients grown in Mateychuck's own backyard.

Watch City also likes to collaborate with their customers. The **Trident's Old Spearhead IPA** was brewed with homebrewer and frequent patron Mike Johnson of Natick. The brewpub has even started a Patron's Appreciation Society; the first beer brewed is called **Stephanie's Cherry Raspberry Wheat,** brewed with customer Alan Muir.

For the less experimental types, there are plenty of "normal beers," such as the **Bitter and Jaded ESB** (extra special bitter), **Skye High Scotch Ale, Bombed Blondshelle Tripel,** and **Brilliant Brunette,** a Belgian strong ale. For those who like lower alcohol beers, **Wee Light** is a lighter version of a Scottish-style wee heavy.

Watch City's burgers are especially good. The oddest—and most likely to clog your arteries—may be the Tick Tock Burger, which consists of a patty deep fried in beer batter and then topped with chipotle lime mayonnaise. You can also get some bacon on the burger if you want. Hey, if you are drinking a bacon beer, you might as well go all out.

Beer Bars

THE ALE HOUSE

33 Main St., Amesbury, MA; (978) 388-1950; www.amesburyalehouse.com
Draft Beers: 30 **Bottled/Canned Beers:** Around 100

Although they do not get as much recognition as other Boston-area bars, the Ale House is one of the best beer bars in all of New England. If you take a look at the draft list and, even more impressive, the bottled list, it would be hard for even the most hard core of beer geeks not to be impressed. Add to the fantastic beer selection a huge and varied food menu, you have a beer destination that everyone should seek out.

The bottled list is simply a thing of beauty. They have one of the largest selections of wild ales and lambics you will ever find. Wild ales, for those who do not know, are typically brewed with wild yeast, which makes the beer sour and/or tart. They have many, including several options from Jolly Pumpkin from Michigan, Cascade Brewing from Washington, and even Haandbryggeriett from Norway. The Ale House also offers several varieties of gueuze, a Belgian ale that is spontaneously fermented with wild yeast and is often sour. The options range from easy to find, like the Lindeman's Framboise, to the harder to find (and expensive) Drie Fonteine Oude Gueuze. Pretty much every other Belgian style of ale is available, including saisons, white ales, dubbels, tripels, and quads.

The draft list has more beers that are meant to turn over quickly, and they are all excellent examples of specific styles. If you like hefeweizens, they typically have Weihenstephan Hefeweiss available. They also have several IPAs, lagers, and seasonals on draft.

The awesomeness that is the Ale House continues to the food side. Starters include Guinness beef stew; Belgian-style frites with a choice of seasonings, toppings, and dipping sauces; fried pickles; lobster corn cakes; and smoked chicken taquitos. Pub food such as American chop suey, a patty melt, and club sandwiches are also available, as are several entrees, which include the lobster quesadilla, which is made with lobster, mozzarella, and guacomole; sesame-crusted tuna; turkey tips; lobster sliders; balsamic braised beef short ribs; and beer-battered fish and chips.

Adding to the Ale House's charm is the location. The bar is located in an old mill, and it still retains a lot of the mill's features, such as the high tin roofs. It also sits on the Powwow River, and the views are amazing. If you're on the north shore for any reason, the Ale House is a place any self-respecting beer lover has to stop.

Massachusetts

ARMSBY ABBEY

144 North Main St., Worcester, MA; (508) 795-1012; http://armsbyabbey.com
Draft Beers: 22 **Bottled/Can Beers:** Around 150

The best beer bar in Massachusetts is not in Boston. It is in central Massachusetts, Worcester to be exact, an area that used to be a beer wasteland. The Armsby Abbey, founded in 2008 by Alec Lopez and his wife, Sherri Sadowski, takes everything to another level.

Sure, there is beer, but that is not the only thing that makes the Armsby Abbey special. They make the best food in Worcester, with almost all locally sourced ingredients. They do not carry name brands. The wines are from small wineries. The spirits are from small-batch distillers. The mixed drink menu is put together with care and a sense of artistry. If you want a Pepsi, you are out of luck. You will have to get a Polar Cola, made in Worcester.

Start with the beer selection. The draft list, posted on a large chalkboard, features 22 hand-selected offerings. Heavy on Belgian ales, but with a great selection of American craft ales, it is a well-put-together list. Even though there are only 22 beers on tap, even the most hard-core beer drinkers will not have any trouble finding something they have never had. The bottled list is also incredibly impressive. Not only does it include beers of nearly every style from every craft brewery producing good beers today, it also features some special, and sometimes pricy, selections from Lopez's beer cellar.

Founder's Breakfast

Each April, the Armsby Abbey hosts a special beer meal. While most beer meals are dinners, this is a breakfast. It makes sense, because at this particular sellout event, Armsby hosts the Founders Brewing Company of Michigan and their collection of excellent breakfast stouts, including the regular Breakfast Stout, the Kentucky Breakfast Stout, and the Canadian Breakfast Stout. These beers are paired with a breakfast prepared by chef/owner Alec Lopez.

If a member of your party is not a beer fan, do not be concerned. The liquor and wine selection is extensive, and the cocktail menu is fantastic, featuring dozens of unique creations made with the small batch liquors.

Food-wise, there are not many beer-centric places, except for the Sierra Grille in Northampton, that can match what the Armsby Abbey does. The menu changes constantly and is based on what Lopez can get locally. Do not go in looking for a quick meal. This is not fast food; it is slow-cooked food, cooked to order and cooked right. The menu always features various cheese plates, local fruits, house-baked breads, desserts, and soups. Entrees can range from a cold duck sausage sandwich to smoked bone marrow.

The pizzas are incredible. If you have a chance, go to the weekend brunch. There are breakfast pizzas (the harvest pizza with pumpkin puree instead of tomato sauce is to die for), gourmet macaroni and cheese, Belgian waffles, different versions of pancakes, toast, and a breakfast slate featuring fruits, local honey, and other condiments and cheeses.

There are many events throughout the year. Lopez, who is also the chef, hosts several beer dinners a year, where a brewery's beers are each paired with a different dish. These sell out quickly. The Armsby Abbey is a must for beer lovers, particularly if you are in the Worcester area. Stop in and be amazed.

BRITISH BEER COMPANY

Ten locations in Cedarville, Falmouth, Framingham, Franklin, Hyannis, Pembroke, Plymouth, Sandwich, Walpole, Westford; (508) 888-6610 (corporate number); www .britishbeer.com
Draft Beers: At least 20 at every location **Bottled/Canned Beers:** Various

The British Beer Company may be a chain (currently with 10 locations and continuing to grow), but the restaurant has never lost its original goal, to provide its beer-loving guests with an experience they won't soon forget.

Modeled after English pubs, most of the bars at the British Beer Company are designed and purchased in England. All of the locations have an extensive beer list, with at least 20 beers on tap. In all, the chain features 290 beers on tap (or draught to keep with the English terminology), and each pub usually features at least 1 cask-conditioned beer. Most of the bars also have a large bottled list of British- and Belgian-imported beers. The beer menu is also arranged in a way that is very helpful to the British Beer Company's customers—they are listed from least complex to most complex.

The British Beer Company also hosts numerous events throughout the year, including tap takeovers, Oktoberfest celebrations, and beer dinners. The Dogfish

Head Tap Takeover is always a favorite, especially when the British Beer Company breaks outs some of their Randall the Enamel Animals (a device that runs a draft beer through fresh ingredients right before it hits the glass, adding fresh flavors). They have also recently started hosting scotch and single-batch bourbon tastings. Throughout the week, the British Beer Company restaurants also host live musicians, so there's always something going on.

The baked brie appetizer, featuring warm brie cheese wrapped in a puff pastry with an apple-mango chutney, is excellent. The Royal Pu Pu includes several of the available appetizers on one plate—the shrimp wontons, crispy panko-encrusted green beans, bourbon sauce wings, bourbon BBQ ribs, sweet potato fries, BBC fries, and onion rings. Of course, there are many British favorites on the menu, including beer-battered fish and chips, bangers and mash, and shepherd's pie. They also have several British pasty pies available, including the popular chicken and leek pasty pie. Burgers are bountiful, and entrees include ribs, steaks, pasta, and the Guinness steak pie.

Their pizzas are also top-notch. If you want to be especially adventurous, try the Over 21 Pizza, which is topped with the brewpub's bourbon sauce, cheddar cheese, steak, peppers, onions, and mushrooms. If that wasn't enough, the pizza is also misted with bourbon tableside. Obviously, the pizza can't be shared with youngsters—let them eat off the kids' menu while you enjoy your bourbon pizza and a nice British ale on draft.

BUKOWSKI'S TAVERN
50 Dalton St., Boston, MA, (617) 437-9909; 1281 Cambridge St., Cambridge, MA, (617) 497-7077; http://bukowskistavern.net **Draft Beers:** Boston, 20; Cambridge, 30 **Bottled/Canned Beers:** Boston, about 100; Cambridge, about 130

Bukowski's Tavern is a Boston classic. If you like good beer and live in the area, odds are you have been there. The Boston and Cambridge locations do have some differences: Boston's Bukowski's is small, a wee bit dingy, and has a limited menu, while the Cambridge location is larger and has a full menu as well as a wine and cocktail list. What they both have in common is great beer, and a rather friendly staff of bartenders.

The draft list features a specially brewed beer by the Wormtown Brewing Company in Worcester called the Buk, which is a rye pale ale. It also features beer from great breweries from around the country, including Brooklyn Brewery, Ithaca Brewing Company, Sierra Nevada, and Brewery Ommegang. They usually feature plenty of New England beers, such as stuff from Pretty Things Beer & Ale Project,

The Annual Kung-Fu Christmas

The holidays can be a stressful time. You're forced to visit family members you have not seen all year, and usually after a couple of hours, you remember exactly why you haven't seen them all year. If you need to escape, head to the annual Kung Fu Christmas at Bukowski's in Cambridge. They open from 5:30 p.m. to 1 a.m. to give you a Christmas free of stress, fruitcakes, and irritating ho, ho, hoing. No Santa hats allowed, and Christmas music will not be blaring in your ear. You will just be drinking a lot of good beer and there will probably be no real kung-fu fighting.

Notch Session, Cisco Brewers, and Smuttynose Brewing Company. Cambridge also has a few imported beers on draft. The bottled and canned list features beers from most of the better breweries around the country, as well as local favorites.

As far as food goes, we'll start with the Boston location. Appetizers include sweet potato fries, fried plantains, mini-mozzarella sticks, and a true Bukowski's original, the White Trash Cheese Dip. The dip is made with a mix of American cheese, green chili peppers, jalapeños, diced tomatoes, and diced onions, served with tortilla chips. Other than starters, burgers, hot dogs, and sandwiches dominate the menu. A particular standout is the gourmet grilled cheese sandwich, which is made with Havarti cheese and sliced tomatoes, pressed between slices of sourdough bread. Burgers include the peanut butter burger, which is a grilled six-ounce burger topped with chunky peanut butter. Another option is the Hangover Helper, which is topped with aged cheddar, bacon, and a fried egg.

The Cambridge food menu is identical save for a few extras, such as PBR onion rings, soup, and even a couple of salads. Entrees include rosemary duck breast served over a smoked gouda risotto; fish and chips; and baked mac and cheese, made with cavatappi pasta and cheddar, Swiss, blue, and mozzarella cheeses. More sophisticated sandwiches, such as the roast beef and brie, are also available.

CAMBRIDGE COMMON RESTAURANT

1667 Massachusetts Ave., Cambridge, MA; (617) 547-1228; www.cambridgecommon
restaurant.com
Draft Beers: 31 **Bottled/Canned Beers:** 12

The Cambridge Common Restaurant may not have the biggest draft selection in the greater Boston area, but it is one of the most fun places to hang out. There is always something going on at the Cambridge Common and the staff, servers, and bartenders are some of the friendliest in town. It is the kind of place you can go to grab a good meal, watch a game (during the World Cup they open early in the morning to allow people to come in and watch their favorite teams and eat breakfast), or take in a beer event.

The beer selection is nothing to sniff at. The staff has a well-thought-out draft list of 31 beers, heavy on locals, but not ignoring beers from other states. Cambridge Common breaks up the draft list into "Always on Tap" and "Rotating Brews." The beers always available include Allagash White, Berkshire Brewing Company's Coffee House Porter, Ithaca's Flower Power IPA, and Victory Golden Monkey. A recent rotating draft list included Massachusetts beers such as Blue Hill's AntiMatter 2, Cambridge Brewing Company's Biere de Gourde, and Jack's Abby Brewing's Copper Legend Oktoberfest. Other beers from the Brooklyn Brewery and Troegs brewery were also available.

Throughout the year, the Cambridge Common hosts several tap takeovers, including a New England tap takeover during Boston Beer Week in June. They also host several beer dinners throughout the year, as well as beer release parties.

The *Improper Bostonian* magazine once said the Cambridge Common had "Boston's Best Bar Food," and the restaurant tries to live up to those lofty standards. Starters include deviled eggs, tater tots, mac and cheese bites, and the huge Middle Eastern platter. The platter includes roasted garlic hummus, Israeli couscous, feta, kalamata olives, tomatoes, greens, pepperoncini, red onions, and pita bread. Comfort foods such as fish and chips and grilled meat loaf are available as entrees, as is the seafood jambalaya that features cod, calamari, mussels, chicken, and chorizo. Healthier options include fish tacos, tofu curry, and numerous salads. A special brunch menu is served on Saturday and Sunday. You can get French toast, pancakes, numerous types of omelets, and breakfast burritos.

Prices are some of the best in the Boston area, and unlike a lot of bars, they do have an on-site parking lot. Drive down the narrow alleyway next to the pub and it opens into a small lot. So many people do not know about it you can often find a spot even if it is standing room only on the inside.

DEEP ELLUM

477 Cambridge St., Allston, MA; (617) 787-2337; www.deepellum-boston.com
Draft Beers: 28 **Bottled/Canned Beers:** 80

Deep Ellum may not have the sheer number of beers as the most famous beer bar in Allston, the Sunset Grill, but it stands up to any beer bar with a great selection of more than 100 beers between its bottled and draft lists. Located just down the street from the Sunset Grill, Deep Ellum has 28 beers on tap, as well as about 80 bottled and canned beers, with several cask options available.

The draft list typically features several beers from Belgium and Germany, as well as occasional visits from Norway and Spain. It is also heavy on New England craft beers, such as Clown Shoes, Element, Haverhill Brewing Company, Jack's Abby Brewing, Pretty Things Beer & Ale Project, and Smuttynose Brewing Company. Beers from other parts of the country are not ignored. It would not be unusual to find beers from Stone Brewing Company and Green Flash Brewing Company from California, or Stoudts from Pennsylvania, on tap.

The bottled list is also well thought out, and separated into either the ale or lager category. The lager selections include some of the best German varieties available. The ale list is further broken down into styles, so it is easy to find a Belgian ale, such as Cantillon, or a wheat beer, such as Schneider Edel Weiss.

To go along with the great beer selection, Deep Ellum features a full menu. Starters include cheese plates, charcuterie plates, and french fries offered in four different styles—Parmesan, chili and pepper jack, malt vinegar and fleur de sel, and truffled gorgonzola. Other options include deviled eggs and the root beer braised pork belly. Burgers are available, as are sandwiches, including the Big Easy, which is a New Orleans' style sandwich made up of cold cuts, provolone cheese, and olives. Another standout is the pork meatball banh mi, which features pork meatballs on French bread, topped with pickled daikon, carrots, srirachi aioli, and cilantro. Other delicious mains include the golden beet and wild mushroom risotto, coffee-braised lamb shank, and chicken schnitzel. Deep Ellum also offers brunch daily. The Fall River French Toast, made with Portuguese sweet bread, and the BBQ Breakfast, which includes braised pork shoulder, cornbread, mustard aioli, and a fried egg, are two of the highlights.

Along with beer, Deep Ellum offers a large selection of cocktails, wines, bourbons, and rye whiskeys. During the summer, make sure to take advantage of the outdoor deck and sit outside while drinking a few beers.

Massachusetts

THE DIVE BAR

34 Green St., Worcester, MA; (508) 752-5802; http://thedivebarworcester.com
Draft Beers: 16 **Bottled/Canned Beers:** More than 100

The Dive Bar is not a pretty place. When you look at it from the outside, it actually looks more like a place where you would go to have a couple of shots of cheap whiskey and then get into a knock-down drag-out fight. It does get better when you walk inside. The walls are a mishmash of beer signs, old-fashioned diving equipment (think full-head diving helmet), and stickers. It is dark inside, and there are not a lot of seats. In fact, the Dive Bar was so divey that *Stuff* magazine once named it one of the best dive bars in America.

But you soon discover the beauty of the bar when you see all the tap handles and the draft list scrawled out on the giant chalkboard. This is not your father's dive bar. This is Alec Lopez's Dive Bar, a bar with a fantastic draft list. The days of dollar draft nights for college students are gone. Lopez also owns the Armsby Abbey. But, except for great beer and a staff that is knowledgeable about beer, there are not many similarities.

There is no food menu, although during the summer, Lopez opens up an outdoor beer garden and throws food on the grill. If you are hungry, a sausage

Beer Event

Dogfish Head Halloween

Every Halloween, the Dive Bar hosts Dogfish Head Halloween, a tap takeover by the popular Delaware brewery. Every single tap is a Dogfish Head beer, and there are also some Dogfish Head spirits available. Do not even consider driving that night. Get a room and take a cab. This is a party to end all parties. Go to the Dive Bar's sister bar, the Armsby Abbey, the next morning for the Dogfish Head brunch to recover.

truck is usually outside. The beer is the star at the Dive Bar, which exclusively features American craft beer on draft. There is a good chance you will find beers from Berkshire Brewing Company, Brooklyn Brewery, Sixpoint, and Southern Tier on draft. The beers are affordable and handled correctly. The staff is friendly and the crowd is loud and raucous, but all are having a good time.

Along with the great beer, the Dive Bar is a haven for local live music enthusiasts. Every Thursday is "Dive Thursday," when local musician Duncan Arsenault and a group of various musicians come together and jam the night away with awesome music. It is loud, so conversation may be tough, but the music will make up for that. Monday usually features live music from the Bob & Pop Jazz Organization, and there are often live bands on other nights.

GREEN STREET GRILLE
280 Green St., Cambridge, MA; (617) 876-1655; http://greenstreetgrille.com
Draft Beers: 10 **Bottled/Canned Beers:** About 30

The Green Street Grille is a restaurant first, and beer bar second. The draft list is small but impressive, and the bottled list features numerous quality beers.

Let's start with the food. With just a quick look at the menu, you will soon realize that the food is a little different than at the average beer bar. Starters include the grilled octopus stew, confit of duck legs, fried goat cheese salad, and an artisanal cheese plate. Dinner highlights include the baked Gloucester haddock that is served with mustard spaetzle, shaved brussels sprouts, bacon, and vinaigrette. The spicy Wellfleet clam stew is made with borlotti beans, jalapeño, bacon, and local kale. The quality continues through the desserts menu, which features such sweet dishes as English toffee pudding cake, house-made ice-cream sandwich, and a banana upside-down cake.

The beer menu is just as well done as the food menu. The list includes an IPA of the Day, Stout of the Day, and Draught of the Day. Some beers that are often on the draft list include Jolly Pumpkin of Michigan, Left Hand Brewing Company of Colorado, Clipper City Brewing Company of Maryland, and Uinta Brewing Company of Utah. The bottled list is also varied, and often offers little-seen beers, such as Prestige Lager from Haiti and Dragon Stout from Jamaica. There are several American craft beers available, too, such as Butternuts from New York, the Bruery from California, and Arcadia Ales from Michigan. Green Street also has a large brandy and rum menu, as well as wine and cocktails, so there is something for everyone.

Massachusetts

HORSESHOE PUB & RESTAURANT

29 South St., Hudson, MA; (978) 568-1265; www.horseshoepub.com
Draft Beers: 80 **Bottled/Canned Beers:** 20

The Horseshoe Pub & Restaurant is the kind of neighborhood bar everyone would want. Take a stroll over, grab your favorite seat at the bar, chit-chat with the bartender and the regulars you see there all the time, and enjoy the game on the televisions. Oh, and enjoy a few of the 80 beers they have on tap.

The Horseshoe Pub is located in downtown Hudson, a working class town, not a place you would normally find a craft beer haven. But the Horseshoe Pub kind of reflects its population. It is a no-frills kind of pub. The bar area is set up like a sports bar, and there is a good size dining area on both the first and second floors. In warmer weather the outside deck is a great place to sit and enjoy a few pints.

Many beer bars go out of their way to get the "proper" glassware for various styles of beer. That is fine, but the Horseshoe offers most of its beers in normal pint glasses. Nothing wrong with that. Sometimes it is nice to get a big glass of an IPA that is not served in a tulip or a snifter. The beer list is heavy on American craft beers. The Horseshoe Pub may not have all the beer geek, hard-to-find beers, but they pretty much have nothing but beers. Beers from Bear Republic, Boulder Beer, Saranac, and Victory always seem to be available. The 'Shoe, as the locals call it, always has a lot of Massachusetts beers on tap. Expect to find beers from Berkshire Brewing Company, the Haverhill Brewery, Mayflower Brewing Company, Wachusett Brewing Company, and Wormtown Brewing Company available most of the time. There are also always a few Belgian ales, English ales, and German lagers and wheat beers available as well.

If you happen to be at the Horseshoe Pub, grab dinner. The menu is a good mix of pub and comfort foods, with some twists thrown in. Appetizers include some tasty house-made potato chips and Reuben eggrolls, stuffed with corned beef, sauerkraut, and Swiss cheese. Or try the Irish nachos, which are topped with Mexican cheese sauce, chopped bacon, and scallions. There are plenty of burgers, sandwiches, and salads on the menu, but the strength of the offerings is really in the entrees. The Horseshoe offers meat loaf and country-style shepherd's pie and beef tips, but they also offer General Gao's chicken. Also available is the Sicilian haddock, which is topped with baby spinach, diced tomatoes, oregano, and shredded Parmesan cheese. If pasta is on your mind, the braised short rib ravioli is a strong contender, as is the butternut squash ravioli and maple butternut chicken.

October is also a good time to be at the Horseshoe Pub. They hold a month long Oktoberfest with a German-style food-heavy menu and extra German beers on tap. *Prost.*

JACOB WIRTH RESTAURANT

31–37 Stuart St., Boston, MA; (617) 338-8587; www.jacobwirth.com
Draft Beers: 32 **Bottled/Canned Beers:** About 30

Jacob Wirth's Restaurant is a true Boston classic. They've been filling glasses with the good stuff for close to 150 years, and to this day it remains a great place to go to have a good German-style meal and grab a half-liter of beer.

Jacob Wirth opened the restaurant in 1868. He and his family owned several breweries and were the sole distributors of Budweiser beers, so they wanted a place to sell the beer locally. Today, you can still find Budweiser at Jacob Wirth's, but you can find so much more. The restaurant has 32 beers on draft and around 30 bottles available at all times. Being a German-style restaurant, Jacob Wirth's has a large number of German beers available.

Although German beer is the star at Jacob Wirth's, that is not all they have. German beer is great, but if you want something different, they do have a fair amount of American craft beer, Belgian ales, and English-style ales, mostly in bottles. They even have two German non-alcoholic beers available in bottles.

Make sure if you're in town in October to head there for the Oktoberfest celebration. Throughout the month there are special events, such as tap takeovers, so it's not to be missed. Other events throughout the year include brewer's nights where the brewers come in and discuss their beer. They have also hosted a mini-golf tournament inside the restaurant.

The food is amazing. You cannot go to a German restaurant and not at least consider getting wursts, or sausages. Jacob Wirth's has several different options—steamed bratwurst, grilled smoked bratwurst, steamed knockwurst, grilled weissewurst, and Jake's Black Label Sausage. The sausages are done right and should be savored with a big glass of a German lager. The appetizers also feature a couple of German standbys, potato pancakes and a bucket of giant soft pretzels. If those aren't for you, they do have nachos, wings, and calamari, which are probably quite popular in Germany. Maybe not. Other German dishes on the menu include the Wiener schnitzel, jaegerschnitzel, and sauerbraten. There are also entree-sized sausage plates.

If German food is not for you, don't worry, there's something for everybody. Non-German entrees include beer-battered fish and chips, vegetable ravioli, and buffalo chicken macaroni and cheese. There are also several salads on the menu, as well as a wide variety of hamburgers. The can't-miss burger is the Bavarian burger, which is topped by red cabbage and cambazola cheese, served with a side of German potato salad.

The atmosphere at Jacob Wirth's is fun. It is set up like a German beer hall with high ceilings and large tables. It gets loud, but it is not annoying. By the time you leave, you'll consider wearing some lederhosen the next time you come in.

LORD HOBO

92 Hampshire St., Cambridge, MA; (617) 250-8454; www.lordhobo.com
Draft Beers: 40 **Bottled/Canned Beers:** About 50

Lord Hobo is one of the many up-and-coming beer bars that takes as much care with every aspect of its food menu as it does its beer. The beer menu, though, is utterly phenomenal. It is changed almost every day, and there is also always at least one cask beer available.

Lord Hobo serves up a fantastic mix of beers. It always has a few New England options, such as High & Mighty Brewing Company or the Smuttynose Brewing Company. It also features many beers from all of the best breweries, such as Founders Beer in Michigan, Victory Brewing in Pennsylvania, and the Avery Brewing Company from Colorado. Also, there always seems to be at least one fresh-tasting German lager on draft, served in a hefty mug. It just seems right to drink a German beer out of a half, or full-liter mug. There are almost always a few rare Belgian ales on draft.

The bottled list is also varied, heavy on large-format bottles such as bombers and 750 ml, which are perfect for sharing. Belgian ales are the stars on the menu, with several great Cantillon beers available (at big bucks), and beers from Achel and Drie Fonteinen. Top-notch American and German beers round out the bottled list.

Your cocktail-inclined friends have a lot of interesting options to chose from, and all of Lord Hobo's drinks are made with fine liquors. They all have eye-catching names, too, such as the Cat Wagon, which is made with Raid Red grape hibiscus vodka, Clear Creek raspberry, Lillet blonde, and fresh lemon topped with Prosecco. Or, give the Soylent Green (it is not people), the Interloper, or the Sloppy Possum a try.

The food is on the pricey side, but excellent. The appetizers include house-made turkey chili, miso baby clams with Chinese broccoli and sticky rice noodles, grilled cheese with cauliflower soup, chicken lollipops, and a cheese board. Make sure to try the Belgian frites with multiple dipping sauces. If you're not in a mood for an entree, Lord Hobo offers several small plates, such as hummus, a beet salad, roasted asparagus, and scallop ceviche.

The entree menu is not large, but has several good options. The pulled pork sandwich is served with cheddar and cabbage, while the mozzarella sandwich includes eggplant caponta and Peppadew tomato. The mac and cheese is one of the best in the greater Boston area, and it is slathered in cheddar, Parmesan, and mascarpone cheeses. The shaved prime rib sandwich with onion jam and bleu cheese is the best sandwich option. Desserts are also available, but the best choice is to get one of the beers as a dessert—a great end to a great night at Lord Hobo.

THE MOAN AND DOVE
460 West St., Amherst, MA; (413) 256-1710; http://moananddove.com
Draft Beers: 21 **Bottled/Canned Beers:** Nearly 200

The Moan and Dove is not the average bar you find in the middle of a college town like Amherst. You know the kind of place: plenty of $4 pitchers of cheap beer and not much else to offer. No, the Moan and Dove is one of the most well-known and most respected beer bars in all of New England. The beer list is just fantastic. No bad beers to be found on the chalkboard. High & Mighty Brewing Company is often available, as are beers from Ballast Point, Laughing Dog, De Ranke, Founders Brewing Company, and Stone. The bottled list includes nearly 200 various beers.

The beer menu (more like a book) is broken down into categories, which makes it much easier to search for a beer you want. In the mood for a sour beer? Just look under sours and pick out something like Monk's Cafe Flemish Sour. The Moan and Dove has beers of almost all Belgian styles, such as lambics, saisons, and Belgian stouts. The menu also has a section on "Strange brews," which are beers made with unusual ingredients, or that do not really fit in the typical categories. Several of Dogfish Head's beers are featured, such as Theobroma and Midas Touch. Stouts are broken up into sweet/coffee stouts, imperial stouts, and stouts. They have several fantastic selections, including Dieu Du Ciel's Peche Mortel and Lion Stout from Sri Lanka. The Moan and Dove also offers what they call the "Nostalgia Series," which includes Pabst Blue Ribbon, Narragansett, Old Milwaukee, and Schlitz.

One thing you should not expect at the Moan and Dove is the ability to order a meal. The only food they have is a big barrel of free peanuts. Although they do not serve food, the Moan and Dove does allow customers to bring in their own food.

MOE'S TAVERN
10 Railroad St., Lee, MA; (413) 243-6637; www.nocoorslight.com
Draft Beers: 13 **Bottled/Canned Beers:** More than 100

Moe's Tavern is the winner for the best website name for a beer bar anywhere—Nocoorslight.com. And although the name of the website for this

Moezapalouza

Each October, Moe's Tavern celebrates its anniversary with a big blowout. Head to Moe's to party and to drink special beers, both on draft and in bottles. Moe's waits until this day to break out some truly amazing treats, or beers rarely found on draft. At its fifth anniversary in 2011, for example, it tapped Dogfish Head's 120 Minute IPA, which is hard to find in bottles or on draft.

western Massachusetts beer bar is funny, it also sets the tone for the kind of bar that Moe's Tavern is. It is a place for those who love good craft beer. There is no Coors, Budweiser, Miller, or even some of the more popular but larger craft beer producers.

No, this is a no-frills bar that offers nothing but some of the best beers brewed in the US. Do not come looking for a beer and a burger—Moe's Tavern does not offer food. Moe's is for beer. And whiskey. Moe's draft list may not be huge, totaling only 13 beers, but the worst beer they have on draft could be as good as the best one at some lesser beer bars. Beers from Brewery Ommegang and Ithaca Brewing Company, both of New York, often find their way onto the menu, as well as the Nebraska Brewing Company and Port Brewing Company. Dogfish Head, Stone Brewing Company, Pretty Things, and Allagash Brewing Company are also usually available.

The bottled and canned beers are truly impressive. Like the draft list, Moe's Tavern's bottled list features all American beer, with the exception of Unibroue from Canada. Almost every great brewery that distributes beers in Massachusetts is available in bottles (or cans) at Moe's Tavern. Breweries often available include Avery, Oskar Blues, and Left Hand from Colorado, Full Sail from Oregon, Goose Island from Illinois, Founders Brewing Company from Michigan, Sixpoint from New York, and Bear Republic, Lagunitas, and Sierra Nevada from California.

Lee might be in the middle of nowhere—about 2 hours from Boston—but Moe's definitely makes it worth the trip.

THE PUBLICK HOUSE & MONK'S CELL

1648 Beacon St., Brookline, MA; (617) 277-2880; http://eatgoodfooddrinkbetterbeer.com
Draft Beers: 34 **Bottled/Canned Beers:** Well over 100

There are a lot of competitors for the best beer bar in the greater Boston area, but one bar that has to be put at the top of that list is the Publick House & Monk's Cell. It is a place where serious beer lovers go to grab fine Belgian ale served in the perfect glass for the style.

The draft list is extremely impressive, and all 34 beers that are on draft are always fantastic offerings. The Publick House is heavy on Belgian ales, with beers from Oud Beersel, St. Feuillien, and Bavik. It also usually features some wonderful Belgian-style ales brewed here in the US, such as Allagash Brewing Company. But not all of the beers are Belgian ales. There are beers from Founders Brewing Company in Michigan, Great Divide Brewing Company in Colorado, and Southampton Publick House in New York. They even have beers from Japan—Hitachino Nest—and Germany. The Monk's Cell, which is right next to the main seating area of the Publick House, serves nothing but Belgian ales.

The bottled list cannot be matched in the Boston area. Just like the draft list, the bottled list is heavy on Belgian beer. They also have all of the Belgian Trappist ales available in the US—Achel, Chimay, Orval, Rochefort, and Westmalle. The Publick House also carries some of the underrated Danish beers, such as Evil Twin

Beer Event

Hophead Throwdown

The Publick House hosts an event made for those who love hops every July called the Hophead Throwdown. The event features nothing but ultra-hoppy beers, paired with extremely spicy food. Needless to say, the entire experience is quite an attack on the taste buds. Even better, the Hophead Throwdown benefits the Multiple Sclerosis Society.

Massachusetts

Brewing. The menu also features several German beers, including several of the Weihenstephan and Ayinger beers. American beers are well represented, with beers from Ballast Point Brewing Company in California, Jolly Pumpkin in Michigan, and local brewery Pretty Things Beer & Ale Project.

The Publick House also has fantastic food. The menu features delicious pots of mussels with a variety of broth options, such as Echte Kriekenbier and herbed garlic butter or Victory Prima Pils with red curry, coconut milk, lime, and sweet chili. Also available are hand-cut Yukon gold potatoes dusted with sea salt served with several house-made dunking sauces. Other starters are a selection of artisanal cheeses, cured meats, house-made pate, and house-made hummus. The entrees are just as good, if not better, than the starters. The Belgian stew is made with mixed seafood in a roasted tomato and herb broth. A can't miss meal is the orrechetti pasta (basically gourmet macaroni and cheese), made with a five-cheese sauce and a list of about 10 different additions such as bacon, mushrooms, or truffle sauce.

SIERRA GRILLE
41 Strong Ave., Northampton, MA; (413) 584-1150; http://thesierragrille.com
Draft Beers: 21 **Bottled/Canned Beers:** About 20

Sierra Grille serves up some excellent food. Not just excellent food for a beer bar, but excellent food for any kind of restaurant. They just happen to be a restaurant that has great beer, too. The 21-beer draft list is fantastic, featuring a good mix of American craft and imported beers. The draft list will often feature beers from Green Flash, Great Divide, and Lagunitas, as well as Chimay and Rodenbach. The bottled list is not as big as those at many places featured, but it is well thought out. Many of the beers are perfect to enjoy with meals, such as several versions of Rochefort or Scaldis. They also have several different J.W. Lee's Harvest Ales, aged in different barrels and of different vintages. They also have something a little different—several meads from Qhilia from South Africa. If you have the inclination, it may be worth experimenting with one of these.

The food menu is not huge, but it is fabulous. Starters include spicy nuts, empanadillas, various cheese plates, and slow-cooked pork shank. The most unusual appetizer they have may be the shrimp with chocolate sauce, which is shrimp sautéed in sherry, orange, chiles, and bittersweet chocolate. Other options include steamed mussels and a loaf of locally baked sourdough bread, served with either butter or olive oil for dipping. The entrees are pretty straightforward. You pick a protein, two sides, and, a sauce. Meat options include chicken, duck, salmon, shrimp, and filet mignon. Sauces include Thai hot basil coconut, fruit barbecue, and citrus salsa,

The Big Game and Big Beer Dinner

This is one of the premier food and beer events in all of New England. Each fall, the Sierra Grille prepares a special menu of meat that you rarely see on a menu, and each course is paired with a big, high-alcohol beers. A past Big Game and Big Beer menu included yak, python, antelope, wild boar, and deer. It is a unique meal, which will please an adventurous palate.

and sides include smashed potatoes, basmati rice, and grilled asparagus. Salads and paninis are available, as are desserts, which include Allagash White Crème Brûlée, chocolate truffles (infused with Framboise), and fruit crisp.

SUNSET GRILL & TAP

130 Brighton Ave., Allston, MA; (617) 254-1331; www.allstonsfinest.com
Draft Beers: 112 **Bottled/Canned Beers:** 380

If you are a fan of good food and good beer, you can't come to Boston without stopping at the Sunset Grill & Tap in Allston. Founded in 1989 by Marc Kadish, the Sunset Grill was an immediate haven for those looking for an alternative to bland, flavorless American macro lagers, offering up what were then rare imports such as Chimay from Belgium and Samuel Smith's from England.

Today, there are dozens of really good bars throughout the greater Boston area, but the Sunset Grill & Tap is still worth a stop, if for nothing else than the pure volume of beers they have available. The problem with a lot of bars with such a large tap selection is sometimes you run into a dirty line, or a past-its-prime beer. That rarely happens at the Sunset. Every draft line is cleaned every two weeks, and with all the colleges in the area, the kegs are emptied fairly regularly.

The beer menu (about a dozen pages long), is easy to get through. The bottles are split up by beer style, so if you want an IPA, it won't be mixed in with dunkelweizens or oatmeal stouts. If you're interested in drafts, flip to the back of the menu. All the current drafts are listed, along with a manager's choice for each style, on the back page. The selection is fantastic with most every big-name craft brewery from around the country represented, such as Dogfish Head Craft Brewery and Victory Brewing Company, sharing space on the beer menu with local favorites like Pretty Things Beer & Ale Project and Smuttynose Brewing Company. If your eyes begin to cross and you're having trouble deciding which beers you want, get a set of four 4-ounce samples, and pick one to order as a full pint.

As far as food, it's mainly pub style, but done really well. The beer-steamed burgers are some of the best in the area (see recipe on page 237), and the chicken wing appetizers are phenomenal. The nacho plate is large and meant for sharing, and there are ample larger entrees such as steaks and fish, as well as Mexican cuisine. Finish it off with ice cream made with beer. A pizza is also a worthy option.

The bartenders are knowledgeable about beer, so if you have any questions, always feel free to ask. The only problem is parking—if you're driving you're going to have to hope a spot on the street opens up. But once inside, you won't worry about the time it took to find a spot. Enjoy.

YARD HOUSE
950 Providence Hwy., Space 200, Dedham, MA; (781) 326-4644; www.yardhouse.com/ma/dedham
Draft Beers: 116 **Bottled/Canned Beers:** 5

Located in the midst of Legacy Place, a large mall that features a giant movie theater, expensive stores, a bowling alley, and many other restaurants, sits the Yard House. Sure, it might be a chain, but Yard House has more and better beers than a lot of bars, and much better than expected food for a typical chain.

The Yard House always prides itself on having the largest beer selection wherever it is located, and the Dedham Yard House is no different, featuring 116 beers on tap. They may not have the hard-to-find rare beers some other beer bars have, but they have many excellent beers available. The draft list is broken up by style, and has several British beers, including Old Speckled Hen; German beers, such as Franziskaner Hefeweizen; and Belgian ales such as Piraat Ale. Most of the draft beers are from American craft breweries, such as Anderson Valley Brewing Company from California, Atwater Block from Michigan, Boulder Beer from Colorado, Goose Island from Illinois, and Troegs from Pennsylvania. The Yard House also has several beers brewed for them as house beers. The menu features several beer blends, from the traditional black and tan made with the house pale ale and Guinness, to the unique, such as the Youngberry Chocolate, which is a blend of Lindeman's Framboise and Young's Double Chocolate Stout. Yummy.

Not in the mood for a big appetizer? Start with a snack-size dish like the truffle fries or deviled eggs. If you're a little bit hungrier than usual, start with the grilled Korean BBQ beef, the onion ring tower, the shiitake garlic noodles, or the seared ahi sashimi, which are all excellent. The sandwich highlight is the blue crab cake hoagie, which includes applewood-smoked bacon, avocado, Swiss cheese, tomatoes, and Cajun aioli served on garlic-toasted French bread. Entrees include the orange peel chicken, which is crispy chicken breast served with baby corn and bok choy, all mixed together in a spicy and sweet orange glaze. Other options include the miso glazed sea bass and the ginger-crusted Norwegian salmon. The Garden menu is a specially created menu that substitutes chicken or beef with soy-based substitutes. Vegetarian versions of boneless wings, chicken strips, spicy Thai chicken pizzas, and burgers are all available.

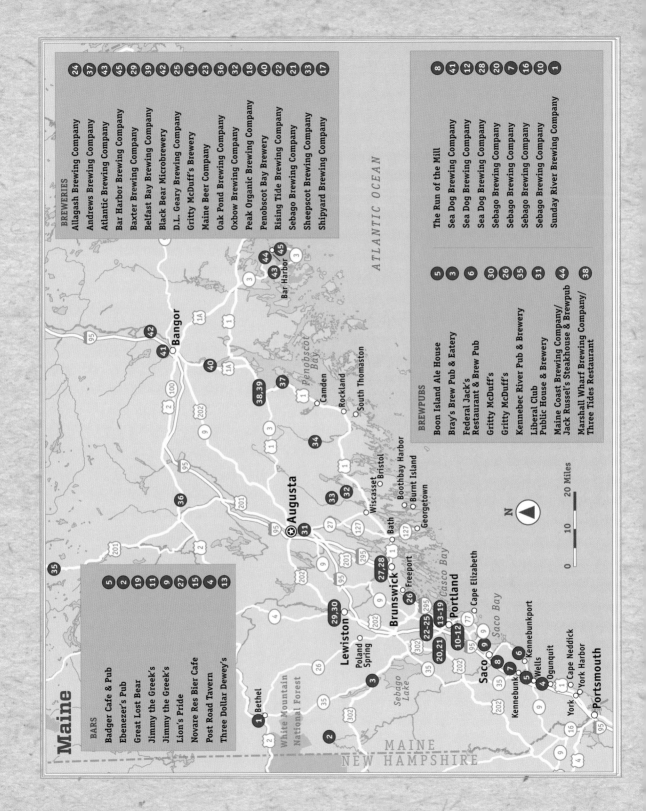

Maine

BARS

5 Badger Cafe & Pub
2 Ebenezer's Pub
19 Great Lost Bear
11 Jimmy the Greek's
9 Jimmy the Greek's
27 Lion's Pride
15 Novare Res Bier Cafe
4 Post Road Tavern
13 Three Dollar Dewey's

BREWERIES

24 Allagash Brewing Company
37 Andrews Brewing Company
43 Atlantic Brewing Company
45 Bar Harbor Brewing Company
29 Baxter Brewing Company
39 Belfast Bay Brewing Company
42 Black Bear Microbrewery
25 D.L. Geary Brewing Company
14 Gritty McDuff's Brewery
23 Maine Beer Company
36 Oak Pond Brewing Company
32 Oxbow Brewing Company
18 Peak Organic Brewing Company
40 Penobscot Bay Brewery
22 Rising Tide Brewing Company
21 Sebago Brewing Company
33 Sheepscot Brewing Company
17 Shipyard Brewing Company

8 The Run of the Mill
41 Sea Dog Brewing Company
12 Sea Dog Brewing Company
28 Sea Dog Brewing Company
20 Sebago Brewing Company
7 Sebago Brewing Company
16 Sebago Brewing Company
10 Sebago Brewing Company
1 Sunday River Brewing Company

BREWPUBS

5 Boon Island Ale House
3 Bray's Brew Pub & Eatery
6 Federal Jack's Restaurant & Brew Pub
30 Gritty McDuff's
26 Gritty McDuff's
35 Kennebec River Pub & Brewery
31 Liberal Club Public House & Brewery
44 Maine Coast Brewing Company/ Jack Russel's Steakhouse & Brewpub
38 Marshall Wharf Brewing Company/ Three Tides Restaurant

ATLANTIC OCEAN

Bangor
Augusta
Lewiston
Brunswick
Portland
Saco
Bethel
Bristol
Wiscasset
Boothbay Harbor
Burnt Island
Georgetown
Bath
Freeport
Poland Spring
Camden
Rockland
South Thomaston
Bar Harbor
Penobscot Bay
Casco Bay
Saco Bay
Sebago Lake
Cape Elizabeth
Kennebunkport
Kennebunk
Wells
Ogunquit
York
York Harbor
Cape Neddick
Portsmouth

White Mountain National Forest

MAINE
NEW HAMPSHIRE

N

0   10   20 Miles

Maine

Maine people with their ol' Yankee ways know what they like—they like Maine potatoes, they like Maine lobster, and they like Maine-brewed beer. Luckily for them, the beer they brew is quite fantastic.

Maine boasts numerous breweries inspired by those in Old England—Geary's Brewing Company, Gritty McDuff's Brewing Company, and Shipyard Brewing Company (all based in Portland) all brew traditional English-style ales, on traditional English-brewing systems.

But not that far from them you have the Allagash Brewing Company, a brewery that specializes in Belgian-inspired brew. And in Lewiston, you have the first brewery, Baxter Brewing Company, that exclusively packages its beers in cans. And the Marshall Wharf Brewing Company is one of the best brewpubs in New England, even though they are not the most well-known one.

Maine has remained one of the brewing hotspots on the east coast.

Breweries

ALLAGASH BREWING COMPANY

50 Industrial Way, Portland, ME; (207) 878-5385; www.allagash.com
Founded: 1995 **Founder:** Rob Tod **Brewers:** Rob Tod, Jason Perkins **Flagship Beer:**
Allagash White **Year-round Beers:** Black, Curieux, Dubbel, Four, Tripel **Seasonals/**
Special Releases: No seasonal beers. Special releases include Confluence Ale, Eleventh
Anniversary, Interlude, Musette, Odyssey, and Tenth Anniversary, as well as the Tribute
Series—Fluxus, Hugh Malone, Victor Ale, Victoria Ale. Other special releases include
the Coolship beers **Tours:** Mon through Fri, 11 a.m., 1 p.m., and 3 p.m.; Sat 1 p.m. and
3 p.m.; free

Can't get to Belgium and try all the wonderful beers brewed there? Don't worry,
look to Portland, Maine, for your Belgian fix. Allagash Brewing Company, founded
by Rob Tod, produces some of the best Belgian-style beer brewed, not just here in
New England or in the US, but in the whole world. When Tod founded Allagash in
1995, Maine was strictly a place for traditional English-style pale ales, bitters, and
other similar beers. Allagash revolutionized brewing in the state, introducing inter-
estingly complex, flavorful beers.

The **Allagash White** is the brewery's most well-known beer, and it's easy to see
why. It's a Belgian-style witbier, a beer brewed with unmalted wheat, coriander, and
bitter orange peel. If you haven't had one, you're missing out. It's the perfect summertime beer, and a great beer to pair with a lobster or steamed clam dinner. The
Dubbel and **Tripel** are spot on for the styles, and are available in both 12-ounce
and 750 ml bottles. The **Four** is a big, appropriately boozy quad, and the **Curieux**
is simply amazing. Aged in bourbon barrels, the Curieux picks up some amazing
flavors, and is pure bliss.

Allagash's special releases are, well, special. The **Odyssey,** in particular, is a
standout. Odyssey is a dark wheat beer aged for 10 months, some in oak barrels and
the rest in steel barrels. The mix of aging in the two different containers forms a
truly unique beer. The **Tribute Series** is perhaps the best group of special releases
in New England. The **Fluxus** might change every year, but what doesn't change is
the quality. The 2011 Fluxus was French farmhouse style ale, while the 2010 was an
imperial chocolate stout.

Also unique (at least here in the US) are the **Coolship** beers. Allagash has built a
coolship, basically a giant flat pan that is kept outside where the wort (a portion of
the early brewing process) is cooled outside, where it is inoculated with wild yeast.
The next morning, the beer is put in wooden barrels to age for however long the

Curieux

Style: Tripel

ABV: 11 percent

Availability: Rotating

The Curieux, aged in bourbon barrels, is one of the best tripels you can get your hands on. It is an exquisite beer. The bourbon flavors really come out in this beer, both in flavor and aroma, and the body has the traditional Belgian-yeast sweetness. It's also full-bodied and malt forward, with fruity flavors and hints of vanilla from the oak barrels. This is a sipping beer, meant to be savored.

Maine

brewers think the beer needs to be ready. The Coolship beers have yet to be sold but have been poured at special events.

The brewery hosts several tours daily that last approximately 45 minutes. Each starts with a tasting, and then the tour leader will bring the guests through the brewery, explaining the brewing, packaging, and barrel-aging process.

ANDREW'S BREWING COMPANY

373 High St., Lincolnville, ME; (207) 763-3505

Founded: 1992 **Founder:** Andrew Hazer **Brewer:** Andrew Hazer **Flagship Beer:** Andrew's Olde English Ale **Year-round Beers:** Andrew's Northern Brown Ale, St. Nick's Porter **Seasonal:** Summer Golden Ale **Tours:** None

Andrew's Brewing Company cares about brewing beer, and only brewing beer. They don't have a brewery store. They don't have a website (although they can be found on Facebook). They don't even offer tours. But what they do is brew beers, and brew beers well. Andrew's offers three year-round beers and one seasonal. The beers are available only in Maine and a small portion of Vermont.

Andrew's Olde English Ale falls somewhere between an American and English pale ale. The hops are present, but not overwhelming. There is a decent malt presence, but the beer is light. It's one of the lighter pale ales, American or English, out there. The **Andrew's Northern Brown Ale** is a more traditional beer. Very little hop presence, which is perfect for the style. This has a nice caramel aroma that carries on into the taste. There is also a pleasant nuttiness to it, and a slight roasted character. Many porters brewed today actually tend to taste like a lighter stout. Not the **St. Nick's Porter.** This is a porter, through and through. It has a much lighter body than a stout, but it does not have as much coffee flavor, with just a hint of sweetness. There is a slight smoky character in this beer. People who like a bigger porter may be surprised by how light this one is. The only other beer is the **Summer Golden Ale,** Andrew's Brewing Company's only seasonal beer. The beer is an exceptional blonde ale. Malty, bready aroma dominates, and that carries on into the taste. The Summer Golden Ale is actually creamy, which you never find in a blonde ale.

As said above, Andrew's Brewing Company does not offer tours. However, if you're trying to complete the Maine Beer Trail pamphlet, call ahead and brewer Andrew Hazer will sign it for you. The Maine Beer Trail is a way to earn prizes from the Maine Brewers Guild while visiting all of Maine's breweries. Andrew's Brewing Company beers are available in 12-ounce bottles and on draft at several restaurants.

Summer Golden Ale
Style: Blonde Ale
ABV: [Unknown]
Availability: Summer Seasonal
Compared to other styles, blonde ales can be a bit boring—they're beers brewed to be easy drinking and not much else. Andrew's Brewing Company's Summer Golden Ale is not boring. There is much more malt aroma and flavor in this summer beer than any other beer in this style, and it finishes with a little kiss of citrusy hops at the back end. It's a summer beer definitely worth seeking out.

ATLANTIC BREWING COMPANY

15 Knox Rd., Bar Harbor, ME; (207) 288-2337; www.atlanticbrewing.com
Founded: 1991 **Founders:** Doug and Barbara Maffucci **Brewer:** James Taylor **Flagship Beer:** Bar Harbor Real Ale **Year-round Beers:** Blueberry Ale, Coal Porter, Island Ginger **Special Releases:** Brother Adam's Bragget, Scottish Ale, Special Old Bitter, Summer Ale, Manly Man Beer Club Series **Tours:** Available 7 days a week between Memorial Day and Columbus Day at 2 p.m., 3 p.m., and 4 p.m.

Blueberry beer fans should thank the Atlantic Brewing Company. In 1992, they became the first brewery to brew and distribute a blueberry beer. Now, most New England breweries and brewpubs brew their own versions of this New England classic.

Although the oldest, Atlantic Brewing Company's **Blueberry Ale** is still one of the best. It's light and refreshing, with the taste of real blueberries, not the overwhelming sweetness typical of blueberry beers that use concentrate. The other year-round beers are also very good. The **Bar Harbor Real Ale** is actually Atlantic's most popular beer. A traditional English-style brown ale, the Bar Harbor is an easy drinking, smooth, and malty beer—a New England classic. The **Coal Porter** is a solid beer. It has chocolaty and coffee notes, with just a slight roastiness. Despite how dark it is, it is not too heavy. The **Island Ginger** is a wheat beer with a twist—it's brewed with gingerroot. The root gives it a flavor reminiscent of a good ginger ale, except with a buzz-inducing kick.

Braggots are an ancient style of beer rarely brewed today. Atlantic Brewing Company's **Brother Adam's Bragget** is an excellent beer, brewed with more than 2,000 pounds of local honey in the beer. This is a sipping beer, coming in at a hefty 11.8 percent alcohol by volume. The honey gives it a pleasant sweetness, and helps counteract the hotness of the alcohol.

The **Scottish Ale** is a traditional, malty version of the style, while the **Special Old Bitter** is a hoppy, English-style bitter. The **Summer Ale** is a blonde ale, which is an easy-drinking, light, summery style of beer.

Atlantic Brewing Company also brews a special line of more complex, higher alcohol beers, called the **Manly Man Beer Club.** The Manly Man Beer Club beers include the **Blackstrapped Molasses** (a brown ale brewed with molasses), the **El Hefe** (a wheat wine), and the **Sea Smoke** (an English-style barleywine). Unlike the rest of the Atlantic beers (except for the Brother Adam's), all of the Manly Man beers come in 22-ounce bottles instead of 12-ounce bottles.

The Atlantic Brewing Company is located in beautiful Bar Harbor, a popular summer destination. If in Bar Harbor, it is definitely worth stopping in at the brewery. Not only are tours available all summer, they have an on-site restaurant that serves barbecue. Atlantic Brewing Company also makes its own sodas, so kids can enjoy something locally made on site while mom and dad enjoy an adult beverage.

Maine

Brother Adam's Bragget
Style: Braggot
ABV: 11.8 percent
Availability: Year-round

The Brother Adam's Bragget isn't for everyone because it doesn't taste or drink like your average beer. This beer is similar to a barleywine, but with the addition of tons of honey, which adds body, sweetness, and alcohol. It has some toffee-like flavors, and hints of sugary sweetness. This is a thick beer—even if you wanted to down one glass, it would be hard to. For the craft beer-inclined, this is a brew to be experienced at least once.

Make sure to stop in the guest shop before leaving. Not only do they sell all of their beers, sodas, and brewery-made mustards, they also sell other local food products. They also sell their own line of wines, the **Bar Harbor Cellars Farm Winery,** which the brewery founded in 2004.

BAR HARBOR BREWING COMPANY

8 Mt. Desert St., Bar Harbor, ME; (207) 288-4592; www.barharborbrewing.com
Founded: 1990 **Founders:** Tod and Suzi Foster **Brewer:** James Taylor **Flagship Beer:** Thunder Hole Ale **Year-round Beers:** Cadillac Mountain Stout, Harbor Lighthouse Ale, True Blue Blueberry Ale **Seasonals/Special Releases:** None **Tours:** Mid-May through Columbus Day, daily, 10 a.m. to 7 p.m.

The Bar Harbor Brewing Company was a family owned brewery until 2009, when fellow Bar Harbor brewery Atlantic Brewing Company purchased it. The purchase meant the consolidation of the breweries into one brewing location, although the Bar Harbor Brewing Company remains open at 8 Mt. Desert St., where there is a tasting room, brewery store, and the pilot brewery.

What didn't change was the four year-round beers that Bar Harbor brews.

Atlantic kept the recipes, and the beers remain as good as they have always been. The **Thunder Hole Ale,** Bar Harbor's first beer and its flagship, is a classic English-style brown ale. At 4.7 percent alcohol, you can afford to have a few of these beers, and with how it tastes, you'll definitely want more than one. This brown ale has flavors of toffee and a hint of molasses. The **Cadillac Mountain Stout** is simply one of the best stouts brewed in New England, and maybe the best that is less than 8 percent alcohol by volume. This American stout is worth seeking out. Buy a bomber if you find one, because you will want more if you only buy a 12-ounce bottle. The **Harbor Lighthouse Ale** fits the definition of a session beer. A session beer should be low in alcohol (4 percent alcohol by volume or less), but full-flavored. It's called a session beer because you can have a few in one session without getting drunk. The Harbor Lighthouse Ale is 3.2 percent alcohol by volume, but it's not your average light beer—it's an English dark mild ale that packs a whole lot of flavor. Bar Harbor's only other beer is the **True Blue Blueberry Ale.** If you're a fan of a blueberry beer, you will like this beer—it's a little more mellow than some other berry-filled ales.

The brewery is open from mid-March through Columbus Day. There you can go to the tasting room and try the beers before deciding which ones you want to bring home. You can also go inside the brewery, walk around, and take a look at the brewing equipment. The brewery store sells beer to go, as well as local food and wine. There are also shirts, hats, and glasses available.

Beer Lover's Pick

Cadillac Mountain Stout
Style: American Stout
ABV: 6.7 percent
Availability: Year-round
The Cadillac Mountain Stout is a classical version of an American stout. This beer has a lot going on—chocolate and coffee notes in the aroma, blended with some earthy smells. This is an amazingly smooth and creamy beer. There's a pleasant sweetness in the flavor, balancing out the roastiness. Seek this out.

BAXTER BREWING COMPANY

130 Mill St., Lewiston, ME; (207) 333-6769; www.baxterbrewing.com
Founded: 2010 **Founder:** H. Luke Livingston **Brewer:** Michael LaCharite **Flagship Beer:**
Pamola Xtra Pale Ale **Year-round Beers:** Stowaway IPA, Amber Road **Seasonals/Special
Releases:** None **Tours:** Thurs through Sun at noon, 2 p.m., 4 p.m.

The Baxter Brewing Company has found itself a niche in the competitive beer market of Maine—they're the first brewery to can all of their beers. This may not seem like a big deal. Why would having a beer in a can make that much of a difference that people would buy it over a bottled beer? The answer is easy: There are a lot of outdoor recreation activities in Maine. Want to go on a hike and have a beer after you reach your destination? Cans are lighter and take up less space than a bottle in your backpack, and will not shatter if you drop your bag. That goes for boating, too. Do you really want to clean up glass while on a lake or the ocean? And a lot of places, such as campgrounds, do not allow bottles. It is also more environmentally friendly than glass bottles. Of course, it wouldn't matter if the beer wasn't any good. But Baxter Brewing Company's beer is quite good, and it would still be worth buying even if they were in bottles.

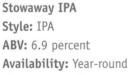

Beer Lover's Pick

Stowaway IPA
Style: IPA
ABV: 6.9 percent
Availability: Year-round
The Stowaway IPA is a west coast IPA without being a huge, high-alcohol beer. This beer is a balanced version of the west coast IPA, with plenty of up-front hops that continue all the way to a relatively dry finish. The malt backbone is present, and you can taste a little sweetness. It is a good, solid IPA that has enough hops to satisfy hopheads and enough balance that those who don't want a tongue scorching beer will like it.

Baxter offers a handful of beers. The first is the **Pamola Xtra Pale Ale.** This 4.9 percent alcohol by volume beer is a light, refreshing pale ale, with just enough of a hop bite to let you know this is a pale ale. It's a crisp, dry-drinking beer. According to a local Native American legend, Pamola is a flying moose with eagle wings that is the god of thunder; no wonder Baxter includes the creature in its brewery logo.

The **Stowaway IPA** is a west coast–style IPA. It's hop forward, with a mix of grapefruit, citrus, and pine aromas that carry into the flavor. At 6.9 percent ABV, it does not cross into the double IPA and remains extremely drinkable. The **Amber Road** is a malty, 5.3 percent ABV amber ale, with a nice little hop bite. Owner H. Luke Livingston, a former beer bloggeer, said he hoped to introduce seasonal beers in 2012 or 2013.

If you're in the Lewiston area, you'll want to stop in at Baxter Brewing to take the tour, offered Thurs through Sun. Their store is also one of the better stocked brewery stores around. They have a lot of the usual items, such as T-shirts and glasses. But, they also have embroidered polo shirts and beanie-style winter hats. The best thing—they all sport Pamola the flying moose. Other items for sale include golf balls, Ultimate Frisbees, Stowaway IPA Body Soap, ice six-pack coolers, temporary tattoos, floating key chains, and spicy mustard made with Pamola Xtra Pale Ale.

BELFAST BAY BREWING COMPANY
100 Searsport Rd., Belfast, ME; (207) 338-2662; http://belfastbaybrewing.com
Founded: 1996 **Founder:** Pat Mullen **Brewer:** Contract brewed by Shipyard Brewing Company **Flagship Beer:** Lobster Ale **Year-round Beers:** Mack Point IPA, McGovern's Oatmeal Stout **Seasonals/Special Releases:** None **Tours:** None

Maine is known for its Maine lobsters—it's hard to find a restaurant that doesn't have steamed lobster, or lobster rolls, or a number of other lobster dishes. So it makes sense that a brewery would come up with a lobster beer. Don't worry, though. Belfast Bay Brewing Company's Lobster Ale doesn't have any lobster in it at all. Rather, it is a beer brewed to go with lobster.

Belfast Bay Brewing Company has gone through a lot of changes throughout the years. It started in 1996 as a brewpub. Now the brewpub is closed, but the beers are being contracted at Shipyard Brewing Company and are available throughout New England. They only sell three beers: the Lobster Ale, the Mack Point IPA, and McGovern's Oatmeal Stout.

The **Lobster Ale** is far and away the most popular and easiest of the three beers to find. It's an amber/red ale that's all about the malt. It is sweet, with just a hint of hops. When pairing beer with a lobster, usually some sort of wheat ale,

Lobster Ale
Style: Amber/Red Ale
ABV: 5 percent
Availability: Year-round

Sure, red ales might not be the most exciting beers in the world, but this is a really well-made one. There is just a hint of hops, and the caramel and toffee flavors work nicely in this beer. It's also relatively light-bodied, which is perfect for a year-round beer.

a Belgian-style witbier, or a German-style hefeweizen, seems like the best choice. However, the Lobster Ale really does pair well with a lobster. The malty sweetness grabs hold of the succulent lobster meat's flavor and works in harmony. And although this is a malty beer, it is not an overly heavy beer, so it does not overwhelm the taste of the lobster. The **Mack Point IPA** is a decent IPA that's appropriately hoppy, decently balanced, and easy to drink. If you find it on tap at a bar in Maine, grab a pint and it will not disappoint you. The **McGovern's Oatmeal Stout** is a great example of the style. It's more chocolaty than most oatmeal stouts, smooth, and creamy, while being full-bodied. It's the perfect beer to pair with your dessert after you finish your lobster (and Lobster Ale).

BLACK BEAR MICROBREWERY

19 Mill St., Suite 4, Orono, ME; (207) 949-2880; www.blackbearmicrobrew.com
Founded: 2008 **Founder:** Tim Gallon **Brewer:** Tim Gallon **Flagship Beer:** Gearhead Ale **Year-round Beers:** Drop Dead Red Ale, Pail Ale, Pirate Bear Ale **Seasonals/Special Releases:** Bad Omen IPA, Black Bear Stout, Blueberry Ale, Liquid Sunshine Ale, Patriot Brown Ale, Tree Tugger Barleywine, Voodoo Porter **Tours:** By appointment only

Tim Gallon likes to talk beer. So, if you happen to be in Orono, Maine, you should stop at his Black Bear Brewery, where he will lead you through a tour of his small brewery, telling you about his beers and the history of Black Bear.

The passion Gallon has for beer really comes out in his product. The brewery, which started brewing in 2008, features four year-round and several seasonal and rotating beers. The year-round beers are the Gearhead, Drop Dead Red, Pail Ale, and the Pirate Bear Ale. The **Gearhead Ale** is a malty, easy-drinking dark amber ale, while the **Drop Dead Red** is another malty beer, which is what you want in a red ale. The **Pail Ale** has the hops that the other two beers are missing. It has a nice hop bite for a pale ale. The **Pirate Bear Ale** is another hoppy pale ale.

Black Bear brews two winter seasonals and two summer seasonals. The winter seasonals are the Stout and the Voodoo Porter. The **Stout** is a smooth, creamy, and slightly bitter (from the roasted malts, not from the hops) stout. The **Voodoo Porter** is robust, well-balanced, and a great cold night beer. The summer seasonals are the Blueberry Ale and Liquid Sunshine. Most New England breweries brew a blueberry

Beer Lover's Pick

Black Bear Stout
Style: American Stout
ABV: 6.3 percent
Availability: Winter
The Black Bear Stout falls somewhere between a traditional stout and an imperial stout. It comes in at a solid 6.3 percent alcohol by volume. The beer has big roasty flavors, with espresso-like coffee flavors, mixed well with cocoa. The beer has a nice head, and it is full-bodied and creamy. It is a really easy-drinking beer, and perfect for a cold Maine night.

Maine

beer, and the **Blueberry Ale** is another solid entry into a long line of such beers. The **Liquid Sunshine** is a Bavarian-style hefeweizen. It has the traditional clove-like flavors, and little lemon notes. The flavors come directly from the yeast, which Gallon brought over from Germany to use in this beer.

Other beers include the Bad Omen IPA and the Patriot Brown Ale, two beers that have some similarities—hops. The **Bad Omen IPA** is brewed with hopheads in mind. It's definitely leaning toward west coast style, and it is a strong beer, coming in at more than 7 percent alcohol by volume. It's also flirting with being a black IPA—it's an extremely dark IPA, which gives it some chocolaty notes from the malts. The **Patriot Brown Ale** is a hoppier than the usual brown ale. The combination of the dark and caramel malts used in a brown ale works nicely with the hops, making it a pleasantly unusual interpretation of the style. Black Bear also brews an annual anniversary beer that comes out in October.

Tours are available as long as Gallon and his assistant have time for them. The tour also includes a tasting, which is always a good thing. In the brewery store, you can buy growlers of any of the beers they have available.

D.L. GEARY BREWING COMPANY
38 Evergreen Dr., Portland, ME; (207) 878-2337; www.gearybrewing.com
Founded: 1986 **Founders:** David and Karen Geary **Brewer:** David Geary **Flagship Beer:** Hampshire Special Ale **Year-round Beers:** Imperial IPA, London Porter, Pale Ale, Wee Heavy **Seasonals/Special Releases:** Autumn Ale, Summer Ale, Winter Ale **Tours:** By appointment

The D.L. Geary Brewing Company is one of the oldest craft breweries in all of New England, and helped to form the early brewing tradition in the region. David and Karen Geary actually incorporated the brewery in 1983, when there were only 13 other microbreweries in the country. But the brewery did not distribute its first beer until 1986, after David Geary went to Scotland and England to learn and research the art of brewing in those two countries.

Geary was a good learner. The D.L. Geary Brewing Company's beers reflect what Geary learned, with high quality English- and Scottish-style ales throughout their portfolio. Geary's first beer was the **Pale Ale,** and it is still one of the best English-style pale ales being brewed today. It makes use of traditional English-style hops to give it a mild, earthy flavor, with a great malt body. The **Hampshire Special Ale** is a stronger beer, at 7 percent alcohol by volume. It's an English strong ale, and it has a big malty body, with great balance from the earthy hop flavors. The **Imperial IPA** is Geary's newest beer, and its most American. It is also the brewery's strongest beer

Wee Heavy
Style: Scottish Ale
ABV: 8 percent
Availability: Year-round

Hoppy beers are awesome, but sometimes a big malty beer is called for. This Wee Heavy is a wonderfully malty beer, sweet and full-bodied. You can taste the alcohol and flavors of molasses, and there's a woody character even though it is not barrel aged. There are also hints of chocolate. Do not expect to taste any hops—this is all about the malts.

Maine

at 8.2 percent ABV. It definitely uses American hops, and you get the citrusy aroma and flavors from them. The caramel malt flavors works well in this beer. The **London Porter** is a classic English-style porter, and the **Wee Heavy** is a perfect example of the Scottish-style ale—robust and malty.

Geary also does a good job with their seasonals beers. The **Autumn Ale** is an excellent nut brown ale, a perfect fall style. The **Winter Ale** is an English-style IPA, much milder than the American version of the style. The **Summer Ale** is closest to a German-style kolsch beer. It is actually a little stronger in alcohol than most summer beers at 6 percent ABV, and a nice change to the numerous bland summer beers being brewed today.

Tours are typically available daily in the afternoon, but by appointment only. Make sure to call ahead before going, because if it is a busy brewing day, tours will not be available. The tour is led by one of the brewery employees, and it ends with a tasting of all the beers they currently have available.

GRITTY MCDUFF'S BREWERY

396 Fore St., Portland, ME; (207) 772-BREW; www.grittys.com
Founded: 1988 **Founders:** Richard Pfeffer, Ed Stebbins **Brewer:** Ed Stebbins **Flagship Beer:** Original Pub Style **Year-round Beers:** Best Bitter, Black Fly Stout, Red Claws Ale **Seasonals/Special Releases:** Christmas Ale, Halloween Ale, Scottish Ale, Vacationland Summer Ale, 21 IPA **Tours:** None

The Gritty McDuff's Brewery is one of the old school New England breweries that brews traditional English-style ales, but still flourishes in the modern beer world. The reason is easy to figure out—Gritty McDuff's brews good beer and people like to drink good beer.

Gritty McDuff's is a combination brewpub/brewery. Many of their beers are bottled and distributed throughout New England. In addition to the original brewpub in Portland (the above address), they also have brewpubs in Freeport and Auburn, Maine. Most of Gritty's bottled beers are actually brewed at the Shipyard Brewing Company, also in Portland. However, they do brew and bottle their own 22-ounce bombers at their Freeport brewery. They also brew all of their own beers on-site at all three brewpubs.

The beers, for the most part, are straight-up English style. Gritty's flagship is the **Original Pub Style,** a classic English pale ale with a nice hop presence that's extremely easy to drink. The **Best Bitter** is a wonderful English-style bitter, perfect for an afternoon drinking session with friends. The **Black Fly Stout** is an Irish dry stout. If your only experience with an Irish stout is Guinness, you will be surprised by how different this beer is. It is creamy and roasty and tasty. The **Red Claws Ale** is a newer beer brewed in honor of the local NBA Developmental League team that started in Maine. Gritty McDuff's also brews several seasonals worth trying. The **Christmas Ale** and the **Halloween Ale** are both extra special bitters. Although they are both the same style, these are not the same beer, so seek them both out to see how one brewery can make two of the same style beers taste so different. The **Scottish Ale** is a robust, malty beer, sweet with very little noticeable hops. The **Vacationland Summer Ale** is one of the few non-British beers brewed by Gritty McDuff's. It is a blonde ale, fine for the style—light and easy drinking. The other non-British beer is the **21 IPA,** an American-style IPA originally brewed for Gritty's twenty-first anniversary.

If you are in Portland, the Gritty McDuff's brewpub is a can't miss. They have all their beers on tap, and several on cask, which is a treat. It's also great place to grab lunch; the burgers are excellent and the sweet potato fries are otherworldly.

Beer Lover's Pick

Halloween Ale
Style: Extra Special Bitter
ABV: 6 percent
Availability: Fall Seasonal
This is basically a stronger and more flavorful version of Gritty's Best Bitter. This extra special bitter is an excellent example of the style. It has a great malt body, with a sharp hop balance and great carbonation that dances on your tongue. There are flavors of dark fruits, a little alcohol, and even some grassy, herbal hops in this beer. Definitely a nice change of pace from an Oktoberfest or pumpkin beer for a fall seasonal.

Maine

MAINE BEER COMPANY
1 Industrial Way, Unit 3, Portland, ME; (207) 221-5711; www.mainebeercompany.com
Founded: 2009 **Founders:** Daniel and David Kleban **Brewer:** Daniel Kleban **Flagship Beer:** Peeper Ale **Year-round Beers:** Lunch IPA, Mean Old Tom Stout, Zoe Ale **Seasonals/ Special Releases:** None **Tours:** Fri, 2 p.m.; free

The Maine Beer Company's motto is "Do What's Right," and they take that motto seriously—there is a lot right with this tiny brewery's beers. MBC's beers are gaining notice very quickly and for good reason—they're fantastic. The **Peeper Ale,** which originally started as a spring-only beer but was so popular the Kleban brothers had to make it year-round, is a must-buy beer. The ale falls somewhere between a pale ale and an IPA, but what sets it apart is the aroma. You will never find a hoppy beer that smells this good. One whiff and you want to drink this beer. And, oh, is it good, so refreshing and flavorful. **Lunch IPA** is the best India pale ale brewed in New England, and stands up to any IPA brewed anywhere in the country, including the land of hoppy beers, the west coast. Fruity and floral hop aromas carry on into the

Peeper Ale
Style: Pale Ale
ABV: 5.5 percent
Availability: Year-round
A pale ale should not be as exciting as Peeper Ale. From the first whiff of the beer in your glass, you'll want to down it immediately, but stop. This is a beer that should be savored. It smells of citrus and grass from the hops. The flavor is fabulous as well, with a light graininess, as well as the ever-present hops.

taste, perfectly balanced with the sweetness from the malts to form a world-class beer. **Zoe** is an amber ale, but not the typical malty amber ale. Sure, it still has the dark malts to provide caramel sweetness, but this is hopped like an IPA. The mix of an amber ale and IPA form a beer that hopheads will enjoy. Maine Beer Company's only other beer is the **Mean Old Tom Stout,** and it's the only beer that doesn't feature hops as a dominant ingredient. The use of dark roasted malts provides this beer with flavors of chocolate and coffee—a perfect after-dinner beer.

Maine Beer Company packages of all of its beers in 500 ml, or half-liter, bottles, which is a popular size in Europe, but not in the US. Sometimes two 12-ounce bottles are not enough, but three are too many. The half-liter solves that problem—two beers, you're done, and you didn't drink too much.

Maine Beer Company does more than brew good beer; they care about the environment. They are a member of 1% for the Planet, a group of businesses that commit financially to help the planet. They donate 1 percent of all sales to environmental nonprofit organizations. Maine Brewing Company is 100 percent wind powered, and all the leftover yeast, grains, and grain bags are donated to local farmers.

Free tours are also offered at the small brewery on Friday at 2 p.m. They are led by one of the Kleban brothers and feature beer samples.

OAK POND BREWING COMPANY

101 Oak Pond Rd., Skowhegan, Maine; (207) 474-3233; www.oakpondbrewery.com
Founded: 1996 **Founders:** Trevor and Pat Lawton **Brewer:** Don Chandler **Flagship Beer:**
Dooryard Ale **Year-round Beers:** Oktoberfest Lager, Nut Brown Ale, Somerset Lager,
White Fox Ale **Seasonals:** Laughing Loon Lager, Storyteller Doppelbock **Tours:** Mon
through Fri, 3 to 5:30 p.m.; Sat, 12:30 to 5:30 p.m.; free

The Oak Pond Brewing Company is housed in a former chicken barn and has a small staff, consisting of owners Don Chandler (brewer) and his wife, Nancy Chandler. But, despite the modest location and staff, the Oak Pond Brewing Company brews several well-done beers. They are also a standout brewer of lagers, perhaps the best at brewing lagers in Maine.

Oak Pond offers five year-round beers: three ales and two lagers. They also offer two seasonals, both lagers. The flagship beer is the **Dooryard Ale.** This is an American pale ale, but on the lighter side for the style. The hops are present, and the malts provide some balance. What makes this lighter than most pale ales is the use of a little wheat malt to make the body lighter. This is almost like a summer pale ale, when you want a quick, refreshing beer after spending the day mowing the lawn. The **Nut Brown Ale** is a spot-on take on the popular British and New England style. A lively head and hints of chocolate and caramel from the roasted malts make this a pleasure to drink. The **White Fox Ale** is a solid IPA, reminiscent of the

Beer Lover's Pick

Laughing Loon Lager
Style: Munich Dunkel Lager
ABV: 6 percent
Availability: Summer Seasonal
A good Munich dunkel lager is a treat. Even though this is a dark beer, it still fits in as a summer seasonal because it is easy drinking and extremely refreshing. The roasted malts give this beer a slight chocolaty flavor, complemented by some doughy, yeasty taste. The hops provide balance and not much else, exactly what you want for the style.

old-school New England IPA style before brewers started adopting the west coast, hop-forward version of the style. If you are a fan of IPAs on the mellow side, this is the one for you. Oak Pond may be the only brewery that has an **Oktoberfest Lager** as a year-round style, which is fantastic. There is always room for more good lagers, and this is just that. A lot of caramel, sweet, and bready flavors from the malts, with just a hint of hops, make this a perfect beer to enjoy in January, July, or October. The **Somerset Lager** is a traditional German-style pilsner.

The seasonals are both tasty. The **Storyteller Doppelbock** is a traditional German-style beer. It takes 10 weeks of aging for this beer to be ready, but it is worth it. This is a malt bomb of a beer, and the 6 percent alcohol by volume is hidden well. The **Laughing Loon Lager** is an excellent Munich dunkel lager.

Oak Pond Brewing Company hosts tours throughout the week. There is no set time. If they are open and not too busy brewing, one of the employees will give you the tour. The tour itself is heavy on brewing education, with a thorough explanation of the brewing process, and the role each ingredient—hops, malts, water, and yeast—plays in the beer. It is concluded with a tasting of the five year-round beers and whichever seasonal is on tap. The tasting is the perfect way to determine which beer to bring home to drink. You can buy growlers of the beer to go at the brewery. Oak Pond Brewing Company beers are also available in bombers and kegs, and are sold at area stores.

OXBOW BREWING COMPANY
274 Jones Woods Rd., Newcastle, ME; (207) 315-5962; www.oxbowbeer.com
Founded: 2010 **Founders:** Tim Adams, Geoff Marshland **Brewer:** Tim Adams **Flagship Beer:** Farmhouse Pale Ale **Year-round Beer:** None **Seasonal/Special Releases:** Freestyle Series, Oktoberfest, Saison Noel **Tours:** Fri, 2 to 6 p.m.

The Oxbow Brewing Company calls itself an American farmhouse brewery, and not just because of their location on an 18-acre farm. They brew saisons, which are known as farmhouse beers. Saisons can be beautifully brewed beers. If done right, these are dry, go fantastically with many foods, and are light tasting, even if the alcohol is high. They have a quality that beer lovers enjoy, and they seem to be one of the styles that wine drinkers adopt as their own.

Oxbow only does a few beers, but they are fabulous American takes on the classic Belgian style. The flagship beer, the **Farmhouse Pale Ale,** is a combination of a saison and a pale ale. It looks like a saison, golden and unfiltered, and it has the typical yeasty flavors found in a good saison. It also has the hops and citrusy aromas you do not usually find in a saison. The **Oxtoberfest** is not the typical

Farmhouse Pale Ale
Style: Saison
ABV: 6 percent
Availability: Year-round
Saisons are typically dry, often complex beers, but lightly hopped. A west coast IPA can be as hoppy as some mild IPAs. What do you get when you blend the two styles? Oxbow's Farmhouse Pale Ale. This is an extremely interesting beer. The saison and pale ale characteristics actually work together instead of clashing. This would be a great beer to pair with many different foods, particularly duck or even a spicy chicken dish.

Maine

fall Oktoberfest lager. This is another saison, but completely different than the Farmhouse Pale Ale. This is more malty and creamy, but still retains its dryness. The use of smooth, subtle German hops gives this an interesting flavor not usually associated with saisons. The **Saison Noel** is a heftier saison brewed to help keep people warm during the cold Maine winters.

Oxbow also brews several beers as part of the Freestyle Series. These beers allow the brewers to stretch their creativity and brew beers not often found, such as a smoked chocolate stout and imperial saison. These are planned as one-time releases, but they could return in the future on a limited basis.

Oxbow beers are available only on draft at a few restaurants and bars throughout Maine. The beers are also available at the brewery on Friday from 2 to 6 p.m. in half-gallon jugs. While at the brewery, people get a chance to sample the beer and hear the brewing process explained by the founders Tim Adams and Geoff Marshland. Oxbow is also aging several of its beers in oak barrels, and plans on offering some of those beers in 750 ml corked and caged bottles.

PEAK ORGANIC BREWING COMPANY

110 Marginal Way, #802, Portland, ME; (207) 586-5586; www.peakbrewing.com
Founded: 2006 **Founder:** John Cadoux **Brewer:** John Cadoux and contract brewing
Flagship Beer: Pale Ale **Year-round Beer:** Amber Ale, Espresso Amber Ale, Hop Noir, IPA, Nut Brown Ale, Pomegranate Wheat Ale **Seasonals/Special Releases:** Fall Summit Ale, King Crimson, Maple Collaboration, Simcoe Spring, Summer Session, Winter Session, Local Series **Tours:** None

The organic food industry is exploding because more and more people care about how their food is treated before they put it in their bodies. But there are not a lot of options when it comes to organic beers. The Peak Organic Brewing Company gives those who care about organics an excellent option of fantastic beer.

The **Peak IPA** is a wonderfully hopped beer. At 7.2 percent alcohol by volume, there are more than enough hops to balance the combination of piney and citrusy hops. This is an underrated IPA, and any hophead should make sure to give this one a try. The **Amber Ale** is a really solid amber with toasty flavors. The **Espresso Amber** is that rare coffee beer that is not a stout or porter. Strong flavors of espresso dominate this beer, but it is lighter than many coffee beers so it does not sit heavy in the stomach. The **Nut Brown Ale** is excellent. The **Pale Ale,** Peak's flagship beer, has big hop flavor when you first take a sip, but then mellows into a slight sweetness. The

Beer Lover's Pick

Nut Brown Ale
Style: Brown Ale
ABV: 4.7 percent
Availability: Year-Round
Peak Organic's Brown Ale is a treat of a beer. Although it's hard to mess up a brown ale, it's even harder to make an exceptional one like this. There are flavors of caramel and chocolate, and the use of German Hallertau hops, which are more earthy than fruity, helps bring out the nuttiness in this beer. Have this with a grilled piece of beef and you will be so happy.

Pomegranate Wheat Ale is not as sweet as a lot of fruit beers, and the pomegranate is subtle, rather than dominating. The **Hop Noir** is a black IPA and one of Peak Organic's biggest beers at 8.2 percent alcohol by volume. The huge amounts of hops used in this beer and the chocolate malts blend fabulously.

The seasonals include four single-hop beers. Each beer is different, but all share the similarity of only one hop being used in each beer, meant to showcase the different hops. Single-hop beers are interesting, because you get to see exactly what flavor each hop adds to a beer. The four single-hop beers are the **Fall Summit Ale** (Summit hops), **Simcoe Spring** (Simcoe hops), **Summer Session** (Amarillo hops), and **Winter Session Ale** (Citra hops).

Special release beers include **King Crimson,** a true imperial red. Many imperial reds taste like a slightly maltier imperial IPA, but this really tastes like a big red ale—huge caramel and toffee-like malt flavors—with a lot of hops added. The **Maple Collaboration** is not a collaboration with another brewery, but with local businesses. Maine oats and fresh Maine maple are used in the ingredients. The **Local Series** also takes advantage of using local ingredients. There are four beers in the series, and each one is brewed with ingredients specifically from one state (Maine, Massachusetts, New Hampshire, and Vermont) to highlight the local products in each state.

PENOBSCOT BAY BREWERY

279 South Main St., Winterport, ME; (207) 223-4500; www.winterportwinery.com
Founded: 2009 **Founder:** Mike Anderson **Brewer:** Mike Anderson **Flagship Beer:** Whig Street Blonde Ale **Year-round Beers:** Half Moon Stout, Humble B, Meadow Road Wheat, Old Factory Whistle **Seasonals/Special Releases:** Red Flannel Ale, Wildfire **Tours:** Mar through Apr, Fri and Sat, 11 a.m. to 5 p.m.; May through Dec, Tues through Sat, 11 a.m. to 5 p.m. Closed Jan and Feb.

The Penobscot Bay Brewery is an arm of the Winterport Winery, a popular Maine winery. Beer and wine deserve equal billing, and at the Winterport Winery and Penobscot Bay Brewery, they get it.

The brewery brews five year-round beers, the Old Factory Whistle, the Whig Street Blonde Ale, the Meadow Road Wheat, the Half Moon Stout, and Humble B. The **Old Factory Whistle** is a Scottish ale, a full-bodied, malty style of beer, which is perfect for cold Maine nights. The **Whig Street Blonde Ale** is just what the name says, a blonde ale, light and refreshing, good for a summertime day of drinking on the porch. The **Meadow Road Wheat** is brewed like a traditional German-style beer, unfiltered. So, when you pour this beer, do not be concerned if you see something floating in the beer. It is yeast, and it is supposed to be there. The **Half Moon Stout**

The Old Factory Whistle

Style: Scottish Ale

ABV: 6.2 percent

Availability: Year-round

Scottish ales are the perfect beer for a cold New England winter. They are hefty, malty brews that will stick to your bones and warm you up. The Old Factory Whistle is spot on

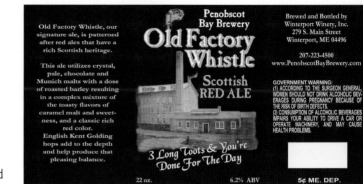

for the style. It is full-bodied, and it has a nice, warming alcohol feel to it. This is a sweet beer, with a hint of burnt sugar. It feels thick in your mouth, but it is not such a high-alcohol beer that you couldn't afford to have more than one.

is based on a historic porter recipe, or a stout porter. Stouts were originally called stout porters, and the porter portion of the name dropped off over the years. The **Humble B** is Penobscot's newest beer. It is a lager brewed with local Winterport honey and ginger. Those two flavors combine to form an easy-drinking beer.

The Penobscot Bay Brewery also brews two seasonals, the Red Flannel Ale and the Wildfire. The **Red Flannel Ale** is a big brown ale brewed for winter. This beer is perfect to drink fresh, or to cellar for the following winter to let it mellow out a bit. The **Wildfire** is a rauchbier, or a German-style smoked beer. Smoked beers may not seem like warm-weather beers, but imagine barbecuing some smoked meat all day, and then pairing it with the Wildfire. The flavors will meld with each other into a beautiful marriage of smoky goodness.

Penobscot Bay Brewery also offers tours, usually led by a brewer, that end with a tasting of the various beers. If you are there, take the time to tour the winery and learn about the differences and similarities of the two beverages. You may be surprised to learn how much they have in common. Beer is also available to go in 22-ounce bombers and growlers.

RISING TIDE BREWING COMPANY

1 Industrial Way, Suite #2, Portland, ME; (207) 370-2337; www.risingtidebrewing.com
Founded: 2010 **Founder:** Nathan Sanborn **Brewer:** Nathan Sanborn **Flagship Beer:**
Atlantis **Year-round Beers:** Daymark, Ishmael, Ursa Minor **Seasonals/Special Releases:**
Polaris **Tour:** Available, call ahead to schedule a tour.

The Rising Tide Brewing Company only brews 90 gallons of beer at a time, but what they do with those 90 gallons is fantastic. Owner/Brewer Nathan Sanborn brews very creative beers, and not one beer in Rising Tide's portfolio is boring. All the beers are twists on traditional styles, and every one of them works.

The flagship beer is **Atlantis,** which is a 5.3 percent alcohol by volume black ale. Although many dark beers are heavy, thick beers, this one is relatively easy to drink with a fair amount of hops giving a passion-fruit flavor and a hint of a applewood smokiness from the smoked malts used. The **Daymark** is an American pale ale with an addition: rye. The rye malts add a spiciness that plays off the fruity hops nicely. Brewing with rye is not easy (it is thick and gums up the brewing equipment), but

Beer Lover's Pick

Daymark
Style: Rye Pale Ale
ABV: 5.1 percent
Availability: Year-Round
A west coast pale ale and rye blended together? That is what Daymark is. A lot of brewers seem to use rye in high alcohol beers, which hides the spiciness associated with rye. Not the Daymark. This is a standard 5.1 percent alcohol by volume pale ale, and the spiciness is in the forefront. The rye does not overwhelm the hops, and vice versa. Good job by Rising Tide.

when it works right, it can make a beer a pleasure to drink. This is one of those beers that works right. The **Ishmael** is a 5.1 percent alcohol by volume German-style altbier. It is copper in color, and thanks to the American hops used in this beer it has some citrusy fruit aromas and flavors. It is quite good. The **Ursa Minor,** named for the constellation, is a dark, black-as-night American stout. What's different about this stout is that Rising Tide uses wheat malt in this beer. The malts create flavors of dark fruits, chocolate, and coffee, but the wheat adds a decidedly wheaty, yeasty flavor not found in many stouts. Another really well-done beer. Rising Tide has also brewed **Polaris,** its only special release beer. The Polaris is the Ursa Minor aged in Jim Beam barrels. You get a lot of booze in the flavor.

All of Rising Tide's beers are available in 22-ounce bombers, but are not easy to find. The beers are in finer liquor stores, as well as on draft in some of the better beer bars in southern Maine. Rising Tide Brewing Company does offer tours, but they request that people call ahead to set up a time because if the employees are too busy, you will be out of luck.

SEBAGO BREWING COMPANY

Production brewery, 48 Sanford Dr., Gorham, ME; Brewpubs located Gorham, Kennebunk, Portland, Scarborough; (207) 856-2537; http://sebagobrewing.com
Founded: 1998 **Founders:** Kai Adams, Brad Monarch, Tim Haines **Brewers:** Kai Adams, Tom Abercrombie **Flagship Beer:** Runabout Red Ale **Year-round Beers:** Boathouse Brown Ale, Frye's Leap India Pale Ale, Lake Trout Stout, Saddleback Ale **Seasonals/Special Releases:** Bass Ackwards Berry Blue Ale, Hefeweizen, Midnight Porter, Slick Nick Winter Ale, Local Harvest Ale, Full Throttle Double IPA, Single Batch Series **Tours:** Mon through Fri, 2 p.m., call ahead; free

Sebago Brewing Company started as a small brewpub in 1998, and now they have taken over the world. Well, not the world, but now Sebago has four brewpubs throughout Maine, and a production brewery that brews and bottles beers for beer lovers throughout New England.

Based in Gorham, Maine, Sebago brews some phenomenal beers, none better than their two IPAs, the Frye's Leap India Pale Ale and the Full Throttle Double IPA. The **Frye's Leap India Pale Ale** is one of the better regular-strength IPAs brewed in New England. It is 6.2 percent alcohol by volume, and is fully packed with hops and caramel malts. The **Full Throttle Double IPA** is a straight-ahead west coast double IPA, packed with juicy hops, with citrusy and piney flavors from the American hops. There are enough malts to balance out this beer, but this is a hop lover's kind of beer. Sebago's flagship beer, the **Runabout Red Ale,** and the **Boathouse Brown Ale** are both solid versions of their respective styles. The **Lake Trout Stout** is an oatmeal

Frye's Leap India Pale Ale
Style: IPA
ABV: 6.2 percent
Availability: Year-round

When introduced in 1998, Sebago's Frye's Leap India Pale Ale was one of the few west coast–style IPAs brewed in New England. All these years later, it still holds up. This is a hop lover's IPA, with strong, fruity hop flavors that are suitably bitter. The use of caramel malts gives it a nice sweetness on the back end of flavor. At 6.2 percent ABV, this is a dangerously drinkable beer.

stout with some extra hops added, and the **Saddleback Ale** is a lighter beer for those with delicate taste buds.

The seasonals are pretty tasty, too. The **Bass Ackwards Berry Blue Ale** is one of the better blueberry beers available. The use of real blueberries instead of flavoring gives it a dryness, instead of the sticky-sweet flavor a lot of blueberry ales have. The **Hefeweizen** is a solid summer beer, and the **Midnight Porter** is a good, English-style porter. The **Local Harvest Ale** is an American pale ale brewed with malted barley and hops grown in Maine. The **Slick Nick Winter Ale** is a personal winter favorite of mine. Unlike many winter warmers, this has no spices added. Instead, caramel malts give it a sweet flavor, with caramel and molasses flavors coming through. Throughout the year, Sebago also brews a **Single Batch Series,** which are various styles only available for a limited time and in limited locations.

Even though you can get Sebago beers in stores, don't forget to stop at one of their brewpubs if you are in the area. They have pubs in Gorham, Kennebunk, Portland, and Scarborough. The pubs are great places to stop to get a Sebago beer on draft and to grab a meal. They all have full menus, and the food is good, so you will not be disappointed.

SHEEPSCOT VALLEY BREWING COMPANY

74 Hollywood Blvd., Whitefield, ME; (207) 549-5330; www.sheepscotbrewing.com
Founded: 1995 **Founder:** Steve Gorrill **Brewer:** Steve Gorrill **Flagship Beer:** Pemaquid Ale **Year-round Beers:** Boothbay Special Bitter, Damariscotta Double Brown, New Harbor Lager **Seasonals/Special Releases:** Sheepscot Valley Stout, Tinky Winky Double IPA
Tours: Tours are available, but call ahead.

Hollywood Boulevard in Whitefield, Maine, is a much different place than the Hollywood Boulevard out in California. Sure, in LA you may run into celebrities being followed by camera-toting paparazzi. But Whitefield's Hollywood Boulevard has something going for it that its more famous counterpart does not—it is home to the Sheepscot Valley Brewing Company. Win goes to Maine in this contest.

The Sheepscot Valley Brewing Company is a brewery that has quietly been going about its business brewing good, solid beers since 1995. It is one of those places in Maine that is popular in its general geographic area, but not easy to find in other areas. The **Pemaquid Ale** is the flagship, a full-bodied Scottish ale. This is a beer that is heavy on the malts and reflects the cold Maine climate. This is a perfect beer to have on a cold night while you are warming up with a big bowl of beef stew; it's a hearty beer meant to go with hearty food. The **Boothbay Special Bitter** is a traditional English-style bitter. It is mild, nicely carbonated with a nice bitterness that plays nicely on your tongue. This beer is often available on cask at better beer bars, and it tastes even better than when served normally. The **Damariscotta Double Brown** is a bigger than average brown ale, while the **New Harbor Lager** is a typical pale lager.

Beer Lover's Pick

Damariscotta Double Brown
Style: Brown Ale
ABV: 6.8 percent ABV
Availability: Year-Round
Brown ales often border on session ale alcohol levels, but not the Damariscotta Double Brown (named for the town of Damariscotta, Maine). This beer is loaded with more malts than the typical brown ale, raising the alcohol to nearly 7 percent ABV. Although it is a sweet beer, it is not too sweet, and this beer has an excellent body and great carbonation. Its extremely pleasant caramel flavors round out this excellent offering.

Occasionally brewed beers include the **Sheepscot Valley Stout.** It is a lighter stout, but it has nice chocolate and coffee notes. The **Tinky Winky Double IPA** is Sheepscot Valley's biggest beer at 9.5 percent alcohol by volume. This is probably the most American of the beers, and worth seeking out.

Sheepscot founder and brewer Steve Gorrill offers tours at his brewery, but make sure to call ahead before going because if he is busy, he will not have time to give you the tour. Growlers of the beers are also available. Other items sold at the brewery are several different Pemaquid Ale T-shirts, including one that features a T. rex on the front. I guess even the most ferocious dinosaur appreciates a nice Scottish ale.

SHIPYARD BREWING COMPANY

86 Newbury St., Portland, ME; www.shipyard.com; 800-BREW-ALE
Founded: 1994 **Founders:** Fred Forsley and Alan Pugsley **Brewer:** Alan Pugsley **Flagship Beer:** Old Thumper **Year-round Beers:** Blue Fin Stout, Chamberlain Pale Ale, Export Ale, Shipyard IPA, Shipyard Light Ale **Seasonals/Special Releases:** Applehead Ale, Summer Ale, Prelude Special Ale, Pumpkinhead Ale, Longfellow Winter Ale, Double Old Thumper, Pugsley Signature Series **Tours:** Guided tours Tues from 5:30 to 7 p.m. (several weeks advance notice needed); video tour daily, every hour between 11 a.m. and 4 p.m.

There is not a more influential brewery in Maine, maybe all of New England, than Portland's Shipyard Brewing Company. Owner/brewmaster Alan Pugsley came from England and brought over the Peter Austin brewing system. He helped set up the signature system at more than 60 breweries across the country, including several other Maine breweries, such as Gritty McDuff's and D.L Geary's. He also brought over Ringwood yeast, from Austin's Ringwood brewery in England. Some beer lovers love it, and some beer lovers hate it. Whatever people think about it, Shipyard makes it work for them, and the brewery has become one of the largest in the country.

Shipyard actually started as the Federal Jack's Restaurant and Brew Pub in Kennebunk (which still exists) in 1992 until it expanded to a full brewery in 1994. The Shipyard Brewing Company specializes in English-style ales. Almost all the year-round beers are British-inspired ales. They include the **Export Ale, Old Thumper, Shipyard IPA,** and the **Chamberlain Pale Ale.** The other two year-round offerings are not English ales; the **Blue Fin Stout** is an Irish stout, and the **Shipyard Light Ale** is a light American blonde ale.

Shipyard is most well-known for one of its three seasonals—the **Pumpkinhead Ale.** For many, the arrival of Pumpkinhead Ale in stores in August means summer is coming to a close and fall is on the way. This is easily the most popular pumpkin ale being brewed today. Shipyard also brews a typical American wheat beer as their

**Pugsley Signature Series
Imperial Porter**

Style: Imperial Porter

ABV: 7.1 percent

Availability: Rotating

The Pugsley Signature Series Imperial Porter is the best beer brewed by the Shipyard Brewing Company. There are a lot of flavors going on in this beer, roasted black coffee, dark fruit, maybe even some raisins and figs, as well as a hint of chocolate. This is not an overly sweet beer, and there is a hint of booze in there, but it is most definitely a winner.

Summer Ale, and the **Prelude Special Ale** is a suitably malty winter beer. The **Longfellow Winter Ale** is a hybrid beer, a blend of a Scotch ale and a porter.

In the past few years, Shipyard has introduced the **Pugsley Signature Series,** a collection of higher alcohol, less traditional beers. The Pugsley Signature Series includes the Barley Wine, Imperial Porter, Smashed Blueberry, Smashed Pumpkin, and XXXX IPA. These beers are quite good. The Barley Wine and Imperial Porter, in particular, are the two best beers being brewed at Shipyard today.

Shipyard also brews beers under several other labels; they own the Kennebunkport Brewing Company, which brews Shipyard beers to put on draft at Federal Jack's. They also own the Sea Dog Brewing Company. Sea Dog has several restaurants in Maine and two in Massachusetts. They also release several fruit beers under the Sea Dog label, including the popular Blue Paws Blueberry Ale, that are easy to find in many liquor stores. Shipyard is also a popular place for other breweries to contract-brew beers. Gritty McDuff's, Geary's, and Peak Organic all bottle their 12-ounce bottled beers there.

Full brewery tours are offered on Tuesday, and are often booked weeks ahead of time, so you have to reserve a space online. If you cannot make it for a full brewery tour, they offer daily video tours and beer tastings at the brewery. Shipyard is part of brewing history, so if you're a beer lover, make a stop there while in Portland.

Brewpubs

BOON ISLAND ALE HOUSE
1677 Post Rd., Wells, ME; (207) 641-8489; www.boonislandale.com
Draft Beers: 4

The Boon Island Ale House is a restaurant first and a brewpub second. There's nothing wrong with that. The problem with many good restaurants is they take great care preparing food, developing a nice wine list and selecting spirits, but then only offer easy-to-get, boring beers. The Boon Island Ale House, on the other hand, has four of its own beers on draft at all times, giving the beer lovers something good to drink while they enjoy their meals.

The four Boon Island Ales are not particularly complex beers. They are meant to be good, easy-drinking beers you can enjoy with a meal. The **Nut Brown Ale** is a traditional English-style brown ale. It has a lot of nutty flavors, along with strong caramel notes and even a touch of chocolate in the finish. The **India Pale Ale** leans toward the English style. The earthy hop and the strong malt base actually work well with seafood because they will not overwhelm it. It is a perfect beer for a Maine restaurant with a lot of seafood. The **Boon Island Light** is the perfect beer for those who are not into craft beer. The **Lager** is Boon Island's best beer; a traditional Czech-style pilsner, it's a clean, easy drink with a frothy head. Again, a good pairing for seafood because it will not overwhelm the delicate flavors.

The real attraction of Boon Island is the food. The appetizers are heavy on seafood related items, such as the Shark Bites, which are actually deep-fried haddock chunks. The fried calamari and the crab cakes are also available, as are the Boon Island Wings, which are hade with a honey lager barbecue sauce (available for purchase). Cheese sticks, a pile of fried mozzarella sticks, are always a crowd pleaser. Or maybe you want something a little heartier. Boon Island offers three different chowder options. You can get the clam chowder, the lobster chowder, or the Boon Island's 1940s Original Fish Chowder, based on a recipe developed by a local housewife in the 1940s.

After the chowder, move on to a burger. The burgers are half-pound patties and feature several topping options. The Harbor Master is topped with roasted red peppers, provolone cheese, caramelized onions, and Boon Island's Special Sauce. Entrees include the lobster mac and cheese, which is macaroni smothered in a special blend of cheeses with chunks of lobster mixed in. Another highlight, the Diver Down, is a dish of pan-seared sea scallops served with a chipotle maple drizzle.

Maine

BRAY'S BREWPUB & EATERY

678 Roosevelt Trail, Naples, ME; (207) 693-6806; www.braysbrewpub.com
Draft Beers: 6 house beers, 26 in all

Maine is full of hidden beer jewels—small breweries and brewpubs no one outside of the general area knows, but that serve some wonderful beer. Bray's Brewing Company in tiny Naples is one of those places. The brewpub isn't far from Portland, where the brewpubs, breweries, and beer bars in the large port city overshadow other worthy beer establishments on the outskirts. But Bray's Brewing Company is an exceptional brewpub; they brew some great beers, have a lot of really good guest taps, and sport a large and varied food menu. It's a worthy destination in its own right.

The draft list is an impressive mix of Bray's own beers, usually 6 of them on draft at one time, along with 20 guest taps. The guest taps feature local beers such as Allagash Brewing Company and Sebago Brewing Company, both from Maine, as well as beers from other parts of the country, such as Victory Brewing Company in Pennsylvania, and even Europe, like St. Bernardus from Belgium.

The house-brewed beers stand up well to these well-known beer heavyweights. Bray's offers two different IPAs, one dark and one light, both coming in at a solid 7 percent alcohol by volume. The **Mt. Olympus Special Ale** is the dark IPA while the **Epicurean IPA** is the light IPA. The **Yammityville Horror** gets extra points by channeling one of the best horror movies of the 1970s, the *Amityville Horror*. Bray's also gets points for brewing this fall beer with yams rather than pumpkin. Other beers include the **Brandy Pond Blonde** (wheat ale), the **Pleasant Mountain Porter,** and the **Muddy River Bog Brown Ale.** Also available throughout the year is the **Songo Lock Scotch Ale,** a 9.4 percent malty monster of a beer, the **Caseway Cream Ale, Graveyard Coffee Stout, Burnt Meadow Mountain Peated Porter,** and the **Viciously Vivacious Vanilla Porter.**

If you make the trip to Naples, you might as well stay for a meal. Bray's offers five different nacho options for appetizers, as well as house-made hummus and grilled shrimp skewers. Or grab the lobster stew for a starter, which features hunks of lobster in a cream sauce with scallions and bacon. If you are not into meat, you may want to skip the pub menu. Except for the veggie burger, the pub menu is designed for those who enjoy meat. It features baby back ribs, the Barbecue Smoked Beef Brisket & Pulled Pork Plate, a sausage platter, sausage sub, and half-pound burgers. The dinner menu is heavy on seafood. You can get baked or fried scallops; baked haddock; or the Broiled Seafood Combo, which features haddock, shrimp, and scallops, panko-encrusted and served in a white wine butter sauce. The mixed grill comes with a 6-ounce sirloin steak, two jumbo shrimp, and some sausage. Bray's also

One Night Stand

Every August, for one night, Bray's clears its taps of all guest beers and puts all the beers they brew on tap at one time. This is the only night of the year that you can get any of the Bray's beers you want. Order a sample platter to make the job of trying all of their offerings a little more manageable.

has a fairly large dessert menu that features freshly made pies, cheesecake, and even a Toll House cookie pie.

Bray's also has live music several nights a week, so there is always something going on there.

FEDERAL JACK'S RESTAURANT & BREW PUB
8 Western Ave., Kennebunk, ME; (207) 967-4322; www.federaljacks.com
Draft Beers: 7

Federal Jack's Restaurant & Brew Pub is the birthplace of one of the oldest and most well-known New England breweries, the Shipyard Brewing Company. Fred Forsley and Alan Pugsley, who went on to found Shipyard Brewing Company in 1994, founded Federal Jack's in 1992. Many of Shipyard's most popular beers were first brewed, and are still available, at Federal Jack's.

Like Shipyard, Federal Jack's concentrates on brewing English-style ales. In fact, most of the beers available at Federal Jack's are members of the Shipyard standard line of beer. The year-round beers include the **Shipyard Blue Fin Stout, Brown Ale, Export Ale, Fuggles IPA,** and **Old Thumper.** The other year-round beers not part of Shipyard's normal rotation include the **Goat Island Light Ale** and the **'Taint Town Pale Ale.**

Federal Jack's also rotates in popular seasonal ales such as the **Longfellow, Prelude,** and **Pumpkinhead** ales. Other seasonals that are not Shipyard beers include the **Sunfish Wheat Ale,** as well as a series of oak-aged beers. The brewpub also often has beers available on cask. Although many of these beers are Shipyard beers, they are as fresh as can be, being brewed in the Kennebunkport Brewery, located right beneath Federal Jack's.

Federal Jack's has a large menu that should have something for everyone. Full meals include sandwiches, burgers, steaks, and turkey, but like many Maine restaurants, Federal Jack's is heavy on seafood options, including crab-stuffed Atlantic haddock, fish and chips, fried clams, Maine shrimp, and potato-encrusted haddock. And, of course, there is lobster. Get a regular steamed lobster, or get the Federal Jack's Feast. The Feast comes with a cup of New England clam chowder, Goat Island mussels, a steamed Maine lobster (twin lobsters are available), fries, cole slaw, and either a pint of beer or homemade root beer.

If you happen to fall in love with a beer while at Federal Jack's, grab a half-gallon growler and bring it home so you can enjoy it again in the privacy of your own living room. It will help to bring back all of those memories of great lobster you ate at Federal Jack's.

KENNEBEC RIVER PUB & BREWERY
1771 US 201, The Forks, ME; 800-765-7238; www.northernoutdoors.com
Draft Beers: 6

After a long day of rafting on the Dead River, you will probably be in need of a beer (or three) and some food. The Kennebec River Pub & Brewery at the Northern Outdoors Resort, located at The Forks, Maine, is exactly the kind of place you need to go. They serve good, simple, filling pub food, and brew better-than-expected beers for a brewpub at a resort.

The Kennebec River Pub & Brewery always has at least six of its beers on tap at all times, and they also distribute three of their beers—**IPA, Sledhead Red,** and the **Summer Ale**—in six-packs throughout New England. Along with those three beers, Kennebec has another 10 beers that they rotate throughout the year. The **Deer-in-the-Head Lite** is Kennebec's version of a mass-produced lager. The **Whitewater Wheat** is a Belgian-style witbier brewed with coriander and orange peel, and the **Kennebec Logger** is a well-made pilsner, while the **Big Mama Blueberry Ale** is your typical blueberry ale. If you like blueberry beers, you'll like Big Mama; if you don't, she won't change your mind. The **Octoberfest** is a solid interpretation of the popular fall seasonal, while the **Hazelnut Brown** is fantastic. The use of hazelnuts in a brown ale is almost always excellent, and this is no exception. The other beers include the **Penobscot Porter** and the **Class V Stout.** They are both really well-done

Spring Raft 'n Brews

Each spring, the Kennebec River Pub & Brewery holds the Raft 'n Brews event. It starts with a day of canoeing on the Dead River, and then continues into the Northern Resort Community Center for a barbecue and tours of the brewery. Different beers are available at special prices and there are live bands to keep the party going all day and into the night.

dark beers, perfect to warm you up after you have fallen out of your raft and gotten soaked several times throughout the day.

Kennebec's burgers are huge, a half-pound each, and can come with a variety of toppings. Other sandwiches include a fried fish sandwich and a grilled meat loaf sandwich. Several different shrimp dishes are available as entrees, but the meal you really should get is the Tornadoes of Beef, which features two 5-ounce filet mignons, char-grilled and topped with homemade herb butter. Desserts are made daily and are different each day. Breakfast is also available in the pub.

LIBERAL CUP PUBLIC HOUSE AND BREWERY

115 Water St., Hallowell, ME; (207) 623-2739; www.theliberalcup.com
Draft Beers: 6

The Liberal Cup Public House and Brewery is what an old-time New England bar should be—a little small, a little dark, nothing but dark wood furniture and beer signs and posters on the wall. It's the kind of place that will make you feel like you belong. The Liberal Cup is located in downtown Hallowell, Maine, fitting into the old-time New England charm that the town gives off with antiques shops and other small establishments.

The beer selection may be small, but it's always rotating, so you should be able to find a beer you like every time you go in there. The beers include a good mix of British styles, with a few others thrown in. The **Alewife Ale** is a red ale, while the

Ex-Wife Extra Bitter (sounds a little personal) is a 6.7 percent alcohol by volume ESB. The **Backhouse Bitter** is also another good British option, as is the **Summer Bitter Summer Not.** Another good choice would be the **For Richer or Poorter,** a solid beer. Other beers include the **Oatmeal Stout, Old Hallow Ale IPA,** and the **Tarbox Stout.** The two standouts, though, are the **Chazmo Altbier,** a solid spot-on German-style alt, and the **Bug Zapper Super Lager,** which is a red or amber lager, full of malty sweetness and flavor. Liberal Cup also offers the **Bug Lager,** which is their interpretation of a mass-produced lager. The Liberal Cup also typically has a beer on cask.

Food-wise, the Liberal Cup offers mainly pub-style food, trying to mimic the English pub culture of simple food with good beer. Appetizer highlights include the Mills Mussels (a recipe stolen from their sister pub, the Run of the Mill) and the Creole Quesadillas. The quesadillas are made with grilled sun-dried tomato tortillas filled with Andouille and chorizo sausages with pepper jack cheese, topped with cilantro-lime sour cream and remoulade for dipping. Starting your meal off with the Liberal Cup's beer cheese soup may be the best decision you'll ever make. Each day a different beer and a different cheese is used, so check with your server before ordering.

Larger meals include the Ale Bird, which is a roasted free-range chicken that has been brewed in Alehouse Ale, served with garlic smashed potatoes. The Drunken Pot Roast is a classic pot roast, slow-roasted in beer. The Haddock Napoleon is beer-battered haddock, served with garlic smashed potatoes, applewood-smoked bacon, and spinach, topped with a mornay cheese sauce. The most unique offering on the menu is the Not Your Mama's Meat Loaf, which is a meat loaf that is stuffed with spinach and mozzarella, then wrapped in applewood-smoked bacon and covered in homemade gravy.

The Liberal Cup is also a great place to hang out to listen to live music. They host bands of all genres most nights of the week, so grab a pint (actually 20-ounce glass) of your favorite beer and relax to some good music.

MAINE COAST BREWING COMPANY
102 Eden St., Bar Harbor, ME; (207) 288-4914; www.bhmaine.com
Draft Beers: 6

The Maine Coast Brewing Company is the house brewery for Jack Russell's Steakhouse and Brewpub. Maine Coast brews a number of beers, year-round and seasonals alike. The beers include the **Bar Harbor Espresso Stout,** which is a perfect after-dinner beer instead of having a coffee. Additional offerings include **Jack Russell's Best Brown Ale,** which is a traditional brown ale and the beer you really should get with all of the beef offered on this menu. The **Wild Blueberry Ale** is the obligatory blueberry ale most Maine breweries brew. The **Precipice Pale Ale** is a solid pale ale, while the **Jordan Pond Ale** is a decent IPA. Other beers include the **Black Irish Stout** and the **Eden Porter.**

But more than any other brewpub in Maine, Maine Coast Brewing Company/Jack Russell's Steakhouse is all about the food. As the name implies, steak is the star at Jack Russell's. Options include the Jack Russell's Filet Mignon that comes in a variety of sizes, from the Ladies' Cut that weighs 6 ounces to the Butcher's Cut, which comes in at 12 ounces. Jack Russell's Maine Maple N.Y. Strip comes with a homemade maple steak sauce, while the prime rib is served as large as 21 ounces. The tenderloin tips are served on skewers, and there are also pork tenderloins on the menu. Not a meat eater or steak lover? No worries—they have you covered with the Vegetarian Platter, which includes roasted veggies, an eggplant cutlet, the vegetable of the day, and a side of hummus with pita bread.

MARSHALL WHARF BREWING COMPANY/THREE TIDES RESTAURANT
2 Pinchy Ln., Belfast, ME; (207) 338-1707; www.marshallwharf.com and www.3tides.com
Draft Beers: 17

The Marshall Wharf Brewing Company is Maine's best kept secret. Marshall Wharf, which is the house brewery for the Three Tides Restaurant, is easily one of the top 10 beer producers in New England, but because they are only available in a few places, they fly under the radar.

Marshall Wharf does not know how to brew bad beers, and has a rotation of more than 30 beers; it's nearly impossible to pick a favorite. Like hoppy beers? Marshall Wharf brews several IPAs/double IPAs. The **Toughcats IPA** is a single-hop IPA, brewed with Palisade hops, which gives it a peachy, apricot-like flavor. The **Big Twitch** is a big, west coast double IPA, coming in at 9 percent alcohol by volume. Then there's the **Cant Dog,** a 10 percent ABV beer. Do you like German-style beers? Go with the **Wiener,** a German-style Vienna lager, or maybe the **Deep Purple,** a smoked ale, or even the **Attenuator Doppelbock,** or maybe the **Illegal Ale-ian,** a Kolsch-wheat beer hybrid. Oh, and don't forget about the stouts. There's the **Danny McGovern's Oatmeal Stout.** Marshall Wharf also brews two great imperial stouts. The first is the **Chaos Chaos Russian Imperial Stout,** a big beast of a beer coming in at a hefty 11.2 percent ABV. The second is the vanilla bean and oak-aged version of the Chaos Chaos, called **Sexy Chaos.** It is a decadent treat. Another stout is the **Pemaquid Oyster Stout,** a traditional style of British stout brewed with 10 dozen oysters. Other beers available include the **Ace Hole Pale Ale, 42 Cream Ale, Bitty**

The Beer and Pemaquid Mussel Fest

Each year, this outside festival is held on the Three Tides Restaurant property. The event features three different bar areas outside, serving more than 30 different Marshall Wharf beers. For the $25 fee, you get a glass and 10 tickets to get beer. All the food, including Pemaquid mussels, is pay as you go. The four-hour event occurs rain or shine.

(a Belgian take on the Illegal Ale-ian), **Cornholio** (blonde ale), **Happy Dock Coffee Porter, Maximillian Imperial Red Ale,** and the **Phil Brown Ale.**

But before going to Marshall Wharf, stop inside Three Tides for some food and to try several of these beers on draft. Not many brewpubs have 17 beers on tap, let alone 17 awesome beers. Three Tides offers a tapas menu that includes garlic pita chips and salsa, a small dish of olives, baked mozzarella sticks, Swedish meatballs, Maine crabmeat or chicken quesadillas, Pemaquid oysters, and rope-grown mussels.

The best part, though, is you can try several of the Marshall Wharf beers before you go inside the brewery portion of the restaurant and pick out which growler of beer you want to take home. Trust me, you will want to take at least one, if not more, home. If you can't make it to Belfast, Marshall Wharf beers are available on draft at several bars in Portland.

THE RUN OF THE MILL
100 Main St., Saco, ME; (207) 571-9652; http://therunofthemill.net
Draft Beers: 7

Despite its name, the Run of the Mill is anything but another run-of-the-mill brewpub. As the sister brewpub of the Liberal Cup Public House & Brewery in Hallowell, it's an exceptional beer destination, with some really good beer and a full menu of tasty food.

Many of the beers available at the Run of the Mill are the same ones available at the Liberal Cup, such as the Bug Lager, Alewife Ale, and the Ex-Wife Extra Bitter, but there are some different offerings. Some of those beers include the **Tented Kilt Scottish Ale** (the name makes me giggle), the **Smelt Cap Strong Ale,** the **Mud Flap Spring Bock,** and the **What's Hoppenin' IPA.** The beers are all solid. There are a variety of styles available, seven, and there should be something for all different beer tastes.

The Run of the Mill's menu also shares several items with the Liberal Cup, but there isn't too much overlap. Start with the croquettes, which are made of potatoes, bacon, and cheddar cheese and then deep-fried. The Maine crab cakes are also delicious, as are the Mussels Dijon, which are sautéed with garlic, onion, red peppers, white wine, and butter and served in a Dijon cream sauce. There are loads of salads available, and Run of the Mill's special house dressing makes them stand out from the usual salad fare. If you're in the mood for a sandwich, there are two standouts. The Indian Island Chicken Sandwich is a grilled chicken breast covered in bacon and cheddar—simple but great. The Grilled Salmon Focaccia features a quarter pound of salmon, a grilled portobello mushroom, tomatoes, and greens, all stacked on focaccia bread and served open faced with a lemon dill aioli.

The menu also offers several comfort food items, such as shepherd's pie and a home-style turkey dinner (perfect if you want to have a taste of Thanksgiving in July). The standout dish, though, is the Mac & Beer Cheese. It is made with macaroni and a triple cheese sauce made with Bug Lager and topped with a blend of pretzels and crackers and a crispy Parmesan cheese wheel.

Beer Event

The Brewer's Dinner

Every May, the Run of the Mill brewers and chefs get together to create a six-course beer dinner. Each course of food is developed especially for the beer dinner and uses their house brew as an ingredient. Then each dish is paired with a Run of the Mill beer, showing the harmony beer and food can have if paired correctly.

SEA DOG BREWING COMPANY

Three locations: 26 Front St., Bangor, ME; 125 Western Ave., South Portland, ME; 1 Bowdoin Mill Island, Suite 100, Topsham, ME; http://seadogbrewing.com
Bangor: (207) 947-8720; South Portland: (207) 871-7000; Topsham: (207) 725-0162
Draft Beers: Various

The Sea Dog Brewing Company is a chain of brewpubs owned by the Shipyard Brewing Company. There are also several Sea Dog restaurants in Massachusetts that do not brew beer. The Sea Dog Brewing Company is most famous for its fruit beers, none more than the ridiculously popular **Blue Paw Wheat Ale,** a blueberry ale. Their other fruit beers are the **Apricot Wheat Ale** and the **Raspberry Wheat Ale,** both light fruit beers, popular among those who like sweet, light beers.

Other Sea Dog offerings include the **Old East India Pale Ale,** the **Old Golly Wobbler Brown Ale,** the **Owls Head Light Ale,** the **Sea Dog Pale Ale,** and the **Sea Dog Stout.** But Sea Dog's best beer is the **Riverdriver Hazelnut Porter.** The hazelnut works fantastically in this beer.

Sea Dog's menu is full of excellent pub fare. Appetizers include the Windjammer Mussels and Frites, which are steamed in Sea Dog's Windjammer Ale. Also available are fried calamari, tuna sashimi, and a cheese plate of local cheeses. The most unusual of the appetizers is the Mexicali Wontons, which are deep-fried wontons filled with blackened chicken, green chili, and cream cheese. They also have tons of sandwiches, including a lobster roll, a grilled crab cake and Havarti sandwich, and the Firecracker Shrimp Roll, made with spicy Maine shrimp, shaved lettuce, and Cajun remoulade.

As can be expected of the location, entrees are heavy on seafood, such as fish and chips and the potato chip–encrusted haddock. There are also fried clams and steamed lobsters, as well as jambalaya. Non-seafood options include fried chicken and mashed potatoes, and wild mushroom and goat cheese ravioli. Another highlight is the Barbecue Bluepaw Short Ribs (recipe on page 242), which is made with a marinade that uses the incredibly popular Bluepaw blueberry beer.

The Sea Dog is also a great option if you're looking for a family restaurant in the area, so if you have the little ones with you, this may be a better option than other brewpubs and beer bars.

SUNDAY RIVER BREWING COMPANY

1 Sunday River Rd., Bethel, ME; (207) 824-3541; www.sundayriverbrewpub.com
Draft Beers: 7

The Sunday River Brewing Company has a special place in my heart—they're the only establishment where you can get beers from the now defunct Stone Coast Brewing Company, the brewery that introduced me to craft beer.

The brewery, located near the Sunday River Ski Resort, offers seven beers on draft, food, and a place to relax after a long day on the slopes. The Stone Coast beers are the 420 IPA, 840 IPA, Jamaican Stout, Black Bear Porter, and the Redstone Ale. They also brew beers under the Sunday River name, including the Sunday River Alt, Sunday River Lager, and the Sunsplash Golden Ale.

The **420 IPA** is a good, solid American-style IPA. It smells of freshly cut grass, and packs a little citrusy punch when you take a sip. If the 420 IPA isn't hoppy enough for you, try its big brother, the **840 IPA.** This is a big, hoppy double IPA. It is also on the sweet side as tons of malts are used to provide balance. At 8.5 percent alcohol by volume, you can feel the burn as it travels down your throat. The **Jamaican Stout** is a traditional foreign export stout, typically brewed for tropical regions. This has huge roasted coffee characters, almost like fresh espresso grounds. It also has some caramel notes, and some bitterness. It's another big beer at 8 percent ABV, however, unlike the 840 IPA, you will not notice the alcohol. Meanwhile, the **Redstone Ale** is a good, solid red ale, malty and sweet, with few hops.

The Sunday River beers are solid. The **Alt** is tasty, if not up to the standards of the top beers in the style. The **Sunday River Lager** is an easy-drinking, flavorful lager, and the **Sunsplash Golden Ale** is a light, refreshing beer and is good for those who are intimidated by heavier beers.

Sunday River's menu mainly consists of tasty pub standards, such as chicken wings, nachos, and onion ring starters. You can also grab a bowl of onion soup to whet your appetite for the main course. Sunday River offers salads, sandwiches such as pastrami and burgers, and fish and chips, as well as lobster; the Memphis-style pulled pork sandwich is a standout, which makes sense because where Sunday River really excels is their barbecue. The meat is slow cooked, and is slathered in tasty sauce. You can get brisket, ribs, and barbecue chicken, or you can get a mixed plate of brisket and ribs, along with fresh corn bread and a baked potato.

If you can only make it to Sunday River one day, try to make it on Wednesday, when the brewery offers $1.50 pints from 3 to 7 p.m. And before you leave, pick up a growler of your favorite beer and save it for the next time you go skiing.

Maine

Beer Bars

THE BADGER CAFE & PUB

289 Common Rd., Union, ME; (207) 785-3336; http://badgercafeandpub.com
Draft Beers: 6 **Bottled/Canned Beers:** 50

Most beer bars in Maine are heavy on finely brewed beers from the immediate area. The Badger Cafe & Pub, though, has a beer list that is heavy on import beer, often only having one or two Maine beers available. Sometimes you just need a bottle of St. Louis Frambois from Belgium, rather than a blueberry ale.

Where the Badger Cafe really excels is their bottled list. There are about 50 bottled options, and there is not one beer on the list that is anything less than stellar. The list features beer from all of the great beer countries—Belgium, England, Germany, and the US, as well as other countries you might not think of when you think about quality beer, like Italy. Some breweries frequently represented include Orval from Belgium, Harvieston and Meantime from England, Unibroue from Canada, Amaracorde from Italy, Schneider from German, and Dogfish Head Craft Brewers and North Coast Brewing Company from the US.

As far as food, the Badger Cafe is a mix of typical pub fare, plus some dishes that you wouldn't expect to see in a pub. Sandwiches include the homemade falafel burger, chicken cordon bleu, and two sandwiches that are pretty much total opposites—the All Veggie and the Barnyard Burger. The All Veggie is made with grilled eggplant, roasted sweet peppers, onions, and fresh greens with garlic and herb cream cheese, while the Barnyard is made with local beef, pork, and lamb. Other entree options include the buttermilk fried chicken, the turkey tetrazzini, and the pork chop Normandy, which is a thick-cut chop served with sautéed apples and a creamy mustard sauce. If you are in Union on Saturday or Sunday, make sure to stop at the Badger Cafe for brunch.

EBENEZER'S PUB

Location: 44 Allen Rd., Lovell, ME; (207) 925-3200; www.ebenezerspub.com
Draft Beers: 35 **Bottled/Canned Beers:** More than 1,000

If you were just to look at Ebenezer's Pub from the outside—it's in half of an old farmhouse—you may pass it up and go to a different bar. That would be your loss. Once inside, Ebenezer's is beer heaven, a bar that people travel from around the country to visit. It's regarded on many beer review websites as one of the best,

Ebenezer's Belgian Beer Dinner

In August, Ebenezer's hosts a week-long Belgian Beer Festival, with people camping on site and enjoying some of the best beers in the world. The highlight of the week is the Belgian Beer Dinner, an 8- to 10-course dinner of gourmet food with Belgian influences. Each dish is paired with a rare, or vintage, beer. The dinner costs well over $200, but it's well worth it.

if not the best, craft beer bars in the world. It's a designation Ebenezer's deserves and has earned.

Owned by Chris Lively and his wife Jen, Ebenezer's Pub has one of the most mind-blowing beer lists ever to be seen. There are rare Belgian ales on draft and in bottles. If an American brewery brews a beer just once and it cannot be found anywhere, there is a good chance Ebenezer's will have it. There are 35 beers on tap and more than 1,000 bottles available. Do you like vintage beers? How about Thomas Hardy ales from England dating back to the late 1960s and early 1970s, or multiple years of Belgium's Cantillon lambics and gueuzes? Although Belgian ales are the specialty, Lively does not skimp on American craft beer. Breweries such as Rogue Brewery from Oregon and Sierra Nevada Brewing Company from California are also available in bottles.

If Lively is working when you stop in, make sure to try to get a few minutes of his time. There are a lot of beer lovers out there, but he is one of the most passionate people about beer there is. You can hear the passion in his voice when he talks about beers, particularly those he loves. And, if you're lucky, maybe he'll give you a tour of his beer cellar, where some of the rarest of the world's rare beers are stored. It really should be some kind of beer museum; he should charge admission to go down there.

Lovell is a small town, and Ebenezer's is one of the few restaurants, so it gets pretty full during the summer. If you want a seat, you may have to call ahead for reservations, or plan on waiting for a while. Beer is obviously what brings people to Ebenezer's, but the food is nothing to ignore. One of the best meal options is the

Caesar salad—order it with lobster on top, and you get nearly a whole lobster. Pizza is always available, and there are plenty of burgers. The star burger is the Chimay Burger, topped with both provolone and Stilton garlic cream cheese, and goes perfectly with a Chimay Red. Entrees include sirloin tips and the Sausage Fest, which includes two foot-long, char-broiled sausages. Fish choices include the Fish 'n Frites and the seafood scampi, which includes lobster, mussels, scallops, and shrimp.

THE GREAT LOST BEAR

540 Forest Ave., Portland, ME; (207) 772-0300; www.greatlostbear.com
Draft Beers: 69 **Bottled/Can Beers:** Macros and retro beers only

You can't talk about the Portland beer scene without mentioning the Great Lost Bear, the granddaddy of New England beer bars. Founded in 1979, the brewery jumped on the craft beer revolution of the mid-1980s and has never looked back.

The Great Lost Bear, which has one of the best bars (a giant horse shoe), features 69 beers on tap, mostly beers from the northeast, heavy on local Maine breweries. They're big fans of the Allagash Brewing Company, also located in Portland. They always have at least five rare Allagash beers on tap as part of "Allagash Alley," and several hand-pumped beers, mainly local beers, served on cask. The Great Lost Bear also has a rotating selection of Belgian beers and extreme beers. Draft beer is the star, but they do have some canned and bottled beers, mainly mainstream beers, or retro cans such as Ballantine, Schlitz, and Narragansett. The beers are rotated often,

Maine Brew Pub Cup

January is an exciting time for Maine breweries. The Great Lost Bear hosts the Maine Brew Pub Cup, where Maine breweries contend against each other to see which brewery sells the most beer during the competition. The best thing about the event for beer fans: The pints are cheap, at $2.99 each for participating breweries. Each pint of the various breweries is tallied, and at the end of the event, a winner is named.

and whenever a Maine brewery releases a new seasonal or a new beer, there's a good chance you'll be able to find it on tap at the Great Lost Bear.

Although they don't host beer dinners, the Great Lost Bear hosts a Brewer's Showcase. The featured brewery's beers will be available at a discounted price, and often the brewers themselves attend the event. The Great Lost Bear also likes to party, and every year they host numerous events. In October they host the Gritty McDuff's Halloween Party and in December they host a "12 Beers of Christmas" event with winter beers available at discounted prices. The first Wednesday of every month is the Shipyard Ale Society night, with all Shipyard pints available for $2.99 each from 5 to 7 p.m. And if you like a game of chance, spin the "Wheel of Destiny." You have to buy whatever beer the wheel ends on.

There's a large menu with mostly typical pub fare, kind of what you'd expect from an old-time bar in Maine. The teriyaki grilled mushrooms and Yippie Thai Yi Yi, fried tortilla chips with Thai dipping sauce, are the stars of the starter portion of the menu. Nachos are offered in nine different styles, from plain cheese to the works. There are plenty of salads and even a vegetarian menu for the non-carnivores.

If in Maine, make sure to stop in at the Great Lost Bear and experience some New England beer history.

JIMMY THE GREEK'S
215 Saco Ave., Old Orchard Beach, ME; (207) 934-7499; www.jimmygreeks.com
Draft Beers: 50 **Bottled/Canned Beers:** About 60

Old Orchard Beach is a summer destination that attracts people from all over New England and a large number of Canadians and bikers. During the summer (and any time of year, really), Jimmy the Greek's is the place for beer lovers to go for craft beer. It's a fun little beer bar, and it has a solid draft list and bottle selection that stands out among the competition.

Jimmy's draft list is heavy on Maine beers, such as Allagash, Baxter, D.L. Geary's, Gritty McDuff's, Sebago, and Shipyard. It also typically has beers from other areas' breweries, such as the Abita Brewing Company in Louisiana and Dogfish Head from Delaware. Imports such as Erdinger from Germany and Delirium Tremens from Belgium are often available. The bottled list also has some more popular mainstays, such as Budweiser and Coors. However, if you're looking for a little more craft in your bottled beer list, Jimmy's has offerings such as Monty Python's Holy Grail Ale and Young's Double Chocolate Stout, both from England, as well as beers from North Coast Brewing Company in California and Victory Brewing Company in Pennsylvania. The bottled list also includes several Belgian ales, such as Kasteel and Chimay. There is also a section for rare beers that includes Samichlaus from Austria and Porterhouse Oyster Stout (made with real oysters) from Ireland. There are also several different meads available, as well as some ciders.

With a name like Jimmy the Greek's, you bet the menu is heavy on delicious Greek food. Appetizers include feta bread sticks, spanakopita, and saganaki. The menu also offers salads, including a strawberry salad that is made up of mixed greens, strawberries, toasted walnuts, goat cheese, and champagne vinaigrette. Main courses include several flat iron steaks, jambalaya, butternut squash ravioli, and fish and chips. Burgers are also available, including the Opa! Burger, which is an 8-ounce patty with tzatziki sauce and zesty spices. Think your stomach is up for a food challenge? Order the King Leonidas Calzone, which is triple the size of a regular calzone. Pick two meats and two veggies and if you can finish it, it's free. If not, you're out about 20 bucks.

It's never a slow night at Jimmy's. Of particular interest to beer lovers, a Brewer's Night is held every Wednesday from 6 to 9 p.m., where patrons get a chance to meet a brewer, drink a lot of good beer, and win some prizes. There's a second Jimmy the Greek's location in South Portland at 115 Philbrook Rd., with a similar menu, similar beer list, and many different daily events, just like the original location.

THE LION'S PRIDE
112 Pleasant St., Brunswick, ME; (207) 373-1840; www.lionspridepub.com
Draft Beers: 35 **Bottled/Can Beers:** 100

The Lion's Pride has a lot in common with another Maine beer bar, Ebenezer's Pub in Lovell. There's a good reason for the similarites: The Lion's Pride is Ebenezer's sister pub, also owned by husband and wife team Chris and Jen Lively. The great beer selection, the excellent food, and knowledgeable staff are there, just as at Ebenezer's.

What is different is the location itself. While Ebenezer's is a bit off the beaten path in Lovell, the Lion's Pride is in the larger town of Brunswick. You can also feel the difference inside the much larger space at Lion's Pride. Take a look at the tap handles if you have a chance. They're all custom-made glass handles and are really pieces of art.

But don't marvel too much at the tap handles—instead, marvel at the beer list. It's an amazing list, full of rare and fantastic beers. There are pretty much guaranteed to be beers you have never tried, or maybe never even heard of. The bottled list is much the same. There are not quite as many vintage ales as there are on the Ebenezer's list, but this list is impressive in its own right. There are plenty of beers from every major American craft brewer and popular Belgian, German, and English imports, as well as beers from smaller American brewers, such as Stillwater Artisanal Ales from Maryland.

Food-wise, just like at Ebenezer's Pub, Lively has created an impressive menu. There are several artisan cheese plates, such as the Chimayo plate featuring cheese made by the same monks who make the Chimay beers. There are plenty of sandwiches, burgers, entrees, and desserts on the menu.

The menu changes from season to season, reflecting the changes in the weather. The summer menu includes such lighter options as crab cakes, lobster rolls, and tuna filets. As the weather turns colder, look for heartier soups and stews. There are also several steak options, ribs, and seafood (it is Maine, after all) available throughout the year. If you have room, grab some mousse for dessert.

The Lion's Pride hosts several events throughout the year, with visiting brewers from the US and Belgium. They lead attendees through tastings of their brewery's beers, discussing the beers and the effort put into brewing the beer. Every Wednesday, there are beer education events; it's a great way to learn about beers and to drink some at the same time. Learning is always easier with a nice beer in your glass!

NOVARE RES BIER CAFE
4 Canal Plaza, Portland, ME; (207) 761-2437; www.novareresbiercafe.com
Draft Beers: 25 **Bottled/Canned Beers:** 500

If you're a beer lover and you don't take the time to go to Novare Res Bier Cafe, you've done yourself a huge disservice. It's a destination bar, to be sure. The bar features 25 hand-selected tap lines, as well as two hand-pumps for casks. There is never a bad beer available.

Novare Res brings together the influences of many different pub and beer cultures. It has the traditional dart boards of the English pubs and always has a couple of cask beers available. It has a somewhat German beer garden feel, with its long tables and excellent German-style beers available, and like a Belgian beer cafe, the draft list is heavy on the Belgians, all served in proper glassware and with a food menu developed to go perfectly with what you have in your glass. So what is Novare Res? It's a uniquely American bar, perfect for nearly anybody.

Whoever chooses the draft list knows their beer. American breweries, such as Rogue from Oregon and Victory from Pennsylvania, share space with Monchshof of Germany and De Struisse from Belgium. There are also plenty of local beers from Allagash and Marshall Wharf available. The bottled list is incredible, and easy to navigate. The menu is organized by style and by country of origin, and then further

Roguepalooza

Every August, Novare Res hosts this event that celebrates the greatness of the Rogue Brewery in Oregon. Rogue brews dozens of excellent beers, and they take over all the taps during Roguepalooza. There you will find some of their rarer or more expensive beers, all available in one location.

by individual styles. For example, IPAs are listed under the American/U.K. Styles, while pilsners are under German Style and lambics are listed under Belgian Style.

On nice days, sit outside in Novare Res's outdoor beer garden. There's nothing better than having a great beer on a wonderful Maine summer day. Well, having some good food with it would probably make it a little better. Novare Res has a small food menu, but it's all tasty. There are plenty of sandwiches, as well as smaller meals, such as fish tacos or the Mediterranean plates. The highlight of the menu is the meat and cheese bar, which has 1-ounce portions of excellent cheeses and meats served with bread and garnishes.

One of the things that sets Novare Res apart from other beer bars is the staff. Every staff member, from bartenders to the wait staff, is a beer geek. They know their beer, and they don't mind helping those having trouble negotiating the beer menu to try to find something perfect for their personal taste.

POST ROAD TAVERN
705 Main St., Ogunquit, ME; (207) 641-0640; http://postroadtavern.com
Draft Beers: 15 **Bottled/Canned Beers:** About 20

At the time of this printing, Post Road Tavern recently began serving house-brewed Rocky Coast Brewery beers, made with a small onsite brewing system. By the time you read this, the Post Road Tavern may be a brewpub. The tavern plans to open the Rocky Coast Brewery by the spring of 2012, which will be housed in, and will brew house beers for, the Post Road Tavern.

The Post Road Tavern is definitely a beer destination worth seeking out in Ogunquit, Maine. They offer 15 different beers on draft and have about 20 different bottle choices and a solid food menu. The draft list at the Post Road Tavern features some excellent beers, such as beers from Allagash, Abita Brewing Company from Louisiana, and Rock Art Brewery from Vermont, as well as beers from England like Fuller's London Pride and Old Speckled Hen. The bottled list is mainly mass-produced stuff you can get in nearly every bar in every state, with some exceptions, such as Samuel Adams, Shipyard, and even more Abita.

The appetizers for the Post Road Tavern are some of the best around. It's all pub food, but excellent pub food. The pub crisps are house-made potato chips, smothered in melted cheddar, bacon, lettuce, tomatoes, sour cream, and scallions. The Disco Fries are covered with melted cheese, house smoked pulled pork, sour cream, scallions, and barbecue sauce. Scotch Eggs, which are boiled eggs wrapped in sausage, coated with panko bread crumbs, and then deep-fried, are an awesome choice (but not for the faint of heart!).

The tavern also offers wings in several styles, including the Chipotle Maple and Moroccan Harissa, which is a north African red sauce made with dried chili peppers, garlic, and spices. Have enough room for a wing challenge? Post Road offers wings in varying degree of heat from "Atomic" through "Toxic Waste." If you can finish 12 Toxic Waste wings without assistance from others, any drinks, any other food, or any dipping sauces, you will receive a $25 gift certificate, a T-shirt, and a pint glass, all for free. Personally, I would have no shot—plain black pepper is my limitation on the hot stuff.

Burgers, sandwiches, and lobster rolls are available, and Post Road also serves several comfort food options, such as shepherd's pie and chicken pot pie, or you can get a steak and kidney pie. The Post Road Tavern also hosts monthly beer dinners, which are six-course meals, each course paired with a different beer.

THREE DOLLAR DEWEY'S

241 Commercial St., Portland, ME; (207) 772-3310; www.threedollardeweys.com
Draft Beers: 36 **Bottled/Canned Beers:** More than 50

Three Dollar Dewey's is a classic Maine pub, originally founded as a haven for those seeking imported beers. Now, while still having several imported beers on draft and in bottles, it has become the best place to buy locally brewed beers.

The draft list itself is impressive. It features many Maine-brewed beers, including Allagash, Bar Harbor, D.L. Geary, and Shipyard. Other beers on tap include offerings from Harpoon Brewery, Long Trail Brewing Company, Samuel Adams, and Victory

Brewing Company. There are also a few imported beers on tap, such as Newcastle Brown, Smithwick's, and Stella Artois. Three Dollar Dewey's also frequently keeps at least seven or eight different rotating seasonal beers on draft. The bottled list features a lot of mass-produced beers, but also includes brew from Baxter Brewing Company and Sebago Brewing Company. Old Speckled Hen and Boddingtons represent imported beers in the bottles. Although the beers are no longer $3 like they were more than 30 years ago, Three Dollar Dewey's does have a daily Happy Hour Special with a different $3 draft available every day from 4 to 8 p.m.

Hungry for a good burger? At Three Dollar Dewey's, you can choose from nine different variations. The highlight is the Cajun Burger, made with "Louisiana" spices and gouda cheese. The menu also features several sandwiches, such as the pastrami sandwich, a Philly cheese steak, Dewey's Gyros, and the traditional Maine falafel sandwich. Okay, maybe not traditional, but tasty. The sandwich is made with a grilled chick pea sesame patty rolled in a tortilla with spinach, tomatoes, cucumbers, and feta garlic dressing. Entrees are strictly seafood—fried clams, clam cakes, fish and chips, beer-battered shrimp, and a real Maine classic, the lobster roll.

Vermont

There is hardly a corner of Vermont that does not have a brewery or a brewpub. From the heavy hitters such as Magic Hat Brewing Company in South Burlington to tiny McNeill's Brewery in Brattleboro, the state has you covered. Heck, if you need a place to stay, some breweries, like Jasper Murdock's Alehouse in Norwich, are located in hotels and inns. There are small hidden jewels hidden throughout the state, such as Lawson's Finest Liquids, which brews some of the hardest-to-find beers in New England, or Hill Farmstead, the hottest brewery in the country.

The state's beer bars are fiercely loyal to Vermont-brewed beers, so you're almost always guaranteed to end up with a good beer when you go out for a night in almost any town. Burlington is also home to one of the best pub crawl locations in New England. All three brewpubs—Three Needs Brewery & Taproom, the Vermont Pub & Brewery, and Zero Gravity Brewpub at American Flatbread—are located within a three-minute walk of each other.

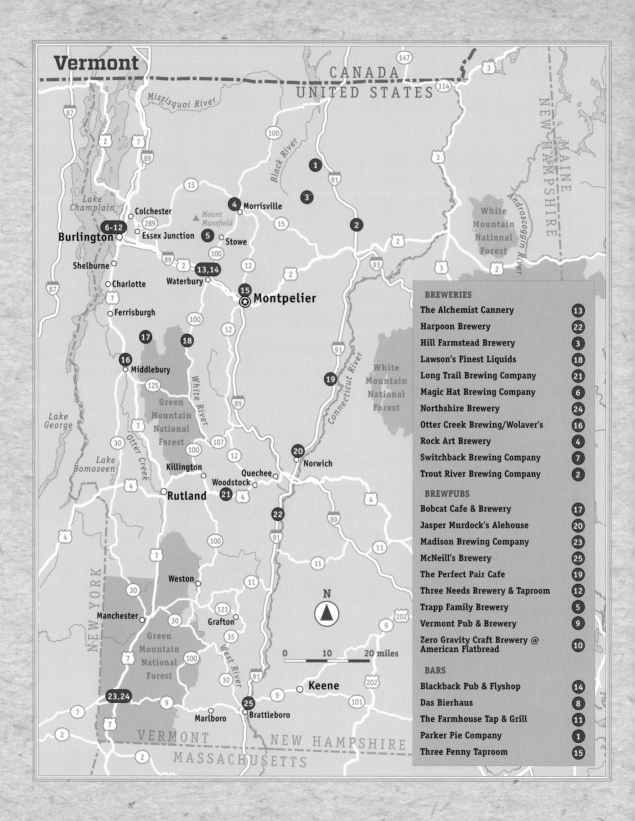

Vermont

CANADA
UNITED STATES

BREWERIES

The Alchemist Cannery	13
Harpoon Brewery	22
Hill Farmstead Brewery	3
Lawson's Finest Liquids	18
Long Trail Brewing Company	21
Magic Hat Brewing Company	6
Northshire Brewery	24
Otter Creek Brewing/Wolaver's	16
Rock Art Brewery	4
Switchback Brewing Company	7
Trout River Brewing Company	2

BREWPUBS

Bobcat Cafe & Brewery	17
Jasper Murdock's Alehouse	20
Madison Brewing Company	23
McNeill's Brewery	25
The Perfect Pair Cafe	19
Three Needs Brewery & Taproom	12
Trapp Family Brewery	5
Vermont Pub & Brewery	9
Zero Gravity Craft Brewery @ American Flatbread	10

BARS

Blackback Pub & Flyshop	14
Das Bierhaus	8
The Farmhouse Tap & Grill	11
Parker Pie Company	1
Three Penny Taproom	15

Breweries

HILL FARMSTEAD BREWERY

403 Hill Rd., Greensboro Bend, VT; (802) 533-7450; http://hillfarmstead.com
Founded: 2010 **Founder:** Shaun E. Hill **Brewer:** Shaun E. Hill **Flagship Beer:** Edward
Seasonals/Special Releases: Ancestor Series, Single Hop Series, Collaboration Series
Tours: None

Brewer Shaun E. Hill may be the most prolific brewer in New England. Since the first brew day in March 2010, Hill Farmstead has brewed about 50 different beers. Some breweries that have been around for decades have not come close to that number. Hill's love of hops shines through in most of his beers. Many of his beers are 85 international bittering units (the unit used to measure how bitter a beer is; double IPAs are usually in the seventies) or higher. He proves brewing hoppy beers is not the exclusive domain of west coast breweries.

Most of Hill Farmstead's beers can be called special releases. Almost none are brewed more than once or twice a year, except for **Edward,** an IPA. Edward is named for Hill's grandfather, on whose land the brewery now resides. Many of the beers are named for Hill's ancestors. **Abner,** named for Hill's great grandfather, is a 170 IBU, double IPA. That level of IBUs is unheard of, and almost insane. At least that's what it looks

Beer Lover's Pick

Iced Coffee Stout (Iced Earl)
Style: Imperial Stout
ABV: 15 percent
Availability: Rotating
The Iced Coffee Stout is one of the most impressive

beers I have ever tried. It might be packing 15 percent alcohol by volume, but you'd never know it. There is no boozy taste, which you'd get with similar higher-alcohol offerings, and faithful to its name, it tastes exactly like an iced coffee. A stunning beer.

like, until you see the IBUs for **Ephraim,** named for Hill's great-great grandfather. The beer is listed at 280 IBUs. It would be impossible for a human to detect that level of bitterness. Other beers named for ancestors include **Anna** (saison), **Earl** (stout), **Edith** (wheat beer), and **Clara** (a traditional ale). Hill Farmstead also brews several single-hop IPAs—they include the **Citra IPA, Galaxy IPA, Nelson Sauvin IPA,** and **Pacifica IPA.**

Not a hophead? Hill Farmstead does brew beers that are not hop monsters. Some of those include **Civil Disobedience** (saison), **Genealogy** (imperial stout), **Phenomena** (saison), and **Twilight of the Idols** (winter porter brewed with coffee and cinnamon and aged on vanilla beans). Hill Farmstead also has done several collaboration beers, including a series of beers with Danish brewer Anders Kissmeyer. The Kissmeyer collaboration beer is called **Fear and Trembling** and it is a Baltic porter. There are three versions, all aged in different barrels—bourbon barrels, French oak barrels, and a Cabernet and bourbon barrel blend. The beer is the same, but the three different barrels add different flavors. Barrel-aging beer is not uncommon at Hill Farmstead. Several of the beers are barrel-aged, mostly in French oak barrels. Some of the beers are released in two versions, barrel-aged and non-barrel-aged.

Tours are not available at the brewery, but Hill Farmstead does have a tasting room and retail showroom that is open Wednesday through Saturday from noon to 5 p.m. You can try the beers that are available in bottles, including limited releases and growlers.

LAWSON'S FINEST LIQUIDS
Warren, VT (not open to the public); (802) 272-8436; www.lawsonsfinest.com
Founded: 2008 **Founder:** Sean Lawson **Brewer:** Sean Lawson **Flagship Beer:** None
Year-round Beers: None **Seasonals/Special Releases:** More than 40 beers; for example, Big Hapi, Chinnoker'd IPA, Crooked Cabin Ale, Fayston Maple Imperial Stout, Gonzie, Hopzilla Double IPA, Farmhouse Ale, Maple Nipple Ale, Papelblonde Ale, Weiss-K. **Tours:** None

The beers from Lawson's Finest Liquids may be the most sought after in all of New England, and they may be the hardest to find. This small artisan brewery, "located high in the hills," only sells its beers in one store. One store in the whole state: the Warren Store in downtown Warren. Owner Sean Lawson delivers a different beer once a week, on Friday. Just one type of beer. The Warren Store limits sales of the beer to two bottles per person, but they are willing to hold a beer if they know you will be there that day.

You can drink Lawson's Finest Liquids beers on draft at the Common Man and the Pitcher Inn in Warren, American Flatbread in Waitsfield, Mad River Glen in Fayston, and the Village Porch in Rochester. The fun thing is, you'll never know what beer is

Gonzie
Style: Pale Ale
ABV: 4 percent
Availability: Rotating

It's easy to brew a hoppy beer with a lot of alcohol in it: Load up on the malt, which increases the alcohol and balances out the bitterness of the hops. What isn't easy is making a balanced low-alcohol beer packed with hops, especially one as tasty as Gonzie. Lawson worked his magic and hopped the Gonzie like a higher-alcohol brew, but found a way to maintain the balance with a lower ABV for the style.

available. Lawson delivers a different beer to each place every week. So one week you may get the Maple Nipple Ale at Mad River Glen, while American Flatbread may have the Red Spruce Bitter.

But the real question is: Is the beer worth it? Most definitely. Lawson may brew beer on a small scale, but it is phenomenal. Many of his beers, such as the **Maple Nipple Ale,** feature local maple syrup. Also brewed with maple are the **Fayston Maple Imperial Stout** and the **Maple Tripple.** Lawson's also brews several IPAs, including the **Chinnoker'd IPA, Big Happi India Black IPA, Hopzilla Double IPA,** and the **Fistful-o-Hop IPA.** Other beers include the **Crooked Cabin Ale** (English brown ale), **Equinox Extra XPA** (a big, high-alcohol pale ale), **Weiss-K** (German-style wheat beer), **292 Ale** (a "Hoptoberfest" Ale), and the **Permagin Rye Pale Ale** (a pale ale brewed with rye malt).

Keeping his brewery so small allows Lawson to spend as much time as he feels he needs on each beer, and the quality shows. Not one of the beers is anything less than stellar. Want a tour of Lawson's Finest Liquids? Not going to happen. Due to the limited space and hours, Lawson does not open his brewery to tours or tastings and there is no store. Instead, make the trek to the Warren Store, buy the beer there, and enjoy it in the privacy of your own home.

LONG TRAIL BREWING COMPANY

5520 US 4, Bridgewater Corners, VT; (802) 672-5011; www.longtrail.com
Founded: 1989 **Founder:** Andy Pherson **Brewer:** David Hartmann **Flagship Beer:** Long Trail Ale **Year-round Beers:** Blackbeary Wheat, Double Bag Ale, Pale Ale, Traditional IPA **Seasonals/Special Releases:** Belgian White Ale, Harvest Ale, Hibernator, Pollinator, Brewmaster Series **Tours:** Daily, 10 a.m. to 7 p.m.

The Long Trail Brewing Company is about more than just brewing good beer; they are about brewing good beer while helping the environment. Long Trail uses thermal energy to use less power at its Bridgewater Corners brewery. It also has cut down on water use, only using two gallons of water to brew one gallon of beer, down from the six gallons of water to one gallon of beer that is the industry standard. They also use a system that turns cow waste into methane gas, which is used to help power the brewery; in turn, they donate the nearly eight tons of spent mash they produce every day to local dairy farms to feed the cows.

Most important—at least for beer lovers—Long Trail manages to do all this without sacrificing the taste of their beers. Long Trail has been around for more than 20 years, and they continue to brew several fantastic beers. The year-round lineup has a good mix of beers you typically do not see as year-round beers. The **Long**

Beer Lover's Pick

Long Trail Ale
Style: Altbier
ABV: 4.6 percent
Availability: Year-Round
Sure this is the brewery's flagship beer, and one of its oldest, but it is still worth trying. Not enough authentic German alts make it to this side of the Atlantic, so when you can find a well-made alt, take advantage. The Long Trail Ale is brownish in color, and there is a mild fruitiness to it, as well as a yeasty flavor. It is a smooth drinking beer. Perfect whenever you want to drink it.

Trail Ale is a German-style altbier, a light-tasting brown ale. The **Double Bag Ale** is basically an imperial version of the Long Trail Ale, and is the strongest of the year-round beers at more than 7 percent alcohol by volume. The **Traditional IPA** and **Pale Ale** are typical of their styles, and are both very solid beers, while the **Blackbeary Wheat** is a light, refreshing beer, perfect for a hot summer day.

Long Trail also brews four seasonals. The **Pollinator** is a slightly hoppy pale ale, and is available during the spring. The **Belgian White Ale** is a traditional Belgian witbier and comes out during the summer. The **Harvest Ale** is a wonderful brown ale, and a welcome non-pumpkin fall seasonal. The **Hibernator** is a nice and malty Scotch ale and comes out when fall turns to winter. Long Trail also has the **Brewmaster series,** which features stronger beers, available in 22-ounce bombers instead of the usual 12-ounce bottles. The Brewmaster Series includes the **Centennial Red,** the **Double IPA,** and the **Imperial Porter.** It also includes the wonderful **Coffee Stout,** which tastes exactly like a well-brewed cup of joe.

Long Trail also has a pub on-site at the brewery and it features mainly pub food like chicken fingers, hot dogs, burgers, and other sandwiches. Several of the dishes do use beer, such as the Long Trail Cheddar Ale Soup and the Double Bag Chili. They also use ingredients from several local farms, and serve Long Trail Tap Water, which was named Vermont's Best Drinking Water by the Green Mountain Water Environment Association.

Harpoon Brewery in Vermont

The Harpoon Brewery is one of the oldest breweries in New England, and a Boston classic. But, they also have a brewery in Windsor, Vermont. In 2000, the brewery purchased the former Catamount Brewing Company and moved some of its production to the Green Mountain State.

Today, the Harpoon Brewery brews beer in the large facility, including much of its Leviathan Series, which are Harpoon's high-octane beers. The Windsor facility is also home to an on-site pub. The pub features a dozen fresh Harpoon beers on tap—year-round, seasonals, Leviathan, and the 100-Barrel Series.

The pub also has seats overlooking the brewery, so as you are enjoying your burger, wrap, panini, or appetizers, you can watch the beer you will soon be drinking being brewed and bottled. They also host tours and tastings, and there is a large brewery store.

MAGIC HAT BREWING COMPANY

5 Bartlett Bay Rd., South Burlington, VT; (802) 658-2739; www.magichat.net
Founded: 1993 **Founder:** Alan Newman **Brewer:** Justin McCarthy **Flagship Beer:** #9
Year-round Beers: Circus Boy, Single Chair **Seasonal/Special Releases:** Hex, Howl, Vinyl, Wacko, IPA on Tour, Flavor Flashbacks, Heart of Darkness **Tours:** Tues through Wed, 3 and 4 p.m.; Thurs through Fri, 2, 3, 4, and 5 p.m.; Sat, 1, 2, 3, 4, and 5 p.m.; Sun, 2 and 3 p.m.

It's safe to say the Magic Hat Brewing Company is a little different than most other breweries. Founded by Alan Newman, the brewery reflects his personality of peace and love, and oddness. After all, his title is Conductor of Cosmic Symphonies. Whatever the title means, Magic Hat has grown to become one of the largest craft breweries in the country, and their flagship beer, #9, can be found in many bars that do not cater to craft beer lovers.

The **#9,** described as a "Not Quite Pale Ale" and flavored with apricots, is also available in every one of the many seasonal mixed 12-packs Magic Hat releases throughout the year. Other year-round beers are the **Circus Boy,** which is a typical

Beer Lover's Pick

Howl
Style: Schwarzbier
ABV: 4.6 percent
Availability: Winter Seasonal
Magic Hat's Howl is a German-style schwarzbier, or a black lager. This is not the darkest black lager out there, but it is still a dark beer. Howl is smooth and has hints of mild chocolate and coffee roastiness. Unlike some other dark beer styles, like a stout, this beer is relatively light bodied and extremely easy to drink.

American wheat beer, and **Single Chair,** a golden ale that is available year-round, only in Vermont. Magic Hat also brews several seasonals. **Vinyl,** an easy-drinking, refreshing amber lager, is the beer of choice for the spring. The summer seasonal is **Wacko,** which has one of the most wacko beer ingredients ever—beets. The beer pours slightly red, and, shockingly, the beets actually work in the beer. Fall brings you Magic Hat's interpretation of an Oktoberfest-style beer, **Hex.** It is not a typical Oktoberfest since it is brewed with ale yeast, but it is still a nice fall beer. **Howl,** the winter seasonal, is a wonderful black lager.

Magic Hat has an interesting way of releasing their four IPAs. Instead of just having them all out at once, they release one every season as part of the **IPA on Tour** series. **Demo,** a black IPA, comes out in the spring; **Blind Faith,** an English-style IPA, is the summer offering; **hI.P.A.,** a straightforward American IPA, is released in the fall; and the winter IPA is **Encore,** which is more of a California west coast–style IPA. Throughout the year, Magic Hat also has **Flavor Flashbacks,** which are special releases of two of their early beers. **Humble Patience,** an Irish red ale and the brewery's first beer, is available from August 1 through October 15. **Ravell,** an English-style porter, takes over from there and remains on the shelves through January. **Heart of Darkness,** a nice oatmeal stout, is released only occasionally.

There are brewery tours daily, either guided or unguided. Growler fills are also available in the brewery store that features a 30-tap growler bar. The bar features year-round beers, seasonals, and sometimes rare, brewery only, or experimental beers. Magic Hat also hosts several events throughout the year, including small concerts and album release parties for new bands. They also host the largest northeast Mardi Gras celebration.

NORTHSHIRE BREWERY

108 County St., Bennington, VT; (802) 681-0201; www.northshirebrewery.com
Founded: 2009 **Founders:** Chris Mayne, Earl McGoff **Brewer:** Chris Mayne **Flagship Beer:** Equinox Pilsner **Year-round Beers:** Battenkill Ale, Chocolate Stout **Seasonals/Special Releases:** Summer Lager **Tours:** Tues through Thurs, 3 to 6 p.m.; Sat, 11 a.m. to 1 p.m.

The Northshire Brewery is the brainchild of homebrewers Chris Mayne and Earl McGoff, who recently made the successful transition from brewing small batches of homebrew to brewing professionally. Their brewery may be small, but they certainly put out a quality product in their three year-round beers and their lone seasonal offering.

The **Equinox Pilsner,** Northshire's flagship beer, is a classic Czech-style pilsner. It is only 4.2 percent alcohol by volume, but it packs tons of flavor. It's a fizzy yellow beer with a classic bready/yeasty taste and a nice touch of grassy hops. The

Equinox Pilsner
Style: Czech Pilsner
ABV: 4.2 percent
Availability: Year-Round

Sometimes fizzy, yellow beers are looked down upon in the craft beer world. The Equinox Pilsner is one of those beers that proves beer snobs wrong. This is a full-flavored, low-alcohol, Czech-style pilsner. The malts provide a malty and bready flavor, while the hops are grassy and floral. This is an easy-drinking, quality beer even for the most discerning of beer lovers.

Battenkill Ale, named for a local river, is a really solid amber ale, although darker than some amber ales. It is also a little hoppier than expected, with grassy hops and a sweet malt balance. The beer has slight diacetyl tastes, giving it hints of butter in the flavor. The body is a little thin, but not offensively so. The **Chocolate Stout** is Northshire's biggest beer at a modest 6 percent alcohol by volume. It is nice and full-bodied, with a full and creamy head. Flavorwise, the chocolate is not overpowering. Instead, the roasted flavors come out first, and the chocolate is more on the finish, which is a nice change from all the in-your-face chocolate stouts that are on the market today. Northshire also brews one seasonal, a light lager called **Summer Lager.** The Summer Lager is light beer with a bready aroma, but has a nice biscuity flavor with just a hint of hops—a perfect beer to enjoy at a cookout. It is similar to the Equinox Pilsner, but with less hops.

Northshire also hosts tours and tastings during the week. The tours of the brewery, led by one of the two owners, is free. Tastings are $3 each, but you get to keep the Northshire sample pint glass. Northshire also brews several house beers for the Mount Snow ski area, so skiers have something good to warm up with after a day on the slopes.

OTTER CREEK BREWING/WOLAVER'S

793 Exchange St., Middlebury, VT; (802) 388-0727; www.ottercreekbrewing.com
Founded: 1991 **Founder:** Lawrence Miller **Brewer:** Mike Gerhart **Flagship Beer:** Copper Ale **Year-round Beers:** Otter Creek: Black IPA, Stovepipe Porter. Wolaver's: Brown Ale, IPA, Oatmeal Stout **Seasonal/Special Releases:** Otter Creek: Otter Summer, Oktoberfest, Winter Red Ale, the Shed Mountain Ale, the Shed IPA. Wolaver's: Alta Gracia Porter, Pumpkin Ale, Wildflower Wheat **Tours:** Self-guided tours, daily, 11 a.m. to 6 p.m.

Otter Creek Brewing and Wolaver's Brewing Company are two breweries in one location in Middlebury, Vermont. Wolaver's purchased Otter Creek in 2002, and kept the Otter Creek line of beers separate from their own. That means there are two separate and distict lines of beer.

The Otter Creek Brewing Company is one of the most well-known names in Vermont brewing. They brew three year-round beers, as well as three seasonals. The **Otter Creek Copper Ale** is a German-style alt, a great choice for a flagship beer. The beer is grainy and has some caramel flavors. It is an easy-drinking beer, yet still has a full body. The **Stovepipe Porter** is an excellent porter and smells of burnt molasses, with some sweet aromas wafting up from the glass. This might be a dark beer, but it drinks very light. The **Otter Creek Black IPA** originally started as a seasonal, but it became so popular, they made it a year-round offering. That

Beer Lover's Pick

Otter Creek Black IPA
Style: Black IPA
ABV: 6 percent
Availability: Year-Round
I held a blind tasting with a dozen of the best black IPAs brewed in the US with several other beer lovers. The Otter Creek Black IPA won easily. This is a phenomenal beer. It has the hoppiness of a good, solid IPA, yet has the chocolate and roasted malts of a darker beer. The flavors all meld together into near perfection.

Vermont

was the smart choice, considering it is an excellent beer. Seasonals include the **Otter Summer,** which is a light, refreshing wheat beer. The **Oktoberfest** is a non-traditional Oktoberfest beer, mainly because it is an ale instead of a lager, while the **Winter Red Ale** is a hoppy red ale. Otter Creek also purchased the iconic the Shed Brewery lineup of beers in 2011 when the brewpub closed. They brew the popular **Shed Mountain Ale** and **Shed IPA.**

Wolaver's brews nothing but organic beers. Their **Brown Ale, IPA,** and **Oatmeal Stout** are all really well-done beers. The brown is nutty and malty, while the IPA is a solid, hoppy beer that does not overwhelm the palate. The Oatmeal Stout is suitably creamy and full-bodied. Wolaver's also brews three seasonals. The **Alta Gracia Porter** is a fantastic coffee beer with huge black coffee flavors, a perfect pick-me-up type of brew. The **Pumpkin Ale** is brewed with locally grown and organic pumpkins, and the **Wildflower Wheat** is a nicely done wheat ale brewed with honey, which provides sweetness and smoothness, resulting in a light, refreshing beer.

Otter Creek offers daily self-guided tours, and has a tasting room where you can sample many of the Otter Creek, Wolaver's, and the Shed's beers.

ROCK ART BREWERY

632 Laporte Rd., Morrisville, VT (802) 888-9400 www.rockartbrewery.com
Founded: 1997 **Founders:** Matt and Renee Nadeau **Brewer:** Matt Nadeau **Flagship Beer:** Whitetail Ale **Year-round Beers:** American Red Ale, Black Moon, IPA, Magnumus Ete Tomahawkus, Ridge Runner, Stock Ale, The Vermonster **Seasonals/Special Releases:** Belgian IPA, Belvidere Big IPA, Jasmine Pale Ale, IPA (II), Pumpkin Imperial Spruce Stout, Double Porter, Hell's Bock, Stump Jumper, Midnight Madness Smoked Porter, Mountain Holidays in Vermont, American-Belgo Style IPA, Infusco, Golden Tripple, The Riddler, Sunny and 75 **Tours:** Fri through Sat, 2 and 4 p.m.

In 2009, Rock Art Brewery played David to Monster Energy Drink's Goliath, when Monster tried to force Rock Art to rename one of its beers—the Vermonster. However, like David, Rock Art prevailed, and Vermonster remains on liquor store shelves unchanged today.

Besides its name, the best thing about **Vermonster,** a big, hoppy barleywine, is that it is an excellent beer. That is not unusual for the Rock Art Brewery, which is one of the best breweries in Vermont and all of New England. They have a large lineup of year-round, seasonal, and specialty beers that even the most hard-core beer fan should be able to enjoy. The **Whitetail Ale,** the brewery's flagship, is a fantastic American pale ale. The **American Red Ale** and the **IPA** are both spot on for their respective styles.

Vermonster
Style: Barleywine
ABV: 10 percent
Availability: Year-round

This was not an easy beer to pick. There are at least five beers that could have been chosen for this spot, but hey, Vermonster won out because it was part of a national news story. But most important, it is a fantastically hoppy barleywine. This is an American barleywine all the way, with 100 IBUs. But, it is also more balanced than you would think. The sweet malt backbone is needed to balance out this monster of a beer, and it works to great effect.

Rock Art is one of the better brewers of hoppy beers in New England. Along with the Vermonster, they also brew a huge black IPA, the **Black Moon,** which is extremely hoppy. The summer seasonal, the **Belvidere Big IPA,** and the winter seasonal, **IPA (II),** are both beers designed for the hop lovers. They also brew a fantastic Belgian-style IPA as part of their Belgian series of beer, the **American-Belgo Style IPA.**

But Rock Art is about more than just the hops. The **Ridge Runner** is a fantastic barleywine, almost on the mild side at only 7 percent alcohol by volume. They also brew two porters as seasonals, the **Double Porter** and the **Midnight Madness Smoked Porter.** The **Mountain Holidays in Vermont** is one of the best bocks brewed anywhere. It is an exquisite beer. Rock Art also brews one of the most interesting pumpkin beers on the market in the **Pumpkin Imperial Spruce Stout.** It is a pumpkin stout, of which there are few, and it is also an imperial stout, of which there are even fewer. Some people may not like the spruce flavor, but most beer lovers should enjoy it. Belgian beer fans rejoice—Rock Art also produces a Belgian series. Along with **Belgian IPA,** there is **Infusco** (a dream for those who like the flavor of anise), **Golden Tripple** (a Belgian triple), **The Riddler** (Belgian dubbel), and **Sunny and 75** (Belgian-style witbier).

Rock Art hosts tours on Friday and Saturday. They also host daily tastings at the brewery, which cost $3 (the cost of the sample glass you get to keep), and sell beer to go, from singles to cases to kegs, as well as other Rock Art gear.

SWITCHBACK BREWING COMPANY

160 Flynn Ave., Burlington, VT; (802) 651-4114; www.facebook.com/switchback brewingcompany
Founded: 2002 **Founders:** Bill Cherry, Ash Roesch **Brewer:** Ash Roesch **Flagship Beer:** Switchback Ale **Seasonals/Special Releases:** Roasted Red Ale, Slow-Fermented Brown Ale, Switchback Porter **Tours:** Sat, 1 and 2 p.m.; free

Ask someone in Burlington what beer you should try while you are in town, they are likely to say you have to try a Switchback Ale. Locals love their hometown brewery because Switchback brews quality, tasty, easy-drinking beers. You won't find wild and crazy experimentation going on here, but you will find finely crafted beers.

The **Switchback Ale** is the brewery's flagship beer, and the only beer Switchback brewed for the first five years of its existence. It really does not fit into any particular style—the closest may be an amber or red ale. This beer is brewed with five different malts and yeast the brewery cultivates itself, which creates some unique fruity flavors. The **Roasted Red Ale** is a wonderfully brewed red ale. A combination of caramel and roasted malts with a bigger-than-expected hop kick all comes together to form this excellent beer. It also ends with a taste of chocolate, which is a nice surprise for the style. The **Switchback Porter** is not a traditional English-style porter. The porter is brewed with several different types of malts, as well as flaked barley, which gives the beer a deeper malt presence. But this beer is not all about the malts. Switchback uses Simcoe hops, a very American hop not found in many British beers, which adds both aroma and bitter flavors, creating a tasty porter. The final beer, introduced in 2010, is the **Slow-Fermented Brown Ale.** Like the porter, this is not a traditional brown ale. Switchback ferments the beer at a much colder temperature than most ales, allowing the yeast to ferment slower, creating a brown ale that has the clean-drinking taste of a lager, but retains the creaminess of a good brown ale.

All of Switchback's beers are available only on draft. Do not get concerned if you get a pint and the beer is cloudy, because all of Switchback beers are unfiltered. Switchback Brewing Company offers tours on Saturday at 1 and 2 p.m. The tours are

Switchback Ale
Style: Pale Ale
ABV: 5 percent
Availability: Year-Round

The original is still the best. This unique tasting beer brewed with a house yeast is just so drinkable that you will want more than one or two. It is flavorful, easy-drinking, and just plain good. The hops are nice and mild, which allows the malt to come through. This is an amazingly balanced beer, which is exactly what you want while spending a night at the bar.

free, but they do recommend calling ahead to reserve a spot on the tour. Participants will get a chance to sample all the beer that is currently available. But do not expect to get beer to go. Switchback does not offer growlers because they feel the beer loses its quality when transferred from keg to growler.

TROUT RIVER BREWING COMPANY

645 Broad St., Lyndonville, VT; (802) 626-9396; www.troutriverbrewing.com
Founded: 1996 **Founders:** Dan and Laura Gates **Brewer:** Dan Gates **Flagship Beer:** Rainbow Red Ale **Year-round Beers:** Chocolate Oatmeal Stout, Hoppin' Mad Trout, Scottish Ale **Seasonals/Special Releases:** Boneyard Barley Wine, Caramel Porter, Dominator Doppelbock, Knight Slayer **Tours:** On-site pub open Fri and Sat, 4 to 9 p.m.

Dan and Laura Gates opened their small brewery in 1996 with the goal of providing good, fresh, and local beer to its customers. All these years later, Trout River Brewing Company is still cranking out those fresh beers, although you now can find them in states other than Vermont.

The brewery only brews four year-round beers. With the exception of one (Chocolate Oatmeal Stout), they are all traditional British styles of beer. The **Rainbow Red Ale,** named for the tastiest of all trouts, is a nicely done red ale. It is slightly

Vermont

toasty, very malty, and full-bodied. The **Hoppin' Mad Trout** is a light pale ale that comes in at 4.7 percent alcohol by volume. This is not a west coast pale ale with a dominant hop flavor, but it is a well-balanced pale ale, where the hops actually come on more in the finish. The **Scottish Ale** is the strongest of the year-round beers at 5.9 percent alcohol by volume. As the style should be, this is a malt dominated beer. There is even a hint of peat smokiness, which adds a little something extra to this beer. The **Chocolate Oatmeal Stout** is on the light side for a stout, but this does not take away from the flavor.

Trout River also brews several beers that are never available outside the brewery, such as the **Boneyard Barley Wine** and the **Knight Slayer,** which is an imperial stout. Those beers are available at the brewery on Friday and Saturday from 4 to 9 p.m., when Trout River's pub is open to the public. Beer lovers can come in and get their growlers filled, as well as sample between 6 and 10 Trout River beers, many only availllable at the brewery. Sourdough pizzas, hand-tossed and made with Dan Gates's own sourdough yeast culture—aged more than a decade—are also available.

Beer Lover's Pick

Chocolate Oatmeal Stout
Style: Oatmeal Stout
ABV: 4.9 percent
Availability: Year-round
Oatmeal stouts are often creamy, have hints of chocolate and coffee from roasted malt, and are on the low end of the ABV spectrum for stouts. Trout River's Chocolate Oatmeal Stout ratchets up the chocolate flavors by actually adding real chocolate. It is one of the lighter stouts you will ever have, but the chocolate creaminess will more than make up for the lack of body. It is by far the best beer currently being brewed by Trout River.

Brewpubs

BOBCAT CAFE & BREWERY

5 Main St., Bristol, VT; (802) 453-3311; www.bobcatcafe.com
Draft Beers: 12

The Bobcat Cafe & Brewery is the place to go in Bristol to get good, locally sourced meals and fresh, house-brewed beer. The brewpub prides itself on fresh food and fresh beer, and the quality of both shines through.

Beer-wise, the Bobcat Cafe offers a mix of traditional and not-so-traditional beers. The **Kolsch** is a traditional interpretation with one twist—it is aged for six weeks on French oak. The **Strawberries & Cream** is brewed with both ale and lager yeast, which is different than most beers. The strawberries are added during fermentation for flavor, and the Bobcat Cafe serves the beer on nitro, giving it a creamier head and body. Another unusual beer is the **Unrepentant,** which is a Belgian-style stout, again with a twist: It is brewed with chocolate and pepper. Many beers brewed with the same ingredients usually tip the scales at a higher ABV, but the Unrepentant comes in at a modest 5.1 percent ABV.

And then there are the traditional beers, which are exciting in their own way just because they are so good. The **Prayer Rock Pale Ale** is a traditional, west coast pale ale packed with a lot of hop flavor and aroma, but not overwhelming for those not into hoppy beers. The **Pocock Pilsner** is a light and refreshing pilsner with just a little hop bite. The **Dauntaun Braun** is a German-style dunkel weizen with hints of banana and chocolate in the flavor. The **Brickwall** is a big double IPA, brewed with hops grown on the side of the Bobcat Cafe, while the **lil Brick** is a quality black IPA.

The food is top notch and heavy on local ingredients. Appetizers include butternut squash bisque, Vermont venison stew, and braised duck spring rolls. A different daily flatbread is also an option. The entrees include ginger tofu tempura, which is fermented black bean and sweet potato cake served with curried coconut broth and sautéed bok choy. The maple-brined grilled pork chop is yet another standout, made with wild rice bread pudding, cider braised red cabbage, and Vermont apple and Riesling pan sauce. If you are not in the mood for such a large meal, order from the pub menu, which features burgers, sandwiches, and nachos.

Oh, make sure to leave room for one of the incredible desserts, such as the chocolate silk pie served in a graham cracker crust with a toasted marshmallow topping; the lavender honey walnut baklava, served with Ben and Jerry's vanilla ice cream; or the maple crème brûlée, made with Hillsboro Sugarworks Maple Syrup.

Vermont

The **Alchemist Pub and Brewery** in Waterbury, Vermont, was one of the best brewpubs in the state, respected for its wide selection of world-class beers, from its flagship double IPA, the Heady Topper, to its number of other beers including sours, stouts, and daily drinking beers.

But in August 2011, Hurricane Irene hit Vermont hard. It caused flooding, destroying homes, roads, and even small bridges. It also destroyed the Alchemist, with several feet of water filling up the basement, where all the brewing equipment was located. The Alchemist immediately had to close its doors, and later announced they would not be reopening.

However, this story has a happy ending. Long before Hurricane Irene's assault on Vermont, the Alchemist's founders, John and Jennifer Kimmich, had already started building a cannery, also in Waterbury. Shortly after the brewpub was destroyed, the **Alchemist Cannery,** located at 35 Crossroad, opened. At the time of this writing, they were only canning one beer, the **Heady Topper,** one of the best beers brewed in New England and one of the best double IPAs available in the world. Fresh 16-ounce cans of Heady Topper are available every week at the Alchemist Cannery in single cans, four-packs, or cases. It is a beer that should not be missed. The beer is also available at several restaurants in Vermont and Massachusetts.

The Alchemist has not announced when they will start brewing new beer, but they say their beer menu from the now defunct brewpub is a "blueprint for the future." It is sad that the Alchemist brewpub is gone, but the Alchemist Cannery may bring this brewery to even bigger heights and expose more people to the awesomeness of its beers. Long live the Alchemist.

JASPER MURDOCK'S ALEHOUSE

325 Main St., Norwich, VT; (802) 649-1143; www.norwichinn.com
Draft Beers: 4

The Norwich Inn is a beautiful little inn in picturesque Norwich, Vermont. It is also the home of Jasper Murdock's Pub, a small English-style brewpub. The brewpub is named for the original owner of the Norwich Inn, Jasper Murdock. The inn itself was built in 1797, and President James Monroe was a guest in 1817.

Jasper Murdock's mainly brews finely crafted English-style ales, and the only beer available at all times is the **Whistling Pig Red Ale,** which is an Irish red ale with a little more hops. The brewpub only has four beers on tap, but they are rotated often. Other British-style beers include the **J & R's Birthday Brown Ale,** the **Stackpole Porter, Oh Be Joyful** (English mild), **Second Wind Oatmeal Stout,** the **Old Slippery Skin IPA, ESB, Another Ale** (English best bitter), **Famous Sidekick** (dark mild), **Ma Walker's Double Strength Stout, 70 Shilling Ale, 90 Shilling Pale Ale,** and **Fuggles & Barleycorn** (English golden ale).

Jasper Murdock's also offers several German-style beers, including the **NORweizINN** (German-style weizen), **Oktoberfest, Bock from the Trail** (Maibock), **Munich Dunkel,** and the **Scwarzpils.** Also offered are a few Belgian-style ales, including **Light Humour** and **Dark Humour.** The Light Humour is a traditional Belgian-style witbier, while Dark Humour is also a Belgian-style witbier, except is dark, not light like a traditional beer. The **Norwich Abbey** is a strong dark Belgian ale.

The Norwich Inn has two areas for eating—the more rowdy and casual brewpub and then the dining room, which takes reservations and is a little quieter. They offer the same menu, so whatever atmosphere you like, the quality food will be there. And don't worry if there is someone in your party that does not like beer. The Norwich Inn has a wine cellar that includes 2,000 bottles.

Start with the Autumn Salad, which is made of baby romaine lettuce, toasted pecans, lardons, fried brie, and dried cranberries topped with sherry rosemary vinaigrette. Appetizers include duck confit egg rolls and the Charcuterie Plate, which includes venison sausage, country pate, pork rillette, cherry sage chutney, and grilled flatbread. Entrees include cashew-encrusted trout filets, the rack of lamb, and chicken roulade. The seasonal menu changes throughout the year—be sure to sample the pumpkin risotto, which includes caramelized apples, gorgonzola, and toasted pumpkin seeds, in the fall.

Unfortunately, if you do fall in love with a Jasper Murdock's beer, you will not be able to bring it home with you—the only place their beers are available is at the brewpub. In that case, you might want to stay an extra night or two.

Vermont

MADISON BREWING COMPANY

428 Main St., Bennington, VT; (802) 442-7397; www.madisonbrewingco.com
Draft Beers: 8

The Madison Brewing Company bills itself as the place where "Fermentation & Civilization are Inseparable." Loosely translated, I think that means it is a brewpub where people like to go eat, drink, and be merry. The brewpub is a Bennington mainstay and they brew several excellent beers that have a full and varied nature.

The Madison Brewing Company features eight beers on tap, six year-round beers and a rotation of two seasonals available at a time. The year-round beers include the **Sucker Pond Blonde,** a beer for those who want something easy to drink, and the **Old 76 Strong Ale,** which is basically the opposite, a stronger, full-flavored, malt-dominated English-style strong ale. The **Buck's Honey Wheat** is a wheat beer brewed with local honey. The rest of the year-round beers include **Willoughy's Scottish Ale,** the **Crowtown Pale Ale,** and **Wassick's White Ale.** The seasonals include the **American Honey Brown Ale,** the **Strawberry Hefeweizen,** and the **Octoberfest.** During the year, you may find a homebrew beer on tap; the Madison Brewing Company takes part in a local homebrewing competition where the winning beer is on brewed and put on tap at the pub.

If you cannot decide what beer to order, order a sampler and get six of them at once in 5-ounce glasses.

Appetizers are straight-up pub classics—chicken tenders, nachos, mussels, and calamari. If you'd rather have something on the lighter side, try the You Had Me at Brie salad, which includes grilled eggplant and brie cheese, stacked with caramelized shallots, wild field greens, diced tomatoes, shredded carrots, and roasted red pepper dressing. Meat lovers will want to order the Brewmaster's Sausage Dinner, which includes bratwurst, knockwurst, and Irish sausage, served with apple chutney, beer sauerkraut, and garlic mashed potatoes.

Once you're done digesting, consider grabbing a growler of one of Madison's beers to bring home.

MCNEILL'S BREWERY

90 Elliot St., Brattleboro, VT; (802) 254-2553; www.mcneillsbrewery.com
Draft Beers: 10 to 12

McNeill's Brewery is an institution. Founded in 1992 by Ray McNeill, this brewpub is one of the most well-known brewpubs in all of New England. They brew tons of award-winning beers in their small Brattleboro pub.

Their beers, more than 30 to choose from, are all pretty much spot-on for their styles. The **Big Nose Blonde** is an aromatic blonde ale, while the **Dead Horse IPA** is one of the best English-style IPAs being brewed in New England. The **Champ Ale** is a fantastic pale ale. McNeill's **Firehouse Amber Ale** is a wonderful amber ale—very easy to drink, with just enough body to make it a step above the average amber ale. The **Duck Breath Bitter** is a really good English-style bitter, the **Ruby Ale** is a quality red ale, and the **Pullman's Porter** is a better-than-average porter. McNeill's also brews several seasonals. They include the **Octoberfest,** the **Maibock,** and the **Summer Brown Ale.** The brewpub also produces a couple of really good, higher octane beers. The **Warlord Double IPA** is a big, hoppy monster of a west coast IPA. Their biggest beer is the **Dark Angel Imperial Stout;** it is 10 percent alcohol by volume, malty, with a lot of chocolate flavors in the beer.

McNeill's also bottles several of its beers, which are brewed and bottled at its nearby production facility. The bottled beers are the Blond Bombshell Ale, Champ Ale, Dark Angel, Dead Horse IPA, Extra Special Bitter, Exterminator (doppelbock), Firehouse Amber Ale, Oatmeal Stout, Octoberfest, Old Ringwood, Professor Brewhead's Brown Ale, Pullmans' Porter, Sunshine IPA, Tartan Ale, and Warlord Double IPA.

McNeill's does offer some food, but it is a very limited menu that includes a few pub items, such as pizza, chili, nachos, and the like. People are welcome to bring in food from other restaurants if they want. The pub is cash-only, so stock up that wallet before you.

THE PERFECT PEAR CAFE
48 S. Main St., Bradford, VT; (802) 222-5912; theperfectpearcafe.com
Draft Beers: 4

Some brewpubs are all about the beer, and offer quick, easy, serviceable pub food and burgers. Other brewpubs, such as the Perfect Pear Cafe in Bradford, are the opposite. The Perfect Pear serves up some delicious food first and foremost—they just also happen to brew some quality beer.

Home to the Vermont Beer Company, the Perfect Pear Cafe offers two house beers on tap. The various beers include the **First Tap India Pale Ale,** the **Devil's Den Brown Porter, Smoked Maple Porter,** and **Walt's River Red Ale.** Other beers include a doppelbock, pilsner, and an Oktoberfest. They also usually have two guest taps from such breweries as McNeill's Brewing Company in Vermont and the Oxbow Brewing Company in Maine.

The beers are exclusively brewed to be served at the Perfect Pear and the pub, where the small brewing system is located, beneath the Pear Café. The beer is brewed by the Perfect Pear's Chef Adam Coulter, who is also a homebrewer.

Their beers are great, but if you are going to the Perfect Pear, you are going for the food. The homemade pickles and crispy pork dumplings are standout options as starters. Also worth trying is the garlic and ale braised mussels, available in different sizes, either for individuals or groups. Paul's Lebanese Plate includes stuffed grape leaves, hummus, tabouli, and warm pita bread. Larger meals include Ale House Fish & Chips and a rosemary and ale lamb stew. The wild mushroom ravioli and the confit duck leg, which is served with braised onions and a cider glaze, are also worth trying, as is the bangers and mash. Along with the usual the Pear Cafe menu, the pub also serves some food. It features a burger and beer special for $10. The pub opens at 2 p.m.

THREE NEEDS BREWERY & TAPROOM
185 Pearl St., Burlington, VT; (802) 658-0889
Draft Beers: 12

There are three brewpubs in downtown Burlington, and each one is completely different. The Three Needs Brewery & Taproom is the place where the younger locals head out to grab a cold beer for cheap. Despite all the bar options in downtown Burlington, Three Needs will often be the only one with a line outside the door with people waiting to get in on a weekend night. The inside is small, dark, loud, and packed. This is a dive bar. But they have some tasty beer, so if you're a bit of a bar snob, you might want to make an exception. Make sure to get food before you go there, though, because they do not serve food. It is all about the beer and loud music.

You will be hard pressed to find cheaper beer at a brewpub. You can get some pints for $3.50. However, do not mistake cheap for bad; Three Needs' beers are very good. The draft list changes quite often. On any given night, you may find Belgian styles, lagers, IPAs, or numerous other styles. Some of the beers include the **Belgian Chocolate Stout** and the **Chocolate Thunder Porter.** They also brew a very good **Belgian Triple.** Three Needs, which brews its beers in the basement, also brews some sour beers, such as the **Sour Red** and the **Wild Blonde.** A standout is the **Ich Bin Ein Berliner Weisse,** while the **Dortmonder-style Lager** is a solid lager. Three Needs also brews a solid koslch.

Three Needs usually has one of its several IPAs on tap. They brew four different IPAs, as well as several different stouts. Other styles brewed include Scottish ale, a rye beer, wheat beers, a honey ale, and a smoked ESB. Often only about half of the taps are Three Needs beers, and the rest of the tap list is made up of guest brewers, mostly other Vermont breweries, although sometimes beers from as far away as California will find their way on tap.

TRAPP FAMILY LODGE BREWERY

700 Trapp Hill Rd., Stowe, VT; (802) 243-7509; www.trappfamily.com
Draft Beers: 4

Does the "Trapp" name sound familiar? This is the same Trapp family featured in one of the most famous movies of all time, *The Sound of Music*. The Trapp Family Brewery is in the Trapp Family Lodge in the mountains of Stowe. The all-lager brewery was opened in 2010 after family patriarch Johannes von Trapp decided to pursue his dream of brewing beer like he remembered from his formative years growing up in Austria.

The brewery, which is a really a brewpub with all of its beer served on the on-site DeliBakery at the resort, brews three year-round beers and one seasonal at a time. The **Golden Helles,** a German-style helles bock, is the flagship. It is also available at bars and restaurants throughout the state. Helles bocks are light and refreshing beers, and the Golden Helles is exactly that—it has a nice malty flavor, with just a hint of hops. The **Vienna Amber** is a darker lager, malt forward and still relatively light. The beer is fuller-bodied than the Golden Helles, and it has a sweeter finish. The sweetness is balanced by just a touch of hops on the tongue. The **Dunkel Lager** is a dark lager, with hints of chocolate. This is an extremely malty beer, with barely any hops present.

Throughout the year, the Trapp Family Lodge Brewery offers several different seasonal beers. The **Summer Lager** is the most American of the beers, a pale lager that tastes like a more flavorful mass-produced beer. The **Oktoberfest** is excellent, extremely traditional for the style. The **Winter Geist** is a stronger, maltier, and bigger beer than the year-round Dunkel Lager.

The DeliBakery has an interesting mix of food. There's a different pizza served daily, as well as meat and vegetarian quiches. Go authentic and order something from the von Trapp family's homeland, like the Austrian bratwurst. Several sandwiches are also available in addition to the main courses, and freshly baked pastries and breads are available every day. If the DeliBakery isn't your thing, order a couple of beers and then go to one of the other on-site dining areas, which include the Lounge and the Main Dining Room.

Vermont

VERMONT PUB & BREWERY

144 College St., Burlington, VT; (802) 865-0500; www.vermontbrewery.com
Draft Beers: 12

The Vermont Pub & Brewery is the oldest brewery in Vermont, founded by the late Greg Noonan in 1988. The beers and the pub are both Vermont classics, and many of the beers originally created during the early days of the brewery are still being produced today. Located within walking distance of two other Burlington brewpubs, the Vermont Pub & Brewery is a must-visit.

The brewpub has a good mix of 12 different beers on tap at all times (including two casks). They do a good job of mixing up their styles so they appeal to people of all tastes. In all, they may brew up to 30 different beers in any given year. Like fruit beers? Grab a pint of the **Forbidden Fruit,** a refreshing 6.2 percent alcohol by volume ale brewed with 500 pounds of fresh raspberries. Like stouts? Get the **Handsome Mick's Irish Stout.** The **Tulack Leis,** a Flemish sour red, or the **Saison d'Automne** are some options if you consider yourself a bit of a Belgian ale fan. Other beers include the **Bombay Grab IPA,** the **Dog Bite Bitter, Milk Stout,** and the **Blue Nile Lotus Gruit.** The Vermont Pub & Brewery also brews several seasonals, including the **Ocktoberfest** and the **Rocktoberfest,** two different versions of a German-style Oktoberfest beer.

As far as food, the Vermont Pub & Brewery has a solid menu of pub fare. The appetizers are heavy on fried seafood such as oysters, calamari, and clam strips. There are tons of sandwiches available, including the Chicken Rolli Polli, which is grilled chicken with jack cheese, sweet and sour jalapeño sauce, lettuce, tomatoes, and onions on a wrap. Want a larger meal? Grab a pulled pork pie, which is a pie full of southern-style barbecued pulled pork, topped with corn and mashed potatoes. The Ploughman's Lunch features hunks of both Vermont cheddar and smoked cheddar, with a house-baked loaf of bread, apple chutney, and honey mustard. The pecan-encrusted trout filet is excellent, and the tequila-honey chicken, which is a chicken breast basted in honey and tequila, is also worth exploring as a dinner option.

Before you leave, make sure to pick up a growler of your favorite beer, as well as tie-dye shirts, glassware, or even some of Noonan's books on brewing.

ZERO GRAVITY CRAFT BREWERY @ AMERICAN FLATBREAD

115 St. Paul St., Burlington, VT; (802) 861-2999; http://americanflatbread.com
Draft Beers: 12 house-brewed beers, 8 guest taps, 2 casks

American Flatbread, host of the Zero Gravity Craft Brewery, is the best at a lot of things in Burlington: They make the best pizzas, they are the best brewpub, and they boast the best beer bar in Burlington, with eight guest taps and around 50 excellent selections in craft bottled beers, which does not include the large selection of ciders and meads.

Zero Gravity's brewers produce some excellent beers. Throughout the year they may brew more than 50 beers, with a rotating selection of seasonals. In fall, for example, they brew the **St. Pauli Boy,** a Munich-style Oktoberfest lager. Zero Gravity also brews beers that represent all of the major brewing countries—Belgium, England, Germany, and the US. They brew some experimental beers, such as the **Deus Aqua,** which is a Belgian-style saison brewed with honey and pink and black peppercorns, or the **Gruit,** which is an ancient style of beer brewed with local herbs.

The guest drafts are usually other beers from Vermont (Long Trail) or from other New England states (Smuttynose Brewing Company). Brewery Ommegang from New York is also frequently available. The bottled list includes several beers from Vermont breweries, such as Rock Art Brewery, Trout River Brewing Company, and Wolaver's. American Flatbread also carries numerous beers from the Allagash Brewing Company in Maine, as well as beers from Dieu du Ciel and Unibroue in Canada. There is always a small selection of vintage bottled ales available. These are typically large-format bottles, bombers and 750 ml, perfect for sharing.

It is strange to say, but even though the beer is excellent, American Flatbread's flatbread pizzas are actually the star at this brewpub. They are stunningly good. They are all made without tomato sauce (unless requested) and are made with fresh, locally grown ingredients and cooked in the large, wood-fire stove located in the middle of the restaurant. There are several different options—the New Vermont Sausage, the Medicine Wheel, and the Revolution Flatbread are just a few of them. Even the plain herb and cheese pizza is great. You can also pick all your own toppings ranging from the normal pepperoni to salsa, corn, goat cheese, and black beans.

Vermont

Beer Bars

BLACKBACK PUB & FLYSHOP

1 Stowe St., Waterbury, VT; (802) 505-5115; http://blackbackpub.com
Draft Beers: 25 **Bottled/Canned Beers:** Small selection of special beers

There may not be a more unique beer bar in the world than the Blackback Pub & Flyshop. After all, have you ever heard of a bar with 25 world-class beers on tap that also sells fishing flies and other fly-fishing equipment and serves sushi a few nights a week?

Owner Rick Binet takes a lot of care picking his beer. The beers on tap are not easy to find beers like Samuel Adams or Long Trail. Instead, he said there are no "half-assed craft beers," and he seeks out beers from Hill Farmstead, or some of the more complex offerings from the Allagash Brewing Company. Stoudt's and beers from Stillwater Artisanal Ales from Baltimore, Maryland, were also some recent offerings. Blackback Pub also has some rare German beers on draft, as well as options from Belgium and other American breweries. The bottled list is minimal, with a few rare beers.

There is more than just beer at the Blackback Pub. They also have a huge selection of wonderful (and sometimes expensive) whiskeys and bourbons. Some of the whiskeys include Laphroaig Quarter Cask, Balvenie Double Wood 12 Year, Macallan Cask Strength, Glenlivet Nadurra 16 Year, and Ardbeg 10 Year.

The menu is not large but it is eclectic. Blackback Pub serves panini sandwiches and a couple of cheese plates. The pub has also recently added Back Country Flat Breads and calzones from local restaurant La Strada. A sushi chef prepares sushi Wednesday through Friday, with some Saturday specials.

If you are not into the beer, whiskey, sushi, or pizza, this still could be the place to go if you are into fly fishing. Binet is a Vermont fly-fishing guide. At the pub, he sells flies designed for those who are on the hunt for trout in local streams and ponds. The pub also gets its name from the local moniker given to the brook trout that live in the mountain brooks that flow into local streams and rivers, blackbacks. Also available for sale are bamboo fly fishing rods and classic fly reels. These rods and reels are not something you buy as a memory of your stop at Blackback. The rods and reels cost up to $2,600.

The pub is small, but a great place to have a conversation. The bar seats about 25 and there are several small tables. There are TVs for watching games. If you find yourself in Waterbury, the Blackback Pub is a must-stop. Heck, while grabbing a beer and some eel sushi, get the fly-fishing report for an early fishing trip the next morning.

DAS BIERHAUS

175 Church St., Burlington, VT; (802) 881-0600; www.dasbierhausvt.com
Draft Beers: 8 **Bottled/Canned Beers:** More than 60

Das Bierhaus takes its love of the German beer culture to higher levels than any other German-inspired pub in New England. The menu is huge on German food, and the beer list is heavy on German beers. All draft beers are always German beers. Not German-style beers, but beers directly imported from Germany.

Das Bierhaus always has classic German styles—pilsners, lagers, hefeweizens—on draft. They also change beers for the seasons, putting on Oktoberfest beers in the fall and doppelbocks in the winter. Most of the best German breweries are represented on draft, such as Ayinger, Weihenstephan, Frankziskaner, and Warsteiner. Draft beers are also available in three different sizes: 0.3 liters, 0.4 liters, and 0.5 liters. The bottled list is also heavy into German beers, with about another 15 to 20 German beers available in bottles. They also have several American beers, such as Rock Art, and beers from other countries, such as Samuel Smith's from England. Das Bierhaus also always has some large-format bombers and 750 ml bottles available, and they are typically Belgian ales, or higher-alcohol American beers.

To go along with all of that German beer, Das Bierhaus has a menu heavily inspired by German food. Appetizers include soft Bavarian pretzels and Schnitz on a Stick. You could also order the Kasespatzle, which is made in-house with dill and onion, as well as Swiss, cheddar, and gruyère cheeses. The Jager Sandwich, an open-faced pork schnitzel sandwich with sauteed mushrooms, onions, jager sauce, and a house, or haus, cheese blend, is a sandwich worth trying. Entrees include three types of schnitzel. You can get the classic Wiener Schnitzel, which is made from a hand-pounded veal cutlet and then pan fried; the Schnitzel vom Schwein, a pork loin butchered on-site and pan fried; or the Jager "Hunter" Schnitzel, which is the Schnitzel vom Schwein, but topped with a house- (or haus-) made mushroom gravy sauce. Of course, a German restaurant would not be complete without wurst. Das Bierhaus offers five different types of sausage: The Bockwurst is mildly spiced pork and veal sausage; knackwurst is spiced, smoked pork and beef sausages; bratwurst is seasoned veal sausage; bauernwurst is a sausage made with mustard seeds and marjoram, making it spicy; and finally the rauchwurst is a smoked sauasge.

Vermont

THE FARMHOUSE TAP & GRILL

160 Bank St., Burlington, VT; (802) 859-0888; http://farmhousetg.com
Draft Beers: 24 **Bottled/Canned Beers:** About 120

The Farmhouse Tap & Grill bills itself as a farm-to-table gastropub, where almost all the food is made from locally sourced ingredients. Many of its beers are also local. They have 24 beers on tap, and have a huge bottle list of about 120 selections.

The draft list usually features Hill Farmstead beers, as well as Allagash Brewing Company from Maine. They have a couple of imported beers available, too. They typically have two beers on cask. The bottled list is varied and it is broken up by country. American bottles usually include both Allagash and Hill Farmstead, but also beers from Maine Beer Company and Stillwater Artisanal Ales. They also have one canned beer, the Alchemist's Heady Topper, which is delivered fresh from the Waterbury cannery every week. The Belgian ales are broken up into two categories—Belgian and Trappist. They have a huge selection of Trappist ales, and the "normal" Belgian list is impressive. The Farmhouse Tap has a large Canadian beer menu, made up mostly of Unibroue and Dieu du Ciel—there is no Molson here. There are plenty of British and German beers on the list, too. Unlike a lot of bars, the Farmhouse Tap & Grill has a cellared beer list that sports many different aged beers, such as Chimay and other Belgian ales.

Beer Event

Allagash Abduction

Every November, the Farmhouse Tap & Grill hosts a special night when Allagash takes over the tap handles, with 17 of Allagash's best beers on draft all at once in one place. Some of the beers are rarer offerings rarely seen on tap, while others are some of their more well-known but still fantastic beers. No matter what, it is a night of Allagash, and that is a night you want to be a part of.

The menu is not huge at the Farmhouse Tap & Grill, but the food they do serve is delicious. You can start with one of the Tap Room Snacks, which include buttermilk biscuits, Nitty Gritty Corn Bread, and maple-rosemary bar nuts. Entrees include the chicken and biscuits made from local chickens, meat loaf made with both beef and pork, and macaroni and cheese made with carmelized onions and local cheeses. The burgers are all made with local grass-fed beef, and the Winding Brook Farm Pasture-Raised Pork is a sandwich made with local pork, eggs, Grafton cheddar, fennel slaw, and a root beer barbecue sauce.

PARKER PIE COMPANY
161 County Rd., West Glover, VT; (802) 525-3366; www.parkerpie.com
Draft Beers: 13 **Bottled/Canned Beers:** 40

Not enough pizza places embrace good beer. It really doesn't make much sense—what goes better together than a good slice and a great glass of craft beer? The Parker Pie Company in tiny West Glover gets it right. They make great pizzas, and have a top-notch beer selection to wash it all down.

The draft list includes 13 excellent beers from a mix of local breweries, such as the Rock Art Brewery, Hill Farmstead, and Wolaver's, and from other parts of the country, such as the Brooklyn Brewery, Rogue Brewery, and Stone Brewing Company. The bottled list is even more impressive. Whoever is in charge of the beer list is obviously a fan of Stone and Rogue, with several beers from both breweries available. There are also several Belgian ales available, such as A'Chouffe, Cantillon, Monk's Cafe, and Bosteels. Beer Here from Denmark, rarely seen at any place except the best beer bars, is also available. The beer menu also features several mass-produced lagers for an affordable $2.75, so even if you are with someone who's not a craft beer lover, he or she will have options. Parker Pie also has a good-size wine menu.

The beer selection alone may be worth making the trip out to Parker Pie, but the real star is the pizza. They offer different sauce choices—tomato sauce, crushed plum tomatoes, pesto, or garlic white sauce. All the typical toppings are available (although many of the toppings are made locally), but Parker Pie specializes in some truly unique pizzas. The Scott's Revenge is slathered in Scott's Oil, a hot housemade oil used on many of the pizzas, and crushed plum tomatoes, topped with mozzarella cheese, spicy shrimp, scallions, and roasted red peppers. Another unique pizza is the Bangkok Disco, which is covered with Scott's Oil, crushed plum tomatoes, mozzarella and cheddar cheese, zesty chicken breast, red onions, and light bleu cheese and dusted with curry powder. Make sure to have a hoppy beer to complement the heat of these pies.

Vermont

THREE PENNY TAPROOM

108 Main St., Montpelier, VT; (802) 223-TAPS; http://threepennytaproom.com
Draft Beers: 24 **Bottled/Canned Beers:** 60

The Three Penny Taproom is the best place to seek out beer in Vermont's capital city. There are 24 rotating beers on tap, as well as an ever-changing selection of 60 bottled varieties. The Three Penny Taproom also has fantastic food, using as many local ingredients as possible in its dishes.

The draft list is impressive. There are always numerous great beers on tap. They are also one of the few places to occasionally get Lawson's Finest Liquids beers on draft. There are plenty of other good beers, such as Hill Farmstead, also from Vermont, and the Alchemist Heady Topper, Dogfish Head, Stone Brewing Company, and Allagash Brewing Company.

The bottled list is also good, with a strong mix of imported beers and craft beers from New England and other parts of the US.

A sign of a really good pub, or a gastropub, is if the food is as good as the beer, and vice versa. The Three Penny Taproom is pretty darn close. The use of local, fresh ingredients makes for a fantastic menu. Most of the cheeses, poultry, vegetables, and other meats come from local farms.

Starters include horseradish pickled beets and the dilly deviled eggs with pea greens. If you want a hearty soup, get the chicken borscht. Salads include the winter wheat berry salad with gold raisins and mint. Larger items include sandwiches, such as the maple roasted pork belly with sauerkraut and grain mustard and the raclette with pickled sun-dried plums. Another sandwich to consider is the Namaste (a wonderful beer from Dogfish Head), which is braised rabbit served on pumpkernickel bread with spring greens. The Three Penny Taproom also has an impressive selection of artisan cheeses, mostly from local producers.

Note: The menu changes frequently, almost every other week, based on the availability of local ingredients.

Closing hours are not set. The Three Penny Taproom is always open until at least midnight, but sometimes it remains open until 2 a.m., depending on how busy it is.

New Hampshire

Portsmouth is the center of the brewing world in the Granite State: The Smuttynose Brewing Company, Red Hook Brewing Company, the Portsmouth Brewery, and even Anheuser-Busch are all in the city. But there are other places to get good beer. Manchester has Milly's Tavern, a fun brewpub. The Squam Brewing Company is making good beer in the lakes region, and the White Birch Brewing Company in Hooksett is making some of the most unique beers being brewed today.

There are also some cool little beer bars, such as the Barley Pub in Dover, or if you want a place to stay, drink beer, or even brew beer, spend the weekend at the Woodstock Inn. New Hampshire is on the upswing as far as beer is concerned, and it will only get better.

New Hampshire's breweries are also on the forefront of "green brewing," with many of them leading the way when it comes to using recycled materials and using as many local and organic ingredients as possible.

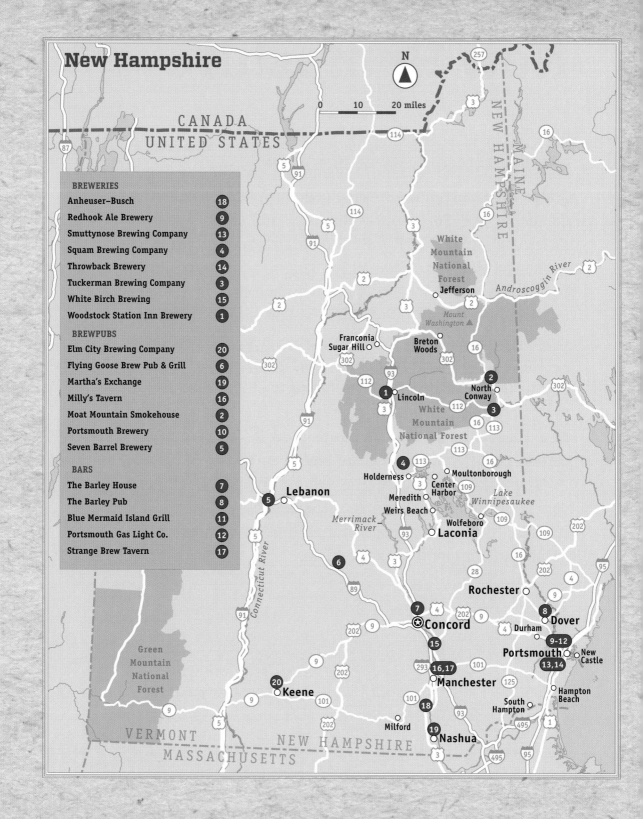

New Hampshire

N

0   10   20 miles

CANADA
UNITED STATES

BREWERIES
Anheuser–Busch — 18
Redhook Ale Brewery — 9
Smuttynose Brewing Company — 13
Squam Brewing Company — 4
Throwback Brewery — 14
Tuckerman Brewing Company — 3
White Birch Brewing — 15
Woodstock Station Inn Brewery — 1

BREWPUBS
Elm City Brewing Company — 20
Flying Goose Brew Pub & Grill — 6
Martha's Exchange — 19
Milly's Tavern — 16
Moat Mountain Smokehouse — 2
Portsmouth Brewery — 10
Seven Barrel Brewery — 5

BARS
The Barley House — 7
The Barley Pub — 8
Blue Mermaid Island Grill — 11
Portsmouth Gas Light Co. — 12
Strange Brew Tavern — 17

MAINE
NEW HAMPSHIRE

White Mountain National Forest

Jefferson

Androscoggin River

Mount Washington ▲

Franconia Sugar Hill
Breton Woods

North Conway

1 Lincoln

White Mountain National Forest

Holderness
Moultonborough
Center Harbor
Meredith
Weirs Beach
Lake Winnipesaukee
Wolfeboro
Laconia

Lebanon

Merrimack River

Green Mountain National Forest

Connecticut River

Rochester

Concord
Dover
Durham

15
Portsmouth
New Castle

16,17
Manchester

20 Keene

18
Milford

19 Nashua

South Hampton

Hampton Beach

VERMONT
NEW HAMPSHIRE
MASSACHUSETTS

Breweries

PRODIGAL BREWING COMPANY

Effingham, NH (closed to public); (603) 539-2210
Founded: 2010 **Founder:** Paul Davis **Brewer:** Paul Davis **Flagship Beer:**
Effinghamburgherbrau **Year-round Beer:** Sacopee Pils **Seasonals/Special Releases:** Rev.
Potter Baltic Porter, 5 different bocks, Oktoberfest **Tours:** None

The Prodigal Brewing Company is a true farmhouse brewery. Owner/founder Paul Davis bought a 20-acre farm to raise his kids and start his own brewery. A professional brewer for years, Davis wanted to brew the beers he wanted to brew, no exceptions. He uses his own hops in the beer, and he grows other ingredients on the farm. His wife is a beekeeper, and they use their own honey in some of their beers.

At the time of this writing, Prodigal only distributed to Dover, New Hampshire, but by the time you read this, they are expected to have increased their distribution. The reason for the slow growth was that Davis was testing his beers, attending beer festivals throughout New England to get feedback on which ones people would enjoy. His brewery, so far, has only brewed lagers because his well water has low mineral content, which is perfect for lager beers.

His **Effinghamburgherbrau**—say that three times fast—is a golden lager. It is a clean tasting, easy beer to drink. For those who say they do not enjoy "fizzy yellow beers," this is the beer to change their minds. The **Sacopee Pils** was originally introduced to be a half-year beer, but it became so popular, Davis has decided to make it a year-round beer. It is a classic German-style pilsner. Prodigal also brews the **Rev. Potter**

Beer Lover's Pick

Effinghamburgherbrau
Style: Lager
ABV: Unknown
Availability: Year-round
This was an easy choice. The Effinghamburgherbrau is an excellent beer, with biscuity notes and a doughy flavor. It also has some grassy, herbal hops. The beer is extremely easy to drink, and if you happen to see it on tap, don't hesitate to order it.

Baltic Porter (porters are typically ales, but Baltic porters are lagers). It is available for a half the year. Davis plans to introduce a second beer that will be available for the other half of the year. Prodigal will also release five different bocks throughout the year, and they recently brewed a traditional Oktoberfest lager. Davis plans to expand the brewery and hopes to start hosting open houses and tours in 2013.

REDHOOK ALE BREWERY

1 Redhook Way, Pease International Turnpike, Portsmouth, NH; (603) 501-3940; http://redhook.com

Founded: Portsmouth location, 1996 **Founder:** Gordon Bowker, Paul Shipman **Brewer:** Andy Swartz **Flagship Beer:** ESB **Year-round Beers:** Copperhead, Long Hammer IPA, Pilsner **Seasonals/Special Releases:** Late Harvest, Mudslinger, Winterhook, Wit, Double Black Stout, Treblehook **Tours:** Mon, 3, 4, and 5 p.m.; Tues, 1 and 2 p.m.; Wed and Thurs, 1, 3, 5 p.m.; Fri and Sat, noon to 6 p.m., hourly; Sun, 1 to 5 p.m., hourly; $1 per person

The Redhook Brewery was already one of the most successful breweries on the west coast when they decided to open up a second brewery on the east coast, which would provide fresh Redhook beers to people on this side of the US. In 1996, they opened up the Redhook Brewery in Portsmouth, and it is nearly a mirror image of the Seattle original.

Redhook's **ESB** is a phenomenal English-style beer full of malty goodness. The **Copperhead** is a really well-done copper ale. The **Long Hammer IPA** is a solid IPA, along the lines of a Harpoon or Longtrail IPA. The hoppiness will not blow you away, but it is still a great representation of the style. The best of Redhook's year-round beers is the **Pilsner.** It used to be a seasonal, but thankfully they listened to their fans and made it year-round. This is the kind of pilsner that I wish big breweries brewed—flavorful, light, with a nice touch of hops on the tongue.

Seasonals include the **Mudslinger,** which is a nut brown ale, a spring beer. The **Wit** is Redhook's summer seasonal, and it is exactly what you want in a Belgian-style wit. Light, but spiced with coriander and bitter orange peel. The **Winterhook** is a spicy winter warmer, and the **Late Harvest Ale** is a nice, malty red ale. Two of Redhook's beers are special releases. The **Treblehook** is a 10.9 percent alcohol by volume, American-style barleywine. It packs a punch with plenty of malts and hops, and is good to drink on a cold winter night. The **Double Black Stout** is an excellent, coffee-flavored stout. It is easy to drink, despite being 7 percent alcohol.

Redhook is also home to a really good on-site brewpub. They have all the typical beers on draft, but it is also where the brewers can experiment with some beers. If you are in the area, definitely stop in for a meal and try the special offerings.

The tour is one of the best in New England. It lasts for almost an hour and includes an in-depth description of the brewing and bottling process. You also get

Double Black Stout
Style: American Double
  Stout
ABV: 7 percent
Availability: Special
  Release, draft only at
  Redhook pub

The Double Black Stout
is an excellent stout
brewed with real coffee.
While many stouts have a
roasty, coffee-like flavor,
this beer is made with real coffee, which makes a big difference. The beer is
full-bodied, dark as night, and with hints of chocolate from the malts. The
roasted malts provide just a hint of bitterness. At 7 percent, it is not a big
imperial stout, but it is bigger than a regular stout.

three to four samples of various beers at the end. Redhook hosts several events
throughout the year, including concerts and a road race. The best is Redhook Fest in
August that features a full day of outdoor music and fun, as well as food and beer.

SMUTTYNOSE BREWING COMPANY

225 Heritage Ave., Portsmouth, NH; (603) 436-4026; www.smuttynose.com
Founded: 1994 **Founder:** Peter Egleston **Brewer:** David Yarrington **Flagship Beer:**
Shoal's Pale Ale **Year-round Beers:** Big A IPA, "Finestkind" IPA, Old Brown Dog Ale,
Robust Porter, Star Island Single **Seasonals/Special Releases:** Pumpkin Ale, Summer
Weizen, Winter Ale, Big Beer Series, Short Batch Series **Tours:** Fri, 3 p.m.; Sat, 11 a.m.

The Smuttynose Brewing Company sometimes gets overlooked when people are
discussing great New England breweries. People always talk about the new,
up-and-coming, hot brewery of the month. Smuttynose has quietly been chugging
along since Peter Egleston founded the brewery in 1994. More than just chugging
along, they've been brewing excellent beers since the mid-'90s, and when other
breweries peak, they stay at the same even level, brewing those excellent beers.

New Hampshire

Smuttynose brews six different year-round beers. The **Shoal's Pale Ale** and **Old Brown Dog Ale** are New England classics. The **"Finestkind" IPA** is a nice, hoppy IPA; if "Finestkind" is not enough for your inner hophead, grab a bottle of the **Big A IPA.** The **Star Island Single** is a unique beer. When most breweries brew a Belgian-style ale, it's usually a dubbel, tripel, or even a quad. Smuttynose went the other direction, brewing basically the equivalent of a Belgian table beer, a beer that you can drink every day. You wouldn't want to do that with a 10.5 percent ABV quad. The **Robust Porter** is just that, big and robust.

The seasonals include the **Pumpkin Ale,** the **Winter Ale,** and the **Summer Weizen,** one of the better New England–brewed wheat beers. Smuttynose also has the **Big Beer Series,** for which a different high-alcohol beer is released each month. These beers are packaged in 22-ounce bombers instead of the usual 12-ounce bottles. The **Baltic Porter** (November release) is absolutely amazing, a beer worth seeking out. The **Maibock** (April) is better than any other maibock brewed anywhere, here in the US or in Germany. Other entries in the Big Beer Series are the **Barleywine Ale,** the **Farmhouse Ale, Gravitation, Homunculus, Imperial Stout, Really Old Brown**

Beer Lover's Pick

The S'Muttonator
Style: Doppelbock
ABV: 8.5 percent
Availability: Rotating
This entry in the Big Beer Series is a German-style doppelbock. This is pretty much the opposite of a hophead's dream. It's all malt, full-flavored, with a thick mouthfeel. There are strong toffee notes, with caramel, coffee, and the flavor of raisins. It is also very smooth and smells incredible, with an almost freshly baked bread quality to it.

The Smuttynose BIG BEER Series

S'muttonator

· Double Bock Beer ·

• The Smuttynose Big Beer Series: big beers in big bottles, released seasonally in very limited quantities.
• S'muttonator is a tasty mixture of German ingredients & good ol' fashioned New England tenaciousness.
• Our brewers take 30 hours to brew a single batch of this traditional Double Bock. Take your time & enjoy its rich, malty & deceptively smooth flavor.

BREWED & BOTTLED BY SMUTTYNOSE BREWING CO.
PORTSMOUTH, NH • WWW.SMUTTYNOSE.COM

Dog Ale, Scotch Ale, S'Muttonator, and the **Wheat Wine Ale.** Smuttynose also does a **Short Batch Series,** which consists of anywhere from 20 to 30 barrels of beer available on draft only. If a Short Batch Series beer is popular and well-received, it may be added to the regular lineup of beers. The Homunculus was the first Short Batch Series beer, when it was known as the Gnome.

The Smuttynose Brewing Company also offers tours on Friday and Saturday and, to top it off, there is a tasting of various beers they have available on draft. Although all the Smuttynose beers are easy to find, you should check out the beers available for sale in the brewery. Oftentimes they have some vintage Big Beer Series beers available.

SQUAM BREWING COMPANY

118 Perch Pond Rd., Holderness, NH; (603) 236-9705; www.squambrewing.com
Founded: 2009 **Founder:** John Glidden **Brewer:** John Glidden **Flagship Beer:** Asquam Amber Ale **Year-round Beers:** Golden IPA, Rattlesnake Rye Pale Ale **Seasonals/Special Releases:** Bobhouse Bitter, No Wake Wheat, Winter Wheat **Tours:** By appointment only

The lakes region of New Hampshire is a great place to go for camping, fun on the water, and good times. And now, thanks to Squam Brewing Company, it's a great place to get a beer. Squam Brewing Company, founded in 2009 by John L. Glidden Jr., bottled its first beer in August 2010, and has produced some fantastic beer from this nanobrewery. How small is Squam Brewing Company? Squam brews about 45 to 50 gallons of beer at a time. That's about one and a half kegs. In his first year, Glidden brewed about 180 gallons. To put that in perspective, that's less than a normal batch of beer brewed at a brewpub at one time.

But what Squam lacks in size, it makes up in the quality of their beer. Currently, Squam brews three year-round beers, the **Asquam Amber Ale,** the Golden IPA, and the Rattlesnake Rye Pale Ale. The **Golden IPA** is one of the best imperial IPAs brewed in New England. The Asquam Amber Ale is a solid amber. It is nearly red in color, with a nice, bready malt flavor and just a touch of hops. The **Rattlesnake Rye Pale Ale** is your standard pale ale with a twist—rye malt. Rye malts add a nice, spicy character to a beer, and that sets it apart from a typical pale ale. Squam also brews three seasonals, the **Bobhouse Bitter** and **Winter Wheat** for the cold months and the **No Wake Wheat** for the warm months. The No Wake Wheat, in particular, is a standout, it's a perfectly light summer beer, great for those hot summer weekends spent grilling with friends or sitting poolside.

Glidden hosts brewery tours by appointment at his brewery, which is also his home. Those taking the tour can try samples of any of the beers Glidden has on hand

Golden IPA
Style: Double IPA
ABV: 8.5 percent
Availability: Year-Round
There are a lot of good double, or imperial, IPAs being brewed in New England, but there are few that are this good. The Golden IPA has a lot of fruity aroma (grapefruit, citrus) that continues into the taste, along with a lot of bittering hops. This beer is not super balanced, but it does not want to be. This is a beer for the hopheads, and the color is much lighter than many double IPAs.

at the time. Bombers of Squam beers are available at the store, or in liquor stores from Concord north. Do yourself a favor and seek these beers out.

THROWBACK BREWERY

121 Lafayette Rd., Unit 3, North Hampton, NH; (603) 379-2317; http://throwback brewery.com
Founded: 2011 **Founders:** Nicole Carrier, Annette Lee **Brewer:** Annette Lee **Flagship Beer:** None **Year-round Beers:** Hog Happy Hefeweizen, Dippity-Do, Maple-Kissed Wheat Porter, Campfire **Seasonals/Special Releases:** Love Me Long Time Bohemian Pilsner, Fat Alberta, Hopstruck IPA, Spicy Bohemian, Stout #3 **Tours:** Thurs and Fri, 4 to 6 p.m.; Sat, 1 to 4 p.m.

Before Prohibition, many small local breweries used local ingredients because they were easy to acquire. The Throwback Brewery wants to take you back to those days (hence the name Throwback), purchasing as many of its ingredients from local sources within 100 miles of the North Hampton brewery as they possibly can.

They then donate the spent grains used in the beer to local farms to be used to feed animals such as cows and pigs. Of course, the best part of Throwback Brewery is the beer. Brewer Annette Lee and her partner, Nicole Carrier, brew an excellent portfolio of creative beers.

The **Dippity-Do** looks like a regular brown ale, but it tastes nothing like it. It is unusually hopped like a pale ale. The sweetness is still the dominant flavor, but the hops come through, particularly in the finish. The **Maple-Kissed Wheat Porter** is different than most porters in several ways. First, wheat malt is used, which is highly unusual in a porter. This gives the beer a lighter, almost smoother taste. And locally produced maple is used during the brewing to give this a pleasant sweetness. It is a really nicely brewed beer. The **Campfire** is another porter, but this one is smoked. It is not as smoky as a German-style rauchbier, but the smoke is ever present. This is the best beer to drink while barbecuing. The **Hog Happy Hefeweizen**

Beer Lover's Pick

Fat Alberta
Style: Imperial Stout
ABV: 9.5 percent
Availability: Year-Round
A peanut butter and chocolate stout is creative and brewing genius. The flavors go together like, well, peanut butter and chocolate. This is a big beer, and the roasted malts and hops used in this beer stand up to these flavors. Many beers that use unusual flavors almost lose their beer-like quality. This does not. This is a phenomenal beer.

is a really well-done German-style wheat beer, and it features flavors of cloves and banana from the yeast. **Fat Alberta** is a big beer, at 9.5 percent alcohol by volume. Do not let that scare you away because you would be missing an extremely good stout. It is a chocolate and peanut butter stout. Let that sink in. It is like a liquid, alcoholic, peanut butter cup. The **Love Me Long Time Bohemian Pilsner** is a traditional pilsner, but the **Spicy Bohemian** is anything but traditional—it's the Love Me Long Time Bohemian Pilsner, but with roasted jalapeños added. Expect a burn in the back of your throat when you drink this. The **Hopstruck IPA** is a red IPA, and the **Stout #3** is an American stout with hints of cocoa and coffee.

Throwback hosts tastings and tours Thursday through Saturday. They also sell beer to go at the brewery, including the coolest-looking growlers ever seen. They are curvy, have a swing top, and, best of all, hold more than 67 ounces, compared to the normal growler that holds 64 ounces. Throwback also sells 22-ounce bombers of some of its beers. They also occasionally sell what they call growlettes, which are 32-ounce bottles of beer.

Throwback Brewery, keeping with their goal of being part of the local canvas, is only available in New Hampshire, so if you are driving through do your best to seek it out.

TUCKERMAN BREWING COMPANY

64 Hobbs St., Conway, NH; (603) 447-5400; www.tuckermanbrewing.com
Founded: 1998 **Founders:** Kristen Neves, Nik Stanciu **Brewer:** Allan Arnold **Flagship Beer:** Tuckerman's Pale Ale **Year-round Beer:** Headwall Alt **Seasonals/Special Releases:** ALTitude, 6288 Stout **Tours:** Sat, 3 p.m.; free

Tuckerman Brewing Company has been quietly brewing excellent beers for more than a decade and building up a dedicated following. The brewery was founded in 1998 by then-24-year-olds Kristen Neves and Nik Stanciu. Their first beer was the **Tuckerman's Pale Ale,** and for the first six years of Tuckerman's existence, this was the only beer they brewed.

The Pale Ale is a nice beer. It has a huge head, and it is easy to drink. It has a pleasant bitterness, with slight citrusy aroma and flavors. The malt is sweet and a tad biscuity. The **Headwall Alt** is a German-style alt, which is a brown ale. It has a fluffy head and it is dark, almost a reddish-brown. Flavor-wise, this is a traditional alt, big on the malt backbone, but with enough hops to offer a nice balance. The **6288 Stout** is named for the height of New Hampshire's Mt. Washington's peak. It is also a wonderful American stout. It is similar to an Irish dry stout, but a little stronger at 5.5 percent alcohol by volume. It still has the creaminess that you want in a stout, and a

Beer Lover's Pick

Headwall Alt
Style: Alt
ABV: 4.75 percent
Availability: Year-round
Alts are the most refreshing dark beer there is,
and the Headwall Alt is
an exceptional example
of the style. The dark malts do not add a roasted character. Rather, this is a
light-tasting beer, creamy and malt-forward, with sweet caramel flavors and a
slight bready taste. The hops are there, but just enough to provide balance to
prevent the Headwall Alt from becoming too sweet. It is an exceptional beer.

bitterness from the roast, not the hops. Tuckerman's only other beer is the **ALTitude**,
which is Headwalt Alt's bigger brother. It is 7.5 percent alcohol by volume, and is
actually closer to being a German-style sticke alt, which is basically an imperial alt.

Tuckerman takes pride in having a "green" company, getting many of its ingredients and other supplies locally, cutting down on transportation costs and gas
consumption. The six-pack holders are manufactured in nearby Hooksett, New
Hampshire. The case boxes are made in Maine and use sustainable forest inactivates.
Most of the malts come from Maine and Canada, which are the closest locations that
grow enough malt for Tuckerman's to brew their beers, and the water is local Conway
water that comes from the Swift River.

Tuckerman Brewing Company hosts tours every Saturday at 3 p.m. The tour
starts with a tasting of Tuckerman's beer, and follows with a tour of the brewery led
by a brewer, who will explain the brewing process and all the ingredients. The tour
then ends with another tasting so you can get a more full appreciation of the beers
after learning how they are brewed.

WHITE BIRCH BREWING
1339 Hooksett Rd., Hooksett, NH; (603) 244-8593; www.whitebirchbrewing.com
Founded: 2009 **Founder:** Bill and Ellen Herlicka **Brewer:** Bill Herlicka **Flagship Beer:**
Hooksett Ale **Year-round Beers:** Belgian Style Pale Ale, Hop Session **Seasonals/Special**

New Hampshire

Releases: Barley Wine Ale, Berliner Weisse, Bohemian Edition Tripel, Cherry Quad, Dubbel, Espresso Stout, Harvest Ale, Indomitus, Indulgence, Night Falls, Quad, Rye Four, Saison, Tavern Ale, Tripel, Wild Ale, Winter Warmer Wrigian, Apprentice Series, Barrel Aged Series, Oak Aged Series **Tours:** Mon and Tues, 10 a.m. to 5 p.m.; Wed through Fri, 10 a.m. to 7 p.m.; Sat, noon to 5 p.m.

There are few breweries as eclectic as White Birch Brewing Company. Founder/ brewer Bill Herlicka likes to give a twist to his beers—almost none are traditional. An avid homebrewer, Herlicka and his wife, Ellen, founded the brewery in 2009, and immediately hit the ground running with a great mix of beers.

White Birch brews three year-round beers—the Belgian Style Pale Ale, the Hooksett Ale, and the Hop Session. The **Belgian Style Pale Ale** may be the closest to traditional that White Birch does. The **Hooksett Ale** blends Herlicka's love of west coast hoppy beers and his love of Belgian ales into a Belgian-style IPA, while the **Hop Session** is a hoppy, west coast–style IPA.

But where White Birch really excels, and where Herlicka's creativity really shows through, is in their rotating releases. The **Cherry Quad** is just that, a Belgian-style quad brewed with cherries. The flavors blend together perfectly. The **Espresso Stout**

Beer Lover's Pick

Berliner Weisse
Style: Berliner Weisse
ABV: 6.4 percent
Availability: Rotating
There aren't many Berliner weisses brewed in the US, so when you see one, you should grab it. This is an excellent Berliner weisse, although much stronger than the typical version. It has a heftier body than the traditional beer, but what it does have is the tartness, which tastes a bit like lemonade. You just want to take a sip.

is a stout brewed with espresso beans, and the **Barley Wine Ale** is a big, burly beer, meant to be sipped, not gulped. The rotating releases also feature beers with some of the most unusual names. The **Indomitus** is a Belgian-style wild ale brewed with both White Birch's house yeast and wild yeast. It forms a tart, fruity beer. The **Indulgence** is brewed with huge amounts of chocolate malts. That's not uncommon in some stouts, but this isn't a stout or a porter, just a dark ale with tons of chocolate malts. The **Night Falls** is a dark wild ale, while the **Wrigian** is a Belgian-style ale brewed with rye.

White Birch also runs an apprentice program. After the program is complete, the apprentice has a chance to brew his or her own beer, which is released in the **Apprentice Series.** Herlicka also brews a **Barrel Aged Series** of beers.

The **Oak Aged Series** of beers are brewed with oak chips or oak spirals in the fermenting stage to impart the oaky, vanilla-like flavors often associated with barrel-aging.

White Birch offers tours Monday through Saturday, led by one of the four employees and featuring a tour of the brewery and education about the history of the brewery and the brewing process. There are also tastings, typically limited to the year-round beers. The brewery store has beer to go in bombers and growlers.

WOODSTOCK INN BREWERY

135 Main St., North Woodstock, NH; (800) 321-3985; www.woodstockinnbrewery.com
Founded: 1995 **Founder:** Scott Rice **Brewer:** Butch Evans **Flagship Beer:** Pig's Ear Brown Ale **Year-round Beers:** Loon Golden Ale, Old Man Oatmeal Stout, Pemi Pale Ale, Red Rack Ale, Through Hiker Double Rye Pale Ale, Scottish Ale, White Mountain Weasel Wheat Ale **Seasonals/Special Releases:** Autumn Brew, Cogsman Ale, Kanc Country Maple Porter, Raspberry Weasel Wheat, Wassail Winter Ale **Tours:** Daily at noon

If you ever want to get away for a weekend, find a nice inn with a nice restaurant, and maybe even enjoy a few good beers, North Woodstock should be one of your top destinations. The Woodstock Station Inn, a 33-room inn spread over five buildings, is also host to the Woodstock Inn Brewery, a small craft brewery that brews some very good beers.

The brewery's most popular beer is the **Pig's Ear Brown Ale,** a traditional English-style nut brown ale. It has a nice nutty flavor, and sweet caramel flavors from the malts. It is an easy beer to savor. The **Red Rack Ale** is Woodstock's first beer, and like the Pig's Ear, is a traditional brewed beer. This Irish red ale is heavy on the malts, just like most of Woodstock's beers. The **Scottish Ale** is a malty beer, but feels much fuller-bodied than a beer that is only 4.75 percent alcohol by volume, while the **White Mountain Weasel Wheat Ale** and the **Loon Golden Ale** are two easy-drinking, light, and refreshing brews. The **Old Man Oatmeal Stout** is smooth and creamy, just as an oatmeal stout should be. The **Pemi Pale Ale** leans toward the English version of the style, with a malt-forward base. However it finishes with a nice hop bite. The **Through Hiker Double Rye Pale Ale** is the biggest of the year-round beers at 7.9 percent ABV. It is a hoppy IPA brewed with rye, giving this beer a nice spicy character.

Where Woodstock really shines is its seasonals. The **Autumn Brew** is brewed with apples and cinnamon and just tastes like fall. The **Raspberry Weasel Wheat** is the same beer as the White Mountain Weasel Wheat, except with raspberries added. The **Kanc Country Maple Porter** is a really well-done porter, brewed with local maple syrup. The maple flavor really comes through, making this a cold weather treat. The **Cogsman Ale** is an English-style IPA with just a touch of English hops pushing through. The brewery's biggest beer is the **Wassail Winter Ale,** which comes in at

Beer Lover's Pick

Kanc Country Maple Porter
Style: Porter
ABV: 6 percent
Availability: Winter Seasonal
The Kanc Country Maple Porter is a wonderful English-style porter, with a twist: the addition of local maple syrup. The porter is malty and has a nice roasty character, with hints of coffee and chocolate. The maple syrup really comes through in this beer, with a pleasant sweetness. If a great breakfast beer ever existed, the Kanc Country Maple Porter would be it.

8 percent ABV. This is a full-bodied beer loaded with a lot of sweet malt. It smells boozy, and that continues on into the taste.

The Woodstock Inn Brewery hosts daily tours that includes an introduction to the brewing process, as well as a sampling of some of their beers. But if you really want to get your hands dirty, you will want to reserve a spot on a Brewer's Weekend. The weekend begins with a welcome reception in the Woodstock Station Inn's restaurant. Work begins on Saturday morning. After a quick breakfast, you will head out to the brewery and help brew beer with brewer Butch Evans. You better be ready to sweat as you start lugging bags of malt and hops around. Top it all off with a nice beer dinner.

New Hampshire

Brewpubs

ELM CITY BREWING COMPANY

Colony Mill Market Place, 22 West St., Unit 46, Keene, NH; (603) 355-3335; www.elmcity
brewery.com
Draft Beers: 9

Keene is one of those small New England towns that you can imagine pictured on a postcard. Not far from Keene State College, in the historic Colony Mill Market Place, is the Elm City Brewing Company. This wonderful little brewpub brews as many as 20 different beers throughout the year and they have 9 beers on draft.

Elm City brews two versions of its kolsch. The regular kolsch is the **Keene Kolsch,** and the second is the **Peachy Keene Kolsch,** which has peaches added. Another fruit beer is the **Raspberry Wheat.** Another interesting beer is the **Oatmeal Pale Ale.** Oatmeal is often used in stouts, but it provides a different depth of character when used in other styles that gives a nice contrast to barley malt that is used in most styles. Other beers include the **Brickhouse ESB, No Name IPA,** the **Porthole Porter, Irish Stout, Monadnock Mt. Ale** (pale ale), and **Vanilla Stout.** Elm City also brews one of the few roggenbiers in New England. Roggenbiers are German-style rye beers, which are hard to find even in Germany! Seasonals include the **Mai Bock, Oktoberfest,** and **Nor'Easter** (wee heavy).

Beer Event

Oktoberfest

Elm City Brewing Company hosts their annual Oktoberfest celebration every September. The outdoor event goes from 1 to 5 p.m. and features German food, German music, games and prizes, and the official first tapping of Elm City's Oktoberfest for the fall season. Grab your lederhosen and head on over.

Elm City has a large dining area, as well as a sunny atrium to sit in, and an outdoor seating area during the summer. Elm City offers many sandwiches, including grilled cheese and tomato, pastrami, BLT, a tuna wrap, and the Spinach and Herb Cheese Sandwich, which is made with spinach, tomato, mushrooms, red onions, bean sprouts, and herb cheese. Entrees include beer-battered fish and chips, vegetable lasagna, and the Brewmaster's Dinner, which includes grilled knockwurst and brat-wurst, served with sauerkraut and a potato pancake. Elm City also offers growlers of its beers to go, as well as glasses, mugs, and T-shirts.

FLYING GOOSE BREW PUB & GRILL

40 Andover Rd., New London, NH; (603) 526-6899; http://flyinggoose.com
Draft Beers: 17

On a road trip through New England, you are bound to drive through some little towns you may never have heard of and come across a little brewpub. That is the case with the Flying Goose Brew Pub & Grill. It is one of those brewpubs people outside of the area may not know, but they will definitely be happy if they stumble across it. The pub has won awards for being environmentally friendly and self-sustaining. They are solar powered, and they use almost all recycled products in the pub.

Flying Goose always has 17 of its beers on tap. The beers include lighter beers like the excellent **Pleasant Lake Pilsner, Heidelberg Hefeweizen, Split Rock Golden Ale,** and the **Wildflower Honey Ale,** which is made with local wildflower honey. Other beers typically available include **Alexandria Alt,** a traditional German-style altbier, the **Hedgehog Brown Ale, Long Brother's Strong Ale,** and **Crockett's Corner Oatmeal Stout.** Other beers occasionally available include the **Berliner Weisse,** a wonderfully tart and refreshing wheat beer, **Mikey's Vyce Black IPA,** the **Rauchbier Lager,** and the **Isle of Pines Barleywine** (definitely get this if you are a hophead).

The food menu is large and varied at the Flying Goose. Starters include the Goose Bread, which is garlic Italian bread topped with parmesan, mozzarella, and blue cheeses, and the Beer Skins, which are potato skins baked in a Hedgehog Brown Ale and butter sauce. Sandwiches include an open-faced prime rib sandwich, steak and cheese paninis, and Emily's Wrap, which features crispy chicken, cheddar and jack cheeses, tomatoes, and barbecue ranch dressing served in a flour tortilla. The burger to get is the New Englander, which is covered in smoked bacon, sautéed onions, and Vermont cheddar cheese.

The entrees are on the creative side, and include pork risotto, country meat loaf, and the Flying Goose Paella, which is made with mussels, shrimp, chicken,

New Hampshire

and chorizo sausage. The Devonshire Delmonico is also worth trying. It is a lightly smoked, hand-cut rib eye steak, dusted in Cajun seasoning, pan baked, and finished with bacon mélange butter.

MARTHA'S EXCHANGE
185 Main St., Nashua, NH; (603) 883-8781; www.marthas-exchange.com
Draft Beers: 8

Nashua is the place where Massachusetts residents go shopping so they can avoid paying sales tax. It is also the home of Martha's Exchange, giving beer lovers a reason to go to Nashua, too. Martha's Exchange brewpub is a historic business. It originally opened in 1932 as Martha's Sweet Shop, where it sold handmade candies. It has also hosted nearly every presidential candidate who has come to Nashua during the campaign every four years.

Martha's Exchange still sells handmade candy in the on-site candy store, but they also sell handmade beer and food in what is now one of New Hampshire's premier brewpubs. Throughout the year, Martha's Exchange will have anywhere between 20 and 25 different beers on tap. The only beer on tap at all times is the **Volstead '33,** a lighter, easy-drinking beer. The beer you have to get if available is the **Velvet Elvis Vanilla Bean Stout.** This is an absolutely amazing beer, and if it happens to be on cask, it would almost be a crime to not get it.

Other beers include **Another Ale** (pale ale), **Biscuit City Pale Ale,** the **Dark Rasputin Stout, Indian Head Red, McGann's London Ale** (English pale ale), **Steeplechase Porter,** and the **Vow of Silence Belgian Stout.** Martha's Exchange also brews several seasonals, including the **Hefeweizen, Magi Winter Warmer,** and **Oktoberfest.** Martha's also brews what they call the **Reserve Series,** which are beers typically only brewed once. Once the keg is tapped, it is gone for good.

If you do not want to eat handmade chocolate for dinner (nothing wrong if you do), grab some food. Appetizers include the pulled pork quesadilla, sweet potato wedges, lemon cilantro mussels, beef tenderloin crostinis, and the Tapas Trio Dip, which includes smoked salmon dip, olive tapenade dip, and a red pepper hummus served with blue and yellow corn chips, carrots, cucumbers, and red peppers for dipping. Also available is a large selection of flatbread pizzas, including the Mexican Fiesta. The Mexican Fiesta is topped with pico de gallo, avocadoes, jalapeños, cheddar and jack cheeses, and a zesty salsa. Salads include two standouts: The lobster salad is lobster with dill mayo over red greens with pita, tomatoes, cucumbers, and roasted red peppers, while the lamb salad is made up of grilled lamb, mixed greens, red onions, tomatoes, pita, kalamata olives, pepperoncinis, and feta cheese.

Entrees include the mango haddock, which is fresh haddock sautéed with a mango/pineapple salsa sauce, served over pasta, and the ginger wasabi steak, a 12-ounce sirloin steak topped with fresh ginger and soy sauce and served with wasabi mashed potatoes.

If you happen to be there on Friday or Saturday, Martha's Exchange turns into a nightclub at 10 p.m. with drink specials and a DJ playing dance music. And if you stop in, make sure to take a look at the bar itself. It was once in one of Al Capone's speakeasies in Chicago.

MILLY'S TAVERN
500 Commercial St., Manchester, NH; (603) 625-4444; http://millystavern.com
Draft Beers: 18

Milly's Tavern is one of the best brewpubs in the Granite State. The beers are phenomenal, and the food is excellent. It is a combination that cannot be beat, particularly when you throw in the abundant live entertainment at this Manchester brewpub.

Their year-round beers are fantastic. The **Fisher Cat Ale** is a light (3.8 percent alcohol by volume) ale made with pale malt, named for the New Hampshire Fisher Cat baseball team located near the brewpub. The **Mt. Uncanoonuc Golden Cream Ale** is a really good cream ale, a style more breweries should brew. **Tasha's Red Tail Ale** is a nicely brewed red ale, with just a hint of a hop kick. Other year-round beers include the **General John Stark Dark Porter,** an exceptional porter, **Milly's Oatmeal Stout**, the **Manch-Vegas IPA,** and **Bo's Scotch Ale,** a type of big beer you usually don't see as a year-round brewpub offering, at 9.5 percent ABV.

The specialty beers are also worth seeking out. Milly's Tavern brews two beers based on the General John Stark Dark Porter. They brew the **Chocolate Porter,** made with Van Otis chocolate, and the **Cherry Porter,** brewed with real cherries. The **Coffee Espresso Stout** is a winner, as is the **Burton Ale** (a classic English-style IPA) and **Hopzilla** (a double IPA). **Milly's Famous Pumpkin Ale** is much sought after by pumpkin beer fans.

But the two beers you have to try are the **Blueberry** and **Raspberry Lambics.** These are not your typical fruit beers, which are usually lighter ales with either fruit flavor or real fruit added. These are traditional Belgian-style lambics. They have a champagne-like carbonation, are extremely tart, and are brewed with a Belgian strain of yeast. Superb beers, both of them.

Food-wise, Milly's Tavern really stands out, particularly for the price. You would be hard-pressed to find better food for a better price. Milly's nachos are huge, big enough for three people to share. Other appetizers include sweet potato fries and stuffed mushrooms, as well as the Espinaca, which is creamy cheese sauce with jalapeños, cayenne pepper, spinach, and salsa served with tortilla chips for dipping. Want a good hearty meal? Grab the Oatmeal Stout Beef Stew, served in a bread bowl (see recipe, page 239). It is a classic beef stew made with Milly's Oatmeal Stout. Milly's also offers 8-inch flatbread pizzas, 12-inch pizzas, burgers, salads, wraps, and quesadillas. There are also plenty of sandwiches. Best bargain? Get two beer-steamed hot dogs for $5. The dogs are steamed in porter. If you have room, grab a brownie sundae or a root beer float for dessert. The chocolate porter and the brownie sundae would be a perfect food pairing.

At night, Milly's Tavern turns into a nightclub, with dancing, live music, and DJs taking over. Don't worry, the beers are still available.

Anheuser-Busch in The Granite State

Although this book is about the great craft beer produced in New England and the places where you can go to get that great craft beer, most people are still likely to choose a mass-produced lager like Budweiser over a hoppy IPA while out at the bar. And there's nothing wrong with that—beer lovers don't have to like just craft beer.

The largest brewing company in the US is Anheuser-Busch—producer of Budweiser, Bud Light, and Michelob, among other beers—and they have 12 breweries in the US, including one at 221 Daniel Webster Hwy., in Merrimac, New Hampshire. The brewery can package eight million 12-ounce bottles or cans a day, if needed. That is more beer than nearly every brewery in New England brews in a year.

The New Hampshire brewery hosts tours throughout the year. The times change by month, so log onto www.budweisertours.com to see when the tour takes place. The in-depth, guided tour is free, and it includes free beer samples, soda, and snacks. It typically lasts about one and a half hours, and photography is usually not allowed. On the first Saturday of the month from 1 to 3 p.m., they allow people take photos of themselves and one of the Clydesdales.

MOAT MOUNTAIN SMOKE HOUSE & BREWING COMPANY

3378 White Mountain Hwy., Rte. 16, North Conway, NH; (603) 356-6481; http://
moatmountain.com
Draft Beers: 6

The Moat Mountain Smoke House and Brewing Company is worth making a trip to North Conway. And you will not have to worry about trying to find a place to stay—you can reserve one of the five rooms they have in their own inn. The Moat Mountain has an eclectic mix of beers that includes several lagers and some higher-alcohol beers.

Year-round beers include the **Moat Czech Pilsner,** the **Moat Ale,** the **Moat Stout,** and the **Hoffman Weiss.** Even better are the seasonals and special releases. The **Moat Pilsner** (a different beer than the Czech Pilsner) and the **Moat Lager** will satisfy those who enjoy lagers. The **Moat IPA** is a 7 percent ABV English-style IPA, and the **Moat Blueberry** is a solid blueberry ale. The **Smoke House Porter** is excellent, and the **Moat Oktoberfest** is spot on for the style. Moat also brews the perfect beer for a pub that specializes in smoked meat, the **Rauchbier,** a German-style smoked ale.

Moat also brews some bigger beers, such as the **Moat Bock,** an 8.5 percent German-style bock. The 8.9 percent ABV **Belgian Triple** is a classic Belgian ale. The **Moat Imperial Stout** is the brewery's strongest beer at 9 percent ABV.

Moat Mountain is more than a brewery; it is also a great place to get some barbecued and smoked meat. The appetizers are different from many restaurants and include the Texas-style brisket and Andouille chili, curried crab and corn bisque, New England–style hush puppies (made with local maple syrup), and the Moat Mountain Pot Stickers. Nachos and quesadillas are also available. Smoke House Burgers are half-pound burgers with tons of toppings available, and there are many sandwiches, such as the blackened catfish and the barbecued Reuben, which substitutes beef brisket for the traditional corned beef.

But if you really like meat, get the Combo Platter, which includes a half-rack of ribs, a quarter chicken, and your choice of beef brisket or smoked pork. It is served with skillet corn bread and cole slaw. All the barbecue sauces used are made on-site.

The great thing about Moat Mountain is that they have the small on-site inn, which makes for an easy overnight trip. All the rooms feature king-size beds and flat-screen televisions. Plan ahead, though—there are only five rooms. Also, if you have pet allergies, keep that in mind because the inn owner's dogs are often inside the inn.

Moat Mountain also sells beers to go in the form of growlers, and you can often find their beers on draft in other bars throughout New Hampshire.

New Hampshire

PORTSMOUTH BREWERY

56 Market St., Portsmouth, NH; (603) 431-1115; www.portsmouthbrewery.com
Draft Beers: 10

The Portsmouth Brewery is known nationally for brewing one of the most sought-after beers in the world, **Kate the Great** (more on her later). Brewmaster Tod Mott and his crew of brewers create some great beer, and the Portsmouth Brewery is one of the five best brewpubs in all of New England.

Founded in 1991 by brother and sister Peter and Janet Egelston, along with Janet's husband, Mark Metzger, the Portsmouth Brewery has set itself above most other brewpubs with a solid lineup of beers from the top to the bottom, as well as several guest taps from other New Hampshire breweries. They also have several Smuttynose Brewing Company beers on tap. Peter Egelston owns Smuttynose, also located in Portsmouth. You'll most likely find something new on top every time you visit. They have a huge list of beers to choose from, from English milds to German alts to Belgian-style ales. Mott brews almost any style you can think of.

The year-round beers include the **Dirty Blonde Ale** and the **Black Cat Stout,** but if you really want to get adventurous, try the other beers on tap. If you're a hophead, the best beer may be the **5 C's,** a west-coast IPA brewed with Cascade, Centennial, Chinook, Columbus, and Crystal hops (and a little Simcoe). Like an

Beer Event

Kate the Great Day

Every February or March, beer geeks from all over gather on the streets of Portsmouth for one reason—Kate the Great. Kate the Great is Portsmouth Brewing Company's Russian imperial stout. It is released on one day each year. There is a lottery ahead of time to get bottles, but people still gather for their chance to taste this beer before it taps out, usually by 5 p.m. the same day.

IPA with a twist? Grab the **Ginga Ninja IPA,** an IPA brewed with ginger. Or, maybe Belgian ales are for you. The **St. Danmon Trippel** is fantastic, and the **Biere de Miele** is a great beer to give to those who say they don't like beer—it has a wine-like quality, and the honey used in the beer is a winning flavor combination. Portsmouth Brewery also has several lagers, including the **Oktoberfest** and the **Pils Von Faust.** But, you cannot talk about the Portsmouth Brewery without mentioning Kate the Great. This 10.5 percent ABV is one of the best beers brewed in the world. Bold, full-flavored, and oh so tasty.

The great thing is, while you're enjoying the beer, Portsmouth Brewery also serves up some really good food. The food is pretty much straightforward pub-style food, but done really well. The crispy fried calamari is a winner for an appetizer, and the nacho plate is perfect for a group of four, and even more. The bratwurst burger is a great sandwich, and the pastrami on rye is as good as any deli's. The Old Brown Dog Hanger Steak, made with an Old Brown Dog beer marinade, is a good option if you want something more than a sandwich (see recipe, page 239).

The Portsmouth Brewery also offers tours, and everyone who takes a tour will get a 50 percent discount on a platter of beer samples. Before leaving make sure to stop at the brewery shop. Growlers of beer are available at the bar, but 22-ounce bottles, as well as shirts, glasses, and other beer-related gear are available in the store.

SEVEN BARREL BREWERY
5 Airport Rd., West Lebanon, NH; (603) 298-5566; http://7barrel.com
Draft Beers: 8

Greg Noonan is most known in New England brewing circles for opening the Vermont Pub & Brewery in Burlington, but he is also the founder of the Seven Barrel Brewery in tiny West Lebanon, New Hampshire. Both pubs have similar qualities—good beer and good food.

The name of the brewery comes from the original brewing system, which was a seven-barrel system. The Seven Barrel Brewery usually has eight beers on draft at all time, which include the **Champion Reserve IPA, New Dublin Brown, R.I.P. Stout, The Red #7,** and the **Quechee Cream Ale.** The cream ale, in particular, is worth trying. It is a light but flavorful beer. Seasonals include the **Octoberfest** and **Spring Ale.** Other beers include the **Double IPA,** the **Mick Jack Porter,** the **Hanover Lager,** and **Al's Bock.** The Seven Barrel Brewery also has a line of higher-alcohol beers called the **Conan the Destroyer Series.** These beers are more high octane than those typically brewed at Seven Barrel and styles include an imperial coffee stout and an imperial brown ale.

Just like the Vermont Pub & Brewery, the Seven Barrel Brewery is heavy on pub-style food. Starters include the Pub Cheese Plate, which includes Grafton Village Cheddar, Gafford's Smoked Gruyère, and Vermont Chevre, served with a crispy baguette, pickled vegetables, house chutney, and honey Dijon mustard. Another standout is a French-Canadian original, poutine, which is french fries smothered in onion gravy and local cheese curds. Entrees include the Cock a'Leekie Pie, which is a pie stuffed with chicken, leeks, carrots, potatoes, and celery and topped with gravy. The Baked Chicken Statler is another possibility. It is a pan-seared, semi-boneless chicken breast with thyme and sautéed mushrooms. You can also get Bratwurst n' Beer, which is a bratwurst steamed in beer, or grab the Toad-in-the-Hole, which is made of pork sausages, sautéed onions, and mild cheddar cheese baked inside a puff pastry.

The Seven Barrel Brewery also frequently hosts live bands, so you can always get a good meal and beer while listening to music. And do not forget to grab a growler of your favorite beer on the way out.

Beer Bars

THE BARLEY HOUSE

132 North Main St., Concord, NH; (603) 228-6363; www.thebarleyhouse.com
Draft Beers: 13 **Bottled/Canned Beers:** 35

The Barley House has a great spot, located right across the street from the New Hampshire State House in Concord. After a day of politicking, a beer and a burger is a must. The Barley House is a great little beer bar that has been voted "Best of . . ." in several categories by local entertainment publications, and it really earns those designations.

Although they only have 13 beers on tap, they are all worth drinking. They typically have beers from Otter Creek, Peak Organic, Lagunitas, and a beer brewed just for them by Harpoon. The bar offers sample platters, and what they call the Dublin Double, which consists of two 10-ounce taster pints of two different beers of your choice. The bottled list is split up between big bottles (22-ounce bombers and 750 ml bottles) and 12-ounce bottles. The larger bottles are a little more geared to beer geeks: they typically have beers from Brewery Ommegang, Brewdog, Chimay, Rogue, Unibroue, and White Birch. The 12-ounce bottles feature mostly mass-produced beers, but Samuel Adams and Long Trail beers are often available.

Food-wise, the Barley House has several decent options. Small plates include crab bacon sliders, which are topped with house-cured bacon, egg, and Cajun mayo on a brioche bun. Other options include wild boar cranberry sausage and Blarney Puffs, which are cheddar, scallions, and potatoes in a fried dumpling, covered with a Guinness cheese sauce. A little too heavy for you? Salads are also available, including the Apple, Craisin, and Spicy Walnut salad, made with mixed greens and cider mustard vinaigrette.

The Barley House is known for making great burgers, which are ground daily. There are several burgers to choose from, including the BBQ bacon bison burger. Another burger to consider is the Bailey Ballpark Burger, which is a pork and beef patty with house beer mustard and smoked Gouda. Many of the entrees offered by the Barley House are made with beer or some sort of liquor. They offer tequila-cilantro-lime sea scallops, Irish whiskey steak, Guinness beef stew, and Smithwick's Curry Fish and Chips. And do not forget to leave room for dessert. The homemade bread pudding with maple whiskey sauce and the crème brûlée with vanilla custard and caramelized sugar are both delightful ends to a good meal.

New Hampshire

THE BARLEY PUB

328 Central Ave., Dover, NH; (603) 742-4226; www.barleypub.com
Draft Beers: 15 **Bottled/Canned Beers:** Varies

Everyone is taught at some point in his or her life this simple adage: "Don't judge a book by its cover." The Barley Pub is a beer bar that epitomizes that adage. It does not look like much—it's small, dark, and could be classified as a bit of a dive—but it is the best place in Dover to grab a great beer and listen to some quality live music.

The beer selection is not the biggest feature here, but beer lovers will never have a problem finding a beer they want to drink. The Barley Pub's draft list is heavy on New Hampshire beers, with beers from the Tuckerman Brewing Company and Moat Mountain, as well as several beers from the Smuttynose Brewing Company. One of the beers often available is the Golden Lady, which is a beer brewed by Smuttynose exclusively for the Barley Pub. Beers from other areas, such as the Sebago Brewing Company in Maine, Green Flash Brewing Company in California, and the Southern Tier Brewing Company in New York, are also often available. The beer prices are relatively cheap, many less than $5 for a pint, but if you want to go even cheaper, Pabst Blue Ribbon is only $2 a mug. The bottled list is not huge, but always features some wonderful beers. Firestone-Walker beers from California have been available, as have Allagash Brewing Company in Maine and Lagunitas Brewing Company in California. Make sure to take a look at the bottled list whenever you come back, because the Barley Pub often has vintage beers available from its cellar.

The food menu is not huge, limited to several types of panini sandwiches, which include the Italian sausage with peppers and onions, grilled cheese with pesto, sun dried tomatoes and fresh pesto, pastrami and Swiss, and homemade meat loaf with American cheese. The Barley Pub also offers cheese and charcuterie plates, which are served with dried fruit and toasted bread points.

One of the things the Barley Pub is most known for is live music. They host live musicians several nights a week. On Thursday they have Bluegrass Night and Sunday is Jazz Night. They also have other events, such as movie nights and pumpkin carving around Halloween.

BLUE MERMAID ISLAND GRILL

409 The Hill, Portsmouth, NH; (603) 427-2583; www.bluemermaid.com
Draft Beers: 8 **Bottled/Canned Beers:** About 20

The Blue Mermaid Island Grill is the closest you will get to the Caribbean without leaving Portsmouth—and they also happen to have great beer. The Mermaid is within walking distance of several other good beer bars, as well as the Portsmouth Brewery, so if you're in town, be sure to make a day of it.

The draft list is on the small side, with only eight beers on tap. The beers, for the most part, are beers from New England, such as Moat Mountain, Shipyard, Smuttynose, and Throwback. They also often switch out the tap list, making sure there are at least a few seasonals available. The bottled list includes Samuel Adams, Sierra Nevada, and imports such as Gulden Draak and Piraat Ale, both from Belgium.

Food-wise, the Blue Mermaid's menu is quite different from most beer bars. That difference is noticeable right away looking at the small plates or appetizers. There are several interesting options, such as wasabi rangoons; orange ginger egg rolls; and the Mermaid Fundito, a dip made with cheddar cheese, pale ale, fire-roasted tomatoes, and chili, served with crusty bread for dipping. Entrees include the plantain-encrusted cod and the Rasta Pasta. The Rasta Pasta is made with penne pasta, sautéed with onions, baby spinach, and roasted tomatoes, served in a chili pesto cream sauce. Other dishes include the New World Paella, made with chicken, shrimp, sausage, and mussels, sautéed in a curried rice; and pan-blackened mahi mahi.

Brunch is also served on Sunday from 10 a.m. to 2 p.m. Items available include lobster frittata, which is three eggs, roasted tomato, goat cheese, spinach, and lobster. Another option is the Green Eggs and Ham, which is made of three scrambled eggs, jack cheese, ham, and jalapeño pesto, served in a tortilla wrap with goat cheese.

PORTSMOUTH GAS LIGHT CO.

64 Market St., Portsmouth, NH; (603) 431-9122; www.portsmouthgaslight.com
Draft Beers: 21 **Bottled/Canned Beers:** About 20

The Portsmouth Gas Light Co. is a multifaceted establishment. It's one part restaurant/pub with good food and beer and one part pizzeria with a big selection of pasta (the outdoor deck also has a smaller menu and live music), and the "Third Floor" is a nightclub. Needless to say, the Gas Light has something for everyone, especially beer lovers.

The pub area has 12 beers on tap, as well as a selection of bottled beers. The pizzeria has another 8 beers on tap, while the deck has 1 additional draft. All the beers and bottles are available throughout the building. The beers are split up between New England beers and beers from other parts of the country. Breweries often available include Allagash, Berkshire Brewing Company, Shipyard Brewing Company, Full Sail Brewing Company, and a brewery I have never seen on tap anywhere else in New England, Hinterland Brewery from Wisconsin.

The menus are different in all three eating locations (the nightclub does not serve food), but the street-level grill serves up some of the best food in Portsmouth. Appetizers include the Louisiana-style grilled sea scallops and the quarter-pound Maine lobster cake. They also offers several salads, including the Tomato and Watermelon Salad, which features tri-colored tomatoes tossed with fresh mint and basil chiffonade, diced watermelon, and feta cheese topped with just a little olive oil. Portsmouth Gas Light also offers a large wood-fired grilled menu. Steaks, ribs, chicken, and mahi mahi are all available from the grill. Downtown Pizza, like its name implies, is all about the pizza. Sure, you can get a regular pepperoni pizza, but why not order one of their specialty pizzas, such as the Congress, which is topped with mounds of pepperoni, sweet sausage, onions, green peppers, mushrooms, and black olives? If you're feeling really hungry, try the Navy Yard, which is topped with cheddar and mozzarella cheese, piles of ground beef, and bacon.

STRANGE BREW TAVERN
88 Market St., Manchester, NH; (603) 666-4292; www.strangebrewtavern.com
Draft Beers: 82 **Bottled/Canned Beers:** 30

The Strange Brew Tavern is a downtown Manchester destination for those looking for good beer and live music. Not only do they feature the most beers on tap in all of New Hampshire, 82 beers over two floors, but the tavern also hosts live bands six nights a week.

The beer selection is large, but for the most part, the beers are more mainstream craft beer, like Magic Hat, Samuel Adams, and Shipyard. They also feature several New Hampshire breweries, such as Redhook, Smuttynose, and Woodstock. Other breweries often featured include Blue Point, Dogfish Head, and Victory. Strange Brew also offers up some a few imports, such as beers from Unibroue, as well as Smithwick's and Dos Equis. Can't decide what beer to get? Order the sampler, in which you can get five small glasses of beers of your choice for $8, only available on Wednesday and Sunday. Most nights, Strange Brew also offers drink specials, with discount beers.

To go along with the beer, Strange Brew also offers some delicious pub food. Appetizers include fried pickle chips or fried artichoke hearts, as well as the Beer

Cheese Platter, which features pub cheese mixed with red ale. If there is a group, the best option is probably the Combo Platter, which features potato skins, jalapeño poppers, mozzarella sticks, and chicken tenders. In addition to the many sandwiches, burgers, and wraps on the menu, there are salads available, including the Strange Brew Chopped Salad, which is made of grilled chicken, bacon, eggs, zucchini, squash, caramelized red onions, Swiss cheese, romaine lettuce, and sweet ranchero dressing. Entrees include Guinness meat loaf and mashed potatoes, Blue Moon Beer Batter Scallops or Blue Moon Beer Batter Fish and Chips, fried fish tacos, and jambalaya.

Along with live music, every Thursday night Strange Brew hosts trivia nights where teams compete for a $100 gift certificate to the Portsmouth Brewery.

Connecticut

BREWPUBS

6	Bru Room at Bar
13	The Cambridge House
15	City Steam Brewery Cafe
12	SBC Restaurant & Brewery–Branford
10	SBC Restaurant & Brewery–Hamden
3	SBC Restaurant & Brewery–Milford
1	SBC Restaurant & Brewery–Stamford
2	SBC Restaurant & Brewery–Southport
18	Tullycross Tavern & Microbrewery
19	Willimantic Brewing Company

BARS

8	The Cask Republic
7	Delaney's Restaurant & Tap Room
16	Eli Cannon's Tap Room
11	MiKro Craft Beer Bar
9	Prime 16

BREWERIES

4	Cavalry Brewing Company
20	Cottrell Brewing Company
5	New England Brewing Company
17	Olde Burnside Brewing Company
14	Thomas Hooker Brewing Company

Connecticut

Connecticut might be a slow starter in the craft beer boom that is taking over New England, but they are showing some signs of becoming bigger and better than ever.

The New England Brewing Company has added some wonderful beers to its already solid lineup, and Thomas Hooker Brewing Company is still chugging along, brewing their old classics while adding some newer beers to appeal to the beginner craft beer enthusiast.

There are plenty of good brewpubs, including the Tullycross Tavern & Microbrewery and the well-established Willimantic Brewing Company to keep Connecticut beer lovers happy. And don't forget about New Haven; a new beer bar seems to pop up in the city at least once a year, adding to an already blossoming craft beer scene.

Breweries

CAVALRY BREWING

115 Hurley Rd., Building 9A, Oxford, CT; (203) 262-6075; http://cavalrybrewing.com
Founded: 2010 **Founder:** Mike McCreary **Brewer:** Mike McCreary **Flagship Beer:**
Marauder IPA **Year-round Beers:** Dog Soldier Golden Ale, Hatch Plug Ale, Nomad Stout
Seasonals/Special Releases: Big Wally Porter, X-Limited Edition series **Tours:** Fri, noon
to 6 p.m.; Sat, 10 a.m. to 3 p.m.

Cavalry Brewing is proof that sometimes something good can come out of something bad. In 2008, founder Mike McCreary lost his job in the declining economy. Instead of just looking for another job, McCreary decided to change his life and he founded Cavalry Brewing. The brewery is a bit of a throwback to New England brewing, concentrating almost exclusively on English-style ales, which is great for those who do not always want high-alcohol or extreme beers. These are all solid beers that will not make your brain fuzzy.

Beer Lover's Pick

Big Wally Porter
Style: Porter
ABV: 4.8 percent
Availability: Year-Round
There is a trend in beer today to imperialize everything and make it bigger. The Big Wally Porter is an example of how good a beer can be when brewed traditionally. This beer has some light roasty undertones, with hints of chocolate and some yeasty flavors. It is a smooth and creamy beer, and the low alcohol means you can enjoy at least one or two more.

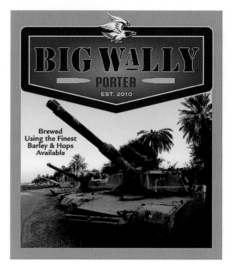

The **Dog Soldier Golden Ale** is a light, refreshing beer with a touch of citrusy aroma. It's also only 4 percent alcohol by volume, making it a perfect session beer. The **Hatch Plug Ale** is a classic English-style bitter. The hops give it a slightly fruity taste, and the malt balance is phenomenal. The **Marauder IPA** is a classic English-style IPA. The hops in this beer provide earthy flavors, more than the citrusy or piney flavors that most American-style IPAs have. The **Nomad Stout** is a fantastic dry stout. It is only 4.5 percent ABV, but it is incredibly roasted. The roasted bitterness blends well with the creaminess; one will find a lot of coffee flavors and slight undertones of chocolate. The **Big Wally Porter** is a classic English-style porter. Again, under 5 percent ABV, it is a wonderful example of how good English-style beers can be if they are brewed right. The **X-Limited Edition** is a new series of beer. The first beer in the series is the **English Nut Brown Ale.** After trying an X-Limited Edition series beer, Cavalry Brewing asks that you go to their website and vote on the beer. If enough people give it a positive review, Cavalry may release it as a full-time beer in the future. If people fail to respond in a positive manner, the beer will disappear.

If you do buy some of the Cavalry Brewing beers, make sure to read the back of the bottles. People McCreary knew while serving in Iraq in 2003 inspire all of the beer names. The back labels give a slight biography of the person featured. Tours are available on Friday and Saturday, and are led by one of the two brewery employees. Make sure to call ahead to make sure someone is available. The tour also includes a tasting of all available beers, and growlers are available to go.

COTTRELL BREWING COMPANY

100 Mechanic St., Pawcatuck, CT; (860) 599-8213; www.cottrellbrewing.com
Founded: 1996 **Founder:** Charles Cottrell Buffum Jr. **Brewer:** Charles Cottrell Buffum Jr.
Flagship Beer: Old Yankee Ale **Year-round Beer:** Mystic Bridge IPA **Seasonals/Special Releases:** None **Tours:** Mon through Wed, by appointment only; Thurs, 3 p.m.; Fri, every half-hour, 3 to 6 p.m.; Sat, every half-hour, noon to 5 p.m.

The Cottrell Brewing Company has to be doing something right. Cottrell has been in existence for 15 years, and during that time, they've been brewing only two beers. If a brewery can succeed for 15 years by brewing only two beers, the beers must be fantastic. Luckily for Cottrell Brewing Company, that is indeed the case.

The **Old Yankee Ale,** in particular, is fabulous. It's an amber ale, which is typically a boring style that a lot of beer lovers ignore. But, do not sleep on this particular amber ale. Old Yankee is probably the best amber ale being brewed in New England today. The **Mystic Bridge IPA** is relatively mellow at 6 percent alcohol by volume. It is not quite a west coast IPA or an English-style IPA—it seems to be somewhere in the middle. It's easy drinking, slightly earthy, but with just a hint of grapefruit character from the hops. The IPA's name came from the local Mystic River Bridge.

The Cottrell Brewing Company is housed in a piece of both Connecticut and Cottrell family history—the former C.B. Cottrell & Sons Inc. factory, a printing press facility that printed nearly every magazine of note in the late 1800s and early 1900s. The founder of that company, Calvert B. Cottrell, is Buffum's great-grandfather. The brewery only takes up about 9,000 square feet of the 350,000-square-foot factory.

To see part of the history, attend one of the several tours Cottrell Brewing Company hosts throughout the week. The tour features a discussion of the brewery's history, as well as the process of brewing the beer, and also includes a tasting. The beer is also available for sale.

Beer Lover's Pick

Old Yankee Ale
Style: Pale Ale
ABV: 5 percent
Availability: Year-Round
The Old Yankee Ale is a classic example of an east coast pale ale. Not as hoppy as its west coast counterparts, this beer is no less complex. The malt is sweet and caramel-like, with a little hint of doughy yeast flavor. The hops are there, providing a wonderful balance to keep the sweetness at a pleasant level without becoming cloying. This beer ends on a sweet note, unlike a lot of dry pale ale. At 5 percent alcohol by volume, this is a great daily drinking beer.

THE HARTFORD BETTER BEER COMPANY

Hartford, CT (corporate office only); (860) 684-5481; www.hartfordbetterbeer.com
Founded: 1991 **Founders:** Mike Harney, Phil Hopkins, Les Sinnock **Brewer:** Contract
brewed **Flagship Beer:** Arch Amber Ale **Year-round Beers:** Arch IPA, Praying Mantis
Porter **Seasonals/Special Releases:** None **Tours:** None

The Hartford Better Beer Company is a nostalgia beer company. It started as Connecticut's first brewpub in 1991, called the Hartford Brewery Limited. However, the brewery went out of business in 2000. But, now, that same brewpub's most popular beers are in 12-ounce bottles and are available throughout the state, which is perfect for those who miss drinking a cold pint of the beers they used to have available on the premises.

The beers are now brewed by the Shipyard Brewing Company in Portland, Maine. Shipyard's master brewer Alan Pugsley trained the original brewers at the Hartford Brewery Limited, and they brewed the beers using the Pugsley system. That means the beers, which are brewed to the original specifications, should taste exactly how people remember them.

Beer Lover's Pick

Praying Mantis Porter
Style: Porter
ABV: Unknown
Availability: Year-round
The Praying Mantis Porter is the Hartford Better Beer Company's best beer. It is a solid, English-style porter. It has nice toasty and roasty aroma, and it tastes of toffee mixed with a little coffee. There is also a hint of chocolate in the flavor, although it is not overwhelming. It is a good, solid beer worth trying.

The **Arch Amber Ale** was by far the most popular beer at Hartford Brewery Limited. It is a decent, if not a little old-fashioned, amber ale. Flavor-wise, the yeast gives it a little bit of a bready taste, while the malts add a little caramel flavor to it. There is also a decent kiss of hops on the finish. This is one of those old New England types of beers that a lot of the older breweries and brewpubs still have. The **Arch IPA** is more of an English-style IPA, in that the hops are not an in-your-face attack on your taste buds. Rather, the hops are a little more subtle, with nice hop aromas. This is a more malt-forward beer. The malt is not overwhelmingly sweet, but still overwhelms the hops. The **Praying Mantis Porter** is a straightforward, English-style porter. It is not an extreme beer, by any means, but it is true to the style.

Since the Hartford Better Beer Company does not brew its own beers, they do not host tours or tastings.

NEW ENGLAND BREWING COMPANY

7 Selden St., Woodbridge, CT; (203) 387-2222; www.newenglandbrewing.com
Founded: 1989 **Founder:** Dick and Marsha King **Brewer:** Rob Leonard **Flagship Beer:** Atlantic Amber **Year-round Beers:** Elm City Lager, Sea Hag IPA **Seasonals/Special Releases:** 668: The Neighbor of the Beast, Gandhi-Bot Double IPA, Imperial Stout Trooper, Wet Willy Scotch Ale **Tours:** Call ahead to make sure someone is available

The New England Brewing Company has the most eye-catching labels or cans in all of New England. They're hard to miss. After all, a robot version of Gandhi kind of stands out on liquor store shelves. You know what else stands out? The beer inside the cans.

The New England Brewing Company has been around for years, brewing solid, sessionable beers, but seem to have really hit their stride in recent years. All three year-round beers are very good. The **Sea Hag IPA** is a well-done, well-hopped, and nicely balanced IPA. The **Atlantic Amber** is an old-school New England beer, and the **Elm City Lager** is an easy drinking beer.

But it's really their special releases that get the New England Brewing Company a lot of attention. The **Gandhi-Bot Double IPA** (mentioned above) is more than just a funny label. It is a phenomenal double IPA. The beer pours a bright orange, and it is aggressively hopped, with aromas of pine and citrus wafting from the glass. Those aromas continue on into the taste. This is a hop bomb, but there is just enough balance to keep this a drinkable hop bomb. The **668: The Neighbor of the Beast** (play some Iron Maiden while drinking) is a spicy Belgian-style strong pale ale. Like Gandhi-Bot, this is a big beer (9 percent alcohol by volume). There are a lot of spices in this beer, and it is sweet, but not cloyingly sweet. This is a great nightcap kind of beer, a sipper. The **Imperial Stout Trooper** was the beer that really put New England Brewing Company on the map for those outside of New England. Again, the labels caught peoples' attention—inspired by Storm Troopers from *Star Wars*—but the beer itself was worthy of the attention. The labels have since changed after a "request" by George Lucas. The beer itself is a remarkable Russian imperial stout. Flavors of coffee and chocolate abound through this complex beer. The **Wet Willy Scotch Ale** is another big beer (10 percent ABV), but it is the best Scotch ale, or wee heavy, brewed in New England today. It is malty beer, with caramel and toffee undertones that are oh so good. Drink this beer only slightly chilled to make sure you get all of the fabulous flavors.

Unlike New England Brewing's other offerings, the Imperial Stout Trooper and Wet Willy Scotch Ale are both bottled. New England Brewing Company also brews several draft-only and brewery-only beers, such as barrel-aged versions of the ones mentioned above. They hold tastings at the brewery, as well as tours (just call ahead to make sure they are not too busy).

Beer Lover's Pick

Gandhi-Bot Double IPA
Style: Double IPA
ABV: 8.8 percent
Availability: Rotating
A big hop bomb in a can? Oh yeah, this is an awesome beer. The Gandhi-Bot is a hoppy assault on the tongue, and a hophead will love that. The hops add citrus and piney flavors, like a classic double or imperial IPA. The malt

is there in the background, but it is just there to provide some body and balance. This is a beer that is all about the hops. If you're eating a spicy dish, this will cut right through it.

Cans vs. Bottles

Bad beer comes in cans. That was the normal thought of craft beer enthusiasts over the years. It gives beer a metallic taste, they would say.

Things have changed. More and more craft breweries are releasing their beers in cans. In New England, Baxter Brewing in Maine cans all of their beers, as does the New England Brewing Company in Connecticut. The Alchemist, a popular Vermont brewery, opened up a cannery to can their Heady Topper double IPA. Even more established breweries, Harpoon Brewery and Cisco Brewers, can some of their beers for summer releases.

Cans offer many advantages over bottles. Light is beer's number one enemy. If a beer gets too much light, it turns the beer skunky. Do you want to drink a skunk? Neither do I. Cans solve that problem. They also take up less space than bottles, they're more portable, and unlike bottles, some beaches and campsites allow beer as long as it's in a can. They're also more environmentally friendly. Another advantage? The pop, fizz noise you hear when crack open a can is so much more satisfying than opening a bottle.

OLDE BURNSIDE BREWING COMPANY

780 Tolland St., East Hartford, CT; (860) 528-2200; www.oldeburnsidebrewing.com
Founded: 2000 **Founder:** Bob McClellan **Brewer:** Joe Lushing **Flagship Beer:** Ten Penny Ale **Year-round Beer:** Dirty Penny Ale **Seasonals/Special Releases:** Amazing Grace Series, Father Christmas Highland Ale, Highland Wild, Penny Weiz, Stone of Destination, Ten Penny Reserve **Tours:** By appointment

A lot of people talk about the different flavors that various yeasts, hops, or malts can add to beers, but perhaps the most important ingredient in beer is water. The Olde Burnside Brewing Company is an extension of owner Bob McClellan's water business. The water he sells has nearly the same mineral quality of Burton-on-the-Trent in England, where the India pale ale was developed. So, in 2000, using his own water, McClellan opened the Olde Burnside Brewing Company, brewing mainly British-inspired beers.

The **Ten Penny Ale,** the brewery's first beer and still its most popular, is a Scottish-style ale. It is a malty beer, but it is not too heavy. It is easy drinking, with slight caramel and roasted flavors. Pick up a growler of this at the local liquor store and share it with friends. Olde Burnside's only other year-round beer is the **Dirty**

Penny Ale, which is one of the few, and the best, commercially brewed black and tans. A black and tan is typically a stout blended with a lighter beer, such as a pale ale or a lager. The Dirty Penny is made up of a blend of 60 percent Ten Penny Ale and 40 percent house-brewed stout. It is a phenomenal beer.

Seasonals include the **Penny Weiz,** which is only available during the summer. It is a Belgian-style witbier, although some heather is added to the traditional coriander and bitter orange peel to give it a little more spiciness. The **Father Christmas Highland Ale** is a big, malty beast of a wee heavy, coming in at 9.2 percent alcohol by volume. This is a sipper, and the perfect beer to leave out for Ol' St. Nick on Christmas Eve to warm him up. The **Ten Penny Reserve,** which is available sporadically at the brewery, is the Ten Penny Ale's big brother. This comes in at a hefty 9.2 percent alcohol by volume. This is a full-bodied, creamy Scotch ale.

Other beers include the **Highland Wild,** a 9.6 percent Scottish wild ale, aged in oak barrels. You will not find this style brewed in Scotland, but the sourness works well with the sweet malts. The **Stone of Destination** is an imperial, or double, black

Beer Lover's Pick

Dirty Penny Ale
Style: Black and Tan
ABV: 5 percent
Availability: Year-round

Usually black and tans are created at home using Guinness and Bass, but this version is made using a stout brewed just for this beer, and mixed with Ten Penny Ale. It is a phenomenal beer. It combines the roastiness of the stout with the sweet, caramel, and malty flavors of the Scottish ale that is Ten Penny. It is creamy and has a great body. It is only 5 percent alcohol by volume, so you can drink a growler by yourself, or you can be nice and share.

and tan ale. The **Amazing Grace Series** is a series of ever-changing beers, usually the Ten Penny Ale aged in various barrels, such as oak barrels used to age Crown Royale. Each one is unique, but worth seeking out (only available at the brewery).

THOMAS HOOKER BREWING COMPANY

16 Tobey Rd., Bloomfield, CT; (860) 242-3111; www.hookerbeer.com
Founded: 1997 **Founder:** Jack Streich **Brewer:** Mike Yates **Flagship Beer:** American Pale Ale **Year-round Beers:** Blonde Ale, Hop Meadow IPA, Imperial Porter, Irish Red, Liberator Doppelbock, Munich-Style, Old Marley Barleywine **Seasonals/Special Releases:** Nor'Easter Lager, Octoberfest, Watermelon Ale **Tours:** Sat, noon to 5 p.m., $5; first and third Fri of every month, open house from 5 to 8 p.m.

Thomas Hooker Brewing Company has been around for a while, and they walk the line of brewing beers for beer geeks and for those new to craft beer. Named for the founder of Hartford and the state of Connecticut, Thomas Hooker has a wide mix of beers, including lagers, fruit beers, and some big malty beers.

Beer Lover's Pick

Liberator Doppelbock
Style: Doppelbock
ABV: 8 percent
Availability: Year-Round
If a double IPA is for hopheads, doppelbocks are for malt heads. This is a big, malty beer with caramel flavors, as well as a toasted, biscuity taste, with hints of dark fruit. It is creamy, and a smooth beer. An 8 percent alcohol by volume beer should not be this easy to drink. Unlike some doppelbocks, you can actually taste the hops in the Liberator, with just a little herbal/grassy notes, particularly in the finish.

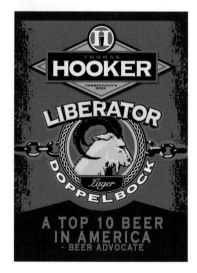

The year-round beers include one of the best New England beers available, the **Liberator Doppelbock.** This is a malty monster of a beer. Along the same lines are the **Imperial Porter** and the **Old Marley Barleywine.** These are the "beer geek" beers—all big beers high in alcohol, complex and flavorful. The **Hop Meadow IPA** is a very good IPA. It is not too bitter and extremely balanced; the **American Pale Ale** is along the same vein, balanced and easy to drink. The **Irish Red** is spot on for the style. It is not an overly exciting beer, but it goes down easy. The **Munich-Style** is a golden lager, a little light, but still with enough flavor to make it enjoyable. The **Blonde Ale** has been considered a kind of beginner craft beer—for those who are just starting to drink craft beer, this is a good place to start.

The seasonals include the fantastic **Octoberfest.** It tastes similar to German-brewed Oktoberfests, and it is easily one of the better Oktoberfest beers brewed in New England. The **Watermelon Ale** is what the name says, a watermelon beer. It is a light beer and kind of tastes like watermelon bubblegum. The **Nor'Easter** is a lager brewed with wintery spices.

On the first and third Friday of every month, Thomas Hooker hosts an open house at the brewery from 5 to 8 p.m. For $10, you get a few drinks and a guided tour and get to take home the pint glass you used during the night. All proceeds go to a local charity. Tours are on Saturday from noon to 5 p.m. For $5 you get a fully guided tour and a tasting of all the available beers. The brewery store sells the beers in 12-ounce bottles and in growlers. Clothing, hats, and several other items are also available in the brewery store.

Connecticut

Brewpubs

BRU ROOM AT BAR

254 Crown St., New Haven, CT; (203) 495-8924; www.barnightclub.com
Draft Beers: 5

The Bru Room at Bar is not just a brewpub. It is part of Bar, a full-service night-club with three separate rooms that fill different roles. The brewpub always has at least five beers on tap.

The year-round beers include the **Toasted Blonde Ale,** which puts a twist on the normally safe style—to get the toasted flavor, brewers throw the malts into the pizza oven and toast them before brewing, giving it a nice, unique flavor never found in a blonde ale. The **AmBAR Ale** is a nice amber ale that features nutty and caramel flavors from the malts, as well as a slight fruitiness from the hops. The **Pale Ale** is a west coast–style pale ale, along the lines of a Sierra Nevada Pale Ale. The **Dam Good Stout** is a nice foreign-style stout, which features undertones of chocolate and coffee. Want more coffee flavor? Grab the **Espresso Dam Good Stout** when it is available. Bru Room features several specialty beers that make occasional appearances. They include the **Big Man IPA,** the **Chocolate Porter,** the **Doctor's Orders Hefeweizen,** the **You Name It IPA,** and the **Raven Haired Beauty,** a 3.7 percent dark mild ale.

The food here is all about the pizza. Except for one salad (which features seasonal greens, pears, pecans, and blue cheese), it's the only type of food available. The pizzas are offered in three bases—the Red Pie, the Red Pie with mozzarella, and the White Pizza with parmesan and garlic. After picking a base, you have 24 options to choose from, including traditional items like pepperoni, onions, and sausage, as well as the not-so-traditional, like mashed potatoes and fresh littleneck clams.

THE CAMBRIDGE HOUSE

357 Salmon Brook St., Granby, CT; (860) 653-2739; http://cbhgranby.com
Draft Beers: 6

The Cambridge House may not be in the most populous area of Connecticut, but this Granby brewpub is worth making a trek. They brew a large selection of varied beers of numerous styles and strengths. For those who are fans of lighter styles, the **Cooper Hill Kolsch, Berliner Weisse,** and the **Czech Yo'Shelf** (a Czech-style pilsner) are definitely for you.

They also brew some hoppy beers, such as the **Abijah Rowe IPA,** or the **BIPA** (Belgian IPA), which are both worth trying. They also brew some malt-heavy beers, such as the **Bock, Pigskin Brown,** and the **Moonbeam Stout,** a 9.8 percent alcohol by volume oak-barrel-aged imperial stout. Other beers brewed by the Cambridge House include the **Alt-45,** the **Farmer's Daughter** (biere de garde), **Oktoberfest,** and **Pumpkin Porter.**

While the beer is obviously what brings people to the Cambridge House, the food will not drive people away. They have a decent-size, if not huge, menu. Starters include seared ahi tuna and the Stout Steak Skewers, which are teriyaki- and stout-marinated steak on a stick. Entrees include the Oh Baby Baby Back Ribs, a stout steak, pan-roasted chicken, and jambalaya. The CBH Mac & Cheese is made with several different cheeses, but what really sets it apart is that you can get a half of a lobster tail mixed into it for just a few extra bucks. Throughout the year, the Cambridge House hosts several beer dinners, and also has live music most Fridays and Saturdays, so it is definitely a place you will want to check out.

CITY STEAM BREWERY CAFE
942 Main St., Hartford, CT; (860) 525-1600; www.citysteambrewerycafe.com
Draft Beers: 8 to 10

Not only does City Steam brew good beer and serve good food, they host a comedy club, Brew HA HA, on site at the brewpub. Little-known (at the time) comedians who have performed there over the years include Kevin James, Denis Leary, Jay Mohr, Ray Romano, and Sarah Silverman.

If comedy is not your thing, don't worry, City Steam is still a brewpub. They always have 8 to 10 beers on tap, as well as guest ciders. The beers always on tap include the **Blonde on Blonde Pale Ale,** the **Colt's Light Lager, Naughty Nurse's Amber Ale,** and the **Export Lager.** Feelings are often mixed when a brewpub puts a light lager on draft, but for a brewpub that also doubles as a comedy club, it makes sense because they attract a large crowd of customers who might not have an interest in craft beer. Other beers that are often available include the **Black Silk Stout** (an oatmeal stout), the **Pugnacious Porter** (a big Baltic porter), **White Wedding** (a hybrid of American, Belgian, and German wheat beers), the **Innocence Ale** (an IPA), and the **City Steam Dark Lager.** There is also usually a special Belgian or another strong ale available on draft at all times, as well as seasonal lagers. Growlers are available to go, but each beer costs a different price, so check with your server.

They also have some unique specialty burgers, including the Reuben, which is a burger topped with corned beef, Swiss cheese, Russian dressing, and Asian slaw. City Steam also has what appears to be the most decadent, heart-stopping burger ever created—the Bacon Triple Decker. It's a bacon cheeseburger sandwiched between two grilled cheese sandwiches. Read that sentence again. If that sounds a little too artery-clogging for you, there is a healthy option section of the menu that includes grilled salmon, grilled fish tacos, and chicken teriyaki skewers. The best seller is the Beer-Braised Pot Roast, braised with house-brewed beer (see recipe, page 241).

SBC RESTAURANT & BREWERY
Five locations in Branford, Hamden, Milford, Southport, and Stamford; Branford, (203) 481-BREW; Hamden, (203) 288-HOPS; Milford, (203) 874-BEER; Southport, (203) 257-BEER; Stamford, (203) 327-BEER; www.southportbrewing.com
Draft Beers: 9

Chain brewpubs can often be a little disappointing. A lot of them have bland beer and boring food. The Southport Brewing Company, or SBC for short, is different. With five locations throughout Connecticut, they do a great job of brewing quality beers and also offer a solid menu.

In all, SBC brews 27 different beers, with 9 different ones on draft at a time. They also make it easy for the novice beer drinker, or those not familiar with the beers. SBC breaks up their beer menu into three tiers. Tier One is light, easy-drinking beers. Tier Two beers are a little more complex, more flavorful, and made to enjoy with food. Tier Three is the more complex beers, designed more for those who are experienced craft beer fans. SBC also lists what mainstream beer the various beers on the menu are most similar to. For example, if you are a fan of Corona, you may want to grab a **SBC Light** from Tier One. If you are a fan of the Samuel Smith's Taddycaster Porter, grab the **SBC Porter** from Tier Three. Harpoon IPA fan? The **SBC IPA** from Tier Two is for you.

The menu is huge and varied. Their mussels are sautéed in the **Big Head Blond Ale,** and SBC offers calamari in three styles: Crispy is the traditional method; the Z-Bar is fried with hot peppers, garlic, and artichoke hearts; and the Sticky is cooked with a sweet chili sriracha glaze with sesame seeds and green onions. Entrees include the SBC Barbecue, a full rack of baby back ribs or a mix of ribs and grilled chicken, all based in beer-infused barbecue sauce. SBC also offers pizza, such as the Loaded Potato Pizza that is topped with mashed potatoes, bacon, scallops, and cheddar and jack cheeses, all topped with sour cream. SBC also has the largest dessert menu of any brewpub I've ever seen. Options include cheesecake, Key lime pie, cinnamon crème brûlée, and chocolate lava cake.

On Sunday from 11:30 a.m. to 2 p.m., SBC offers brunch. Brunch options include many different egg Benedicts, breakfast burritos, omelets, breakfast quesadillas, breakfast sandwiches, steak and eggs, and several different champagne cocktails.

TULLYCROSS TAVERN & MICROBREWERY

1487 Pleasant Valley Rd., Manchester, CT; (860) 644-2739; www.tullycrosstavern.com
Draft Beers: 9

Award-winning homebrewer Brian Flach is the first head brewer at Tullycross, which was founded in 2011 by Sean Wansor. The small brewpub offers eight beers on draft at all times, as well as a rotating guest tap.

The standard beers are the **Tavern Light,** a light beer with a slight hop kick; the **TCT Pale Ale;** the **Tully's Irish Red;** and the **Silk City Irish Stout.** They also have a different IPA on draft at all times—named the **Batch "X" IPA,** Flach brews a different one each time, using different combinations of hops to bring different flavors to the beer.

The Tullycross Tavern also has a list of seasonals planned. The pumpkin and Oktoberfest will be for the fall, while the hefeweizen will be a summer release. The double IPA will be available in the winter. Other seasonals and special releases include a brown ale, an imperial stout, a Belgian pale ale, and a Scottish ale. Growlers of the beer are available to go, ranging in price from $13 to $15.

The menu can be described as upscale pub fare, perfect for an up-and-coming pub. House-made clam chowder and chili made with their Silk City Stout are tasty options as starters. It's when you look at the entree and seafood menu that you see the more upscale food. There are comfort foods such as TCT's Shepherd's Pie and the Tavern Meatloaf. There is more adventurous fare, such as the bacon herb encrusted mussels and the Maine lobster grilled cheese. The "Seafood" section of the menu includes the Fisherman's Pie, which is a "traditional" Irish pie filled with cod, garlic, baby shrimp, carrots, peas, onions, and white cream sauce, topped with mashed potatoes and cheddar cheese.

WILLIMANTIC BREWING COMPANY

967 Main St., Willimantic, CT; (860) 423-6777; www.willibrew.com
Draft Beers: 8 to 10 house beers, 40 overall

The Willimantic Brewing Company is located in a historic post office. It has one of the best mixes of beers around—8 to 10 house-brewed beers and another 30 to 32 guest craft beers.

The only flagship beer is the **Certified Gold,** but the rest are a rotation of IPAs, stouts, porters, red ales, amber ales, blonde ales, wheats, sours, and barrel-aged beers. Get the sampler platter of beers when you go—it is by the far the best way to try as many of the beers as you possibly can. Highlights include the **E-Mail IPA,** an

English-inspired hoppy IPA; the **Dyvil Hopyard Double IPA,** a Belgian-style double IPA; and the **Autobahn Mail Alt,** a German-style altbier. They also try to introduce a new beer at least once a month using different combinations of hops, malts, yeast, and what founder David Wollner describes as "esoteric ingredients" (such as vanilla, tea, and pineapple).

Guest drafts include several beers from local breweries, as well as Belgian ales and beers from throughout the US. Sierra Nevada Brewing Company, Stone Brewing Company, and Dogfish Head Craft Brewery often find their way onto the tap list.

The menu is huge, and there's also a large number of gluten-free items available. Don't want an entree? Grab one of the many flatbread pizzas or sandwiches available. The Beer Tap Beef Sandwich is one of the better options. The sandwich is made up of thinly shaved steak, melted Swiss cheese, and balsamic beer-glazed onions, served on a kaiser roll. Willimantic uses beers in many of their dishes. Along with the onions, they make Beer-B-Que sauce, onion soup, brewer's bread, and sweet beer butter from their house-brewed beers.

Willimantic Brewing Company's beers are also available to go in the form of growlers. Growlers start at $12.95 each, but they can increase in price for the some of the higher-alcohol beers.

Beer Bars

THE CASK REPUBLIC

179 Crown St., New Haven, CT; (475) 238-8335; http://thecaskrepublic.com
Draft Beers: 53 plus 1 cask line **Bottled/Canned Beers:** More than 125

The Cask Republic has become a beer destination for Connecticut beer lovers. The 53-beer draft list is impressive, featuring a wide variety of beers from the US and beyond. If there is an American brewery that you enjoy, and it is available in Connecticut, they have it.

The draft list is broken up by style, so it's easy to navigate. They also have a good mix of big beers and easier to drink, lighter beers. They also have plenty of quality imports. The menu always features some draft specials, when a beer is available at a lower price. The Cask Republic also features several different flights of beers, in which you get four 5-ounce beers, such as the IPA Flight, or the Stone Brewing Company Flight. The bottled beer list is even more impressive. They also have a large imported bottle selection, including a bigger-than-average selection of Italian craft beers (an extremely underrated beer country), and several Japanese beer options. The Cask Republic also has a large selection of Belgian ales and has a few gluten-free beers on the menu.

The Republic also has separate lunch and dinner menus. The lunch menu features smaller, quicker meals, with salads, soups, small plates, sandwiches, and burgers. The Grilled Sausage Plate, which features bratwurst, knockwurst, apple bacon, sauerkraut, and potatoes steamed in lager, is a highlight. If you skipped breakfast, grab the Breakfast Burger, which is topped by a fried egg, applewood-smoked bacon, and tomato jam. Dinner appetizer highlights include the oyster sliders and the seared ahi tuna. There are also plenty of salads, including the warm duck confit salad, which is made up of endive, arugula, red onions, grapes, Granny Smith apples, goat cheese, and caramelized honey vinaigrette. The sandwich you have to try is the German Pretzel Sandwich, which is composed of a breaded pork cutlet, German sauerkraut, and Chimay cheese sauce, all on a giant pretzel bun. One of the standout entrees is the Grilled Extra-Hoppy-Beer-Marinated Half Chicken, served with grilled mash potatoes, sautéed greens, and herb pan gravy (see recipe, page 240).

Connecticut

DELANEY'S RESTAURANT & TAP ROOM

882 Whalley Ave., New Haven, CT; (203) 397-5494; www.delaneystaproom.com
Draft Beers: 54 **Bottled/Canned Beers:** 150 to 200

Delaney's Restaurant and Tap Room is a major part of New Haven's burgeoning craft beer scene. This small pub, founded in 2001, started as a mecca for those in the New Haven area that did not want to drive more than 40 minutes to find a good beer on tap. Delaney's has 54 draft lines, along with one cask. The beer is always handpicked to make sure there are a good variety of beers available. There are always at least six American IPAs; two to four each of German pilsners, Belgian ales, stouts and imperial stouts, and pale/amber ales; and three to six German-style hefeweizens.

There are also always a few rarities on tap, such as the 2007 Smuttynose Brewing Company Barleywine from New Hampshire and the Leipziger Gose, a rare German style of wheat beer. The selection is top notch. Make sure to peruse the large bottle list that includes 150 to 200 different beers, and you just may find a hidden jewel. There are definitely some rarities, including several vintages of J.W. Lee's Harvest Ale, brewed as far back as 1999. There are also aged lambics, gueuzes, stouts, and other Belgian ales. It is much easier to buy a pre-aged beer at a bar than it is to control yourself from drinking a beer you're trying to save, so consider splurging.

There is a wide variety of food, ranging from $6 dishes to $30 entrees, so everyone should find something they like. Appetizers are pretty much what you expect at a pub—fried mozzarella, fried calamari, and stuffed mushrooms. The burger choices include a Guinness burger made with maple stout sauce and the Meatless Burger, which is made with a portobello mushroom instead of beef. Entrees include filet mignon, lobster ravioli, and a scrumptious Argentinian rib eye.

Delaney's also hosts tap takeovers every six months, and samplers are available daily. They also host beer dinners about four times a year. Typically the dinner features a four-course meal, each course paired with a beer from a specific brewery, and costs $40 a person.

ELI CANNON'S TAP ROOM

695 Main St., Middletown, CT; (860) 347-3547; www.elicannons.com
Draft Beers: 33 **Bottled/Canned Beers:** About 40

Eli Cannon's is probably the best beer bar in the great state of Connecticut, but what really sets it apart from other bars is the dessert menu. Yes, that's right, the dessert menu. There are many great beer bars throughout New England,

Every November, Eli Cannon's hosts a Christmas Tree Lighting ceremony. Along with a tree lighting ceremony, there's snow, "hot elves," and presents for the kids. People are also asked to bring a toy to donate to local charities, and there will be much merry and mirth happening as you enjoy the numerous beers available.

but none offer the truly creative desserts that Eli Cannon's serves up on a regular basis. Not only does the dessert menu include adult-only and kid-friendly floats, it includes the Fried Cheese Cake Burritos, the Gourmet Pop Tart Sandwiches, which are chocolate Pop Tarts stuffed with white chocolate pretzel peanut butter, and the S'Mores Bread Pudding.

Okay, now for the beer.

Eli Cannon's has 33 beers on tap, and the choices change nearly daily, which will make you want to come back every day to see what you might be missing. The draft list is a good mix of American, Belgian, British, and German beers. They typically have beers from some of the best breweries in the country, such as Dogfish Head, Flying Dog, and Brooklyn Brewery. They also have beers not often available in New England, such as Cooperstown Brewing Company from Cooperstown, New York. New England is usually well-represented with beers from Allagash, Redhook, and Bar Harbor on draft. They also have beers from Ayinger, Delirium Tremens, Wells & Youngs, and Corsendonk. The bottled list is just as varied, so if you can't find a beer you like at Eli Cannon's, you're not really trying.

Now, back to the food.

If you can hold off eating dessert to start your meal, start with a real appetizer. Eli Cannon's has wings, which is not unusual for a bar. What is unusual is the number of different sauces they have available—14, from mild and sweet to hot and spicy, or hot and sweet—pretty much every heat level up to Atomic. Be careful, if the sauce is too hot, no returns. Their baskets of fries are almost as varied—they are served in nine different styles, including Smokers, which are topped with chipotle sauce, jalapeños, cheese, and ranch dressing. Another option is the Porkies Revenge, which are fries covered in barbecue pulled pork and cheese.

Sandwiches include a half-dozen different types of Philly cheesesteaks, as well as the Yogi's BLT, which is made with bourbon teriyaki grilled salmon, bacon, greens, tomatoes, and lemon caper mayonnaise. Burgers are also available. Entrees include macaroni and cheese made with smoked gouda, gruyère, cheddar, Monterey jack, and Parmesan cheeses. Garlic shrimp and shepherd's pie are also options, as is the Caribbean Pasta, which is sautéed chicken tossed in a creamy Caribbean jerk sauce served over pasta. Or do what I would do—order a dessert and a stout and enjoy.

MIKRO CRAFT BEER BAR
300 Whitney Ave., Hamden, CT; (203) 553-7676; www.mikrobeerbar.com
Draft Beers: 18 **Bottled/Canned Beers:** About 100

The MiKro Craft Beer Bar is proof that good things can come in small packages. The bar only seats 58 people. But, if you are lucky enough to be one of those select few to get a seat inside, you will be treated to a superb draft and bottled list of beer.

MiKro has 18 beers on draft, heavy on New England beers, including Cavalry Brewing Company from Connecticut, Cisco Beer and Harpoon Brewery from Massachusetts, Long Trail Ales and Otter Creek Brewing Company from Vermont, and Sebago Brewing Company from Maine. Other breweries often featured include River Horse Brewing Company from New Jersey, Rogue Brewery from Oregon, and Rodenbach Grand Cru from Belgium. The bottled list includes beers in almost every single style from almost every major American brewery, as well as several larger-format bottles, 750 ml and even 3-liter bottles, from Europe, mainly Belgium.

Throughout the year, MiKro hosts several tap takeovers, where a particular brewery will have several of its beers on tap, often at discounted prices. They also host beer dinners where a brewery will work with the chef to create a dinner in which each beer is matched perfectly with the dish being served. MiKro takes pride in creating a menu that is beer-friendly. Each and every dish is perfect to eat with the various beers on tap.

Start light with a snack, such as deviled eggs, fried chick peas, house-made pretzels, and charcuterie plates, or order small plates. Small plates include beet salad; poutine; chicken wings; and Local Burrata, which is made with cream-filled mozzarella, olive oil confit tomatoes, arugula, basil oil, and balsamic vinaigrette. MiKro also has several whole-wheat flatbreads, with toppings like Yukon Gold potatoes, mushrooms, and pork belly. Sandwiches are always an option, including the

Kobe beef hot dog or the P.B.L.T., which is topped with roasted pork belly, smoked bacon, Bibb lettuce, tomatoes, and roasted garlic mayonnaise.

Entrees, or, as MiKro calls them, "Large Plates," include smoked trout with dill crème fraîche, pickled red onions, squash puree, local apples, and crispy sweet potatoes. Highlights are the Shrimp + Grits, which is cheddar grits served with shrimp, smoked bacon, green onions, and pickled green tomato relish; and pan-roasted chicken breast, which is served with roasted sweet potato, quinoa, Swiss chard, and cilantro-pumpkin seed pesto. There is a different dessert available daily.

PRIME 16
172 Temple St., New Haven, CT; (203) 782-1616; www.prime16.com
Draft Beers: 20, plus 2 casks **Bottled/Canned Beers:** More than 40

Enjoying a good beer while munching on a burger is a time-honored tradition, but Prime 16 takes the pairing to an all-new level: they combine great craft beer with grass-fed beef burgers. Talk about a perfect pairing.

This relatively new bar, only opening in 2010, has 20 beers on draft, as well as more than 40 different craft beers in bottles and cans. Combine that with one of the best burger menus around, and it makes for a perfect night. They also typically have two beers on cask at all times. The draft list is varied, with beers for all tastes, ranging from fruit beers to hoppy American IPAs to many different Belgian ales; if you can't find a beer that you like, you really aren't trying that hard. The bottled list features many of the top breweries in the country, as well as local favorites.

The burgers are the star of the menu. There are several beefless burgers, including the lamb burger and the wasabi-glazed salmon burger. Of course, if you call yourself a burger place, you'd better have some unusual, but tasty, burgers on the menu. Prime 16 does. The Maui Burger has pineapple, Maui onions, tropical mayonnaise, and applewood bacon. The New York Steak Burger is another interesting creation. It's topped with cracked pepper, wilted spinach, blue cheese crumble, and tobacco-fried onions. If there isn't a burger on the menu that catches your attention, you can always build your own burger—pick the toppings of choice to make the perfect burger just for you.

Prime 16 hosts plenty of special events throughout the year. They do a tap takeover at least every other month, and they host both beer and bourbon dinners. In addition, Monday is $3 beer night, and there are free beer tastings every Wednesday starting at 9 p.m. Happy hour, Monday through Friday from 4 to 7 p.m. and Saturday 2 to 4 p.m., features half-price beers. Prime 16 is a perfect night out; just make sure to get there early on a Saturday night or risk standing up all night, then grab a burger and a beer and have fun.

Rhode Island

MASSACHUSETTS

BREWERIES
Coastal Extreme Brewing Company **6**

BREWPUBS
Coddington Brewing Company **7**
Mohegan Cafe & Brewery **8**
Trinity Brewhouse **2**
Union Station Brewery **3**

Woonsocket

RHODE ISLAND
CONNECTICUT

Pawtucket **1**

Providence **2–5**

Scituate
Reservoir

Cranston

Warwick

Fall River

Exeter

Portsmouth

Middletown

Little
Compton

West Kingston

South Kingston

6,7 Newport
9

Narragansett Bay

Rhode Island
Sound

Block Island
Sound

N

0   5   10 miles

BARS
Doherty's East Avenue Irish Pub **1**
English Cellar Alehouse **4**
Julians **5**
Pour Judgement Bar & Grill **9**

8 Block Island

Rhode Island

Rhode Island is New England's smallest state in terms of size and the beer scene, but it isn't without merit. The Coastal Extreme Brewing Company, brewers of Newport Storm beers, brews several excellent beers, from their year-round beers to their special releases, while Narragansett Beer is growing and trying to regain the popularity of its heyday of the 1950s. Meanwhile, Providence is quickly developing a growing beer scene with a pair of brewpubs and several beer bars, making it a nice weekend stop for visitors and a beer haven for local beer lovers.

Breweries

COASTAL EXTREME BREWING COMPANY

293 JT Connell Rd., Newport, RI; (401) 849-5232; www.newportstorm.com
Founded: 1999 **Founders:** Brent Ryan, Derek Luke, Mark Sincliar, Will Rafferty **Brewer:** Derek Luke **Flagship Beer:** Newport Storm Hurricane Amber Ale **Year-round Beer:** Rhode Island Blueberry Ale **Seasonals/Special Releases:** Regenschauer Oktoberfest, Spring Ale, Summer Ale, Winter, Cyclone Series, Annual Release Series **Tours:** Every day except Tues, noon to 5 p.m.; guided tours at 3 p.m., $7 per person, plus tax

The Coastal Extreme Brewing Company, better known as Newport Storm, is the only full production brewery in the state of Rhode Island, and an excellent brewery at that. Coastal Extreme does not get as much love from beer geeks as they really should. They produce some of the most drinkable beers available in New England.

The brewery's flagship offering, the **Newport Storm Hurricane Amber Ale,** is a remarkably drinkable beer. It might be the best amber ale being brewed anywhere; it is a beer that can attract those casual beer drinkers, and still have enough flavor that craft beer lovers will still want to seek it out. Newport's only other year-round beer is the **Rhode Island Blueberry Ale,** which is better than most other beers for the style.

Coastal Extreme brews four seasonals, called the **Storms of the Season.** The **Summer Ale** is a really nice, hoppy summer beer. The **Winter** is a dark, roasty porter, while the **Spring Ale** is a roasty red ale. The **Regenschauer Oktoberfest** is a traditional German-style Oktoberfest, rich and malty. Throughout the year, Coastal Extreme also brews the **Cyclone Series.** Each one of the beers is produced in limited qualities, is a different style, and is named for different Atlantic hurricanes. The styles vary and in the past have included various types of pale ales, a winter warmer, and even a rum barrel-aged beer. At the end of the year, Coastal Extreme brews an anniversary beer, and the name is simply the year—'09, '10, '11, etc. The beers are usually higher octane beers, packaged in 750 ml, strikingly blue bottles, with a waxed top so the beer can be cellared and enjoyed for years, to see how the beer ages and matures.

Also at Coastal Extreme is the Newport Distillery, which produces Thomas TewRum. Coastal Extreme hosts tours daily (except for Tuesday). A guided tour begins at 3 p.m., but self-guided tours are anytime from noon to 5 p.m. The tours cost $7, and you get to try four different beers and get a Newport Storm tasting

Hurricane Amber Ale
Style: Amber Ale
ABV: 5.2 percent
Availability: Year-Round

The Hurricane Amber Ale may be what many people consider a boring style (amber ale), but this is one fantastic beer. It is darker than many amber ales, and it has a full body thanks to the sweet malts, with a creamy head and mouthfeel. At the same time, there is just a hint of hops, which is just enough to give this beer a nice balance.

glass. You can also tour the distillery, which costs an additional $9. Coastal Extreme also hosts several events throughout the year, such as the Hoppy Holiday, which is an on-site beer festival.

NARRAGANSETT BEER

60 Ship St., Providence, RI (corporate office); (401) 437-8970; www.narragansettbeer.com
Founded: 2005 **Founders:** Mark Hellendrung **Brewers:** Contract brewed **Flagship Beer:** Narragansett Lager **Year-round Beers:** Narragansett Light **Seasonals/Special Releases:** Narragansett Bock, Fest Lager, Narragansett Porter, Summer Ale **Tours:** None

"Hey neighbor, grab a 'Gansett." That saying was synonymous with the former Narragansett Brewing Company in the 1950s and 1960s. Pittsburgh had Yuengling, but New Englanders had Narragansett. That was our beer.

But as breweries started consolidating, Narragansett was sold, and eventually it went away, until 2005 when Mark Hellendrung and a group of investors bought back the rights to the name, hired back former brewer Bill Anderson to re-create the original recipe, and brought the 'Gansett name back home. Narragansett is actually brewed in New York, but Hellendrung is trying to sell enough beer that he can open a full brewery in Rhode Island. Until then, more and more bars throughout the state are carrying the classic Narragansett "Tall Boys," the 16-ounce cans.

The classic **Narragansett Lager** is cheap, easy to drink, and just plain tasty. Nothing flashy here. This is a straightforward American lager, but with more flavor than you see from the big boys in St. Louis, Milwaukee, and Golden, Colorado. However, where Narragansett really excels is their seasonals. They have found a niche of doing quality, straightforward interpretations of relatively simple styles. Again, no flash, no twists, just darn good beer. The **Fest Lager** is an Oktoberfest-style beer, available during the fall. It is the kind of beer that goes down easy. It may not be as full-bodied as the German counterparts, but it is about half the price, and it will

Beer Lover's Pick

Narragansett Bock
Style: Bock
ABV: 6.5 percent
Availability: Spring Seasonal
This is close to a traditional German bock, but a little more hoppy. Narragansett excels at doing no-frills, simple styles of beer, and the Narragansett Bock is a perfect example of their brewing philosophy. There is a yeasty, biscuity quality to it, with hints of herbal hops. It is creamy and slightly sweet. Overall, it is a fantastic beer.

not be a letdown. When snow begins to fall, you will see the **Narragansett Porter** popping up on liquor store shelves. This is Narragansett's strongest beer, 7 percent alcohol by volume, and it is a perfect winter beer, dark, creamy, full-bodied with just a hint of heat from the alcohol, just what you want while sitting in front of a fire (or space heater) on a cold January night. The spring seasonal, the **Narragansett Bock,** is their best beer. This is a traditional German-style bock, which is a pleasure to drink. The summer seasonal, **Summer Ale,** is a light, refreshing blonde ale with a touch of hops. It is not uncommon to see someone leaving a liquor store with a few cases of these for a cookout.

Narragansett may be more active than any other New England brewery in terms of getting their name out there. It is almost impossible to find a night on the calendar when there are no in-store tastings of 'Gansett beers in New England. Every year, Narragansett hosts several contests. One of the most popular is one where entrants submit a tie design. The winning design is then turned into ties and inserted into 12-packs and cases for Father's Day. They also release a "Gansett Girls" calendar, which features women in 1950s-style pinup clothing and poses.

Brewpubs

CODDINGTON BREWING COMPANY

210 Coddington Hwy., Middletown, RI; (401) 847-6690; www.newport-brewery.com
Draft Beers: 7

The Coddington Brewing Company provides an option for those who want to visit beautiful Newport, but do not want to pay the high prices that most of the restaurants in the area charge. Add the fact that Coddington brews some quality beer, and you have a good alternative to the expensive Newport dining scene.

The Coddington Brewing Company offers a rotating selection of seven different beers on tap at all times. The selection is varied, ranging from lighter beers to heavy beers and pretty much everything in between. For those who prefer the lighter end of the beer spectrum, the **Golden Ale,** the **Blueberry Blonde,** the **Raspberry Cream Ale, Watermelon Ale,** and the **Vienna Lager** should be right up your alley; although light, they pack plenty of flavor. If you'd rather have a bigger beer, go for the **ESB, IPA, Irish Red Ale, Maibock,** or the **Nut Brown Ale.** Coddington also offers seven bigger beers, such as the **Belgian Triple,** the **Barley Wine,** and the **Doppelbock,** which are all higher than 7 percent alcohol by volume.

Stout lovers will rejoice in the fact that Coddington offers two of the most traditional stouts brewed in New England: Their **Irish Stout** and **Oatmeal Stout** are both under 4 percent ABV, which are traditional levels for the styles. Although low in alcohol, they both retain their flavor. Other beers available include the **Chocolate Porter, English Mild, Maibock, Oktoberfest, Scotch Ale, Scottish Heavy, Winter Lager,** and **Winter Wheat.**

Worked up an appetite? Codington sports a rather large food menu. William Coddington's Turkey Platter is a cross between an entree and a sandwich. The platter has roasted sliced turkey breast, served with red bliss mashed potatoes, stuffing, gravy, and cranberry sauce, all served on top of toast points. If you can handle the heat, try the hot and spicy Calamari Fra Diavolo, which is made of fried calamari tossed in a hot and spicy tomato broth with peppers and onions, all tossed in linguine. Coddington also serves 14-inch pizzas, perfect for two people to share. All traditional toppings are available, or get one of the special pizzas, such as the Chourico & Peppers, which is topped with chourico, green peppers, onions, mushrooms, mozzarella cheese, and red sauce.

Coddington also sells growlers of most of their beer, although some of the higher-alcohol beers and the stouts may not be available.

MOHEGAN CAFE & BREWERY

213 Water St., Block Island, RI; (407) 466-5911
Draft Beers: 6

Mohegan Cafe & Brewery provides a much-needed service to Block Island residents and visitors: They brew quality beer, offering an alternative to the usual mass-produced lagers that dominate the local landscape. The brewpub typically has six rotating drafts from 12 different Mohegan beers. These beers include some lighter offerings, like the **Amber Ale, Apricot Amber** (the amber with apricot flavor added), and the **Summer Wheat.** The **BIPA (Block Island Pale Ale)** is a popular beer, while the **Block Island IPA** is a decently hopped, easy-drinking beer. The **Mohegan Pilsner** is a pretty, golden beer, and goes down easy.

Other beers include the **Black Buck Porter,** the **Black Buck Stout,** and the **Striper English Ale.** Mohegan's strongest beer is the **Joe's High Octane,** an 8 percent alcohol by volume English strong ale. Or perhaps you enjoy spicy food. How about spicy beer? Why not order the **Chili Pepper Ale** and find out?

The Mohegan Cafe & Brewery serves some of the best seafood on the island. The Lone Star Crab Cakes, coconut shrimp, fried calamari, shrimp cocktail, and mussels Chardonnay are all standout starters, as is clam chowder. Lunch options include fish and chips, a fried clam plate, and an open-faced steak sandwich. Burgers are also available all day. Entrees (available at dinner), include seafood scampi, cedar-smoked salmon, baked stuffed tilapia, and curried eggplant risotto.

TRINITY BREWHOUSE

186 Fountain St., Providence, RI; (401) 453-227; www.trinitybrewhouse.com
Draft Beers: 10

The Trinity Brewhouse is in the perfect location in Providence to grab a beer and a bite to eat on your way either to or from an event. Trinity is located right across the street from the Dunkin Donuts Center, just down the street from the Trinity Repertory Theater, and across from the Rhode Island Convention Center.

The Trinity may not be as well-known as Boston-area brewpubs, but do not let their lack of name recognition fool you. Trinity has an eclectic mix of excellent beers always on tap, making it a beer destination. They have 10 house beers on tap, with a featured guest tap from time to time. One thing is for sure: Trinity's beers are never boring. Even common styles are often brewed with a twist.

For example, the **Kolsch,** a wonderfully light German style of beer, is brewed with a Japanese variety of hops called Sorachi Ace, which adds lemon flavors that

Trinity Christmas Party

Joining the Trinity Brewhouse Mug Club gets you many advantages (including large beers at pint prices), and one of the best things you get as a Mug Club member is an invite to the Trinity Christmas Party. Held in December, this event features special winter beers and food prepared for Mug Club members.

you would never find in a traditional German kolsch, resulting in some fantastic flavor. The **Rhode Island IPA** pushes the boundaries between a regular IPA and a double IPA. The beer is only 7 percent alcohol by volume, which is at the top range of what most breweries consider a regular IPA, but this beer is hopped like a double IPA with big citrus notes and a lot of bitterness. And somehow, the Trinity Brewhouse balances this beer without putting more fermentable sugars in the beer to raise the alcohol. Like the Kolsch, the **Bruins Brown Ale** is a traditional style brewed with untraditional hops. In this case, Trinity uses Galaxy hops, which are known for creating passion-fruit flavors and aromas. This works with the brown ale, giving it a fruity essence not typically found in the beer.

Some of the other standouts include the **White Electric Stout,** which is a coffee-infused stout, the **Russian Imperial Stout,** which comes in at 8.5 percent ABV with huge coffee and chocolaty flavors, and the **Belgo-American Saison.** Other occasional beers include the **Imperial Pilsner, Dark Wheat, REDRUM Imperial Red Ale,** and the **Wolf's Breath Winter Warmer,** a huge malty barleywine.

Food-wise, Trinity Brewhouse does not offer entrees, but they have a large selection of appetizers, soups, salads, pizzas, burgers, and sandwiches. Appetizers include the Double Loaded Ravioli, which are deep-fried pasta-potato raviolis stuffed with cheddar cheese and chives, baked with Monterey jack and Colby cheddar, and topped with sour cream, crumbled bacon, and scallops. The Zuppa di Brew is locally harvested black-shell mussels served with chorizo, onions, and roasted garlic, simmered in a pilsner-seafood broth. Fittingly, several of the sandwich options include items prepared with beer. The barbecued pulled pork sandwich features a barbecue sauce that is made with house beer, and the corned beef served on the Reuben is slowly braised in stout.

Trinity also offers growlers of all of its beers to go. In addition, you do not have to be in Rhode Island to get the Trinity IPA. The IPA is bottled and distributed in other states.

UNION STATION BREWERY
36 Exchange Terrace, Providence, RI; (401) 274-2739; www.johnharvards.com
Draft Beers: 8

The Union Station Brewery is part of the John Harvard's chain of brewpubs. Some of the same beers are on tap at both the John Harvard's location in Massachusetts and at Union Station but there is some room for the local brewers to be creative.

A handful of beers you may run into include the **Triple Hop,** which is a hybrid of a Belgian-style tripel and an American IPA. **Ken's Breakfast Stout,** made with coffee, oatmeal, and hints of chocolate, is also worth trying. Union Station has two different porters: the **College Hill Porter** is a typical, straight-ahead porter, while the **Vanilla Bean Porter** is made with vanilla beans and has strong vanilla notes. The **Friar Brown Ale** is a really good brown ale, the **Lucky Penny IPA** is a nicely hopped beer, and the **Hersbruck Pils** is a good, solid pilsner. Buy a growler of your favorite on the way out.

Union Station may not serve up the most adventurous fare in the world, but the menu boasts good pub and comfort-food dishes. Sandwiches include the Lentil Pocket, which is in Syrian bread with feta cheese, shredded lettuce, diced tomatoes, and yogurt dressing. Another tasty option is the fontina and grape grilled cheese sandwich, which also includes rosemary and is served on sourdough bread. Pub-style pizzas and burgers are pretty darn good at Union Station. The Fungus is a burger topped with garlic aioli, crumbled blue cheese, and portobello, white, and shitake mushrooms, while the Three Amigos is a burger made for those who like a little heat with their meat. It is topped with fried cherry peppers, capicola, chipotle and chili aioli, and pepper jack cheese. But the best meal may be the Rhode Island Clam Bake, which includes cod, littleneck clams, mussels, chorizo, corn, potatoes, onions, tomatoes, and herbs. Make sure to leave room for some apple crisp, or the butterscotch bread pudding.

Beer Bars

DOHERTY'S EAST AVENUE IRISH PUB
342 East Ave., Pawtucket, RI; (401) 725-1800; http://dohertys.com
Draft Beers: 82 **Bottled/Canned Beers:** Around 60

There are tons of faux Irish pubs throughout New England. Heck, you can't walk a block in Boston without seeing one. The problem is most of them have a boring atmosphere, and the only thing Irish about them is Guinness on tap and green beer on St. Patrick's Day. Doherty's East Avenue Irish Pub is a step above those pubs. This is a beer destination worth seeking out in Pawtucket.

Doherty's has more than 80 beers on draft (yes, Guinness is one of them), but they also have plenty of good beers from breweries such as Harpoon, Samuel Adams, and Coastal Extreme Brewing. Beers from Heavy Seas and Brooklyn Brewing Company also often find themselves on the draft list. The bottled list is just as good as the draft list.

Food-wise, Doherty's is mainly pub-style food, and there really is not much as far as Irish cuisine available, except for shepherd's pie and bangers and mash.

Appetizers include chicken wings and chicken tenders, fried calamari, and jalapeño poppers. Also available are Chinese pot stickers and Mussels Zuppa, which are Prince Edward Island mussels served in a zesty zuppa sauce. Doherty's also has several burgers and grilled chicken sandwiches on the menu. The highlights include the Old Smoker, which is meat braised with barbecue sauce, topped with your choice of cheddar cheese and bacon or mushrooms and Swiss.

ENGLISH CELLAR ALE HOUSE
165 Angell St., Providence, RI; (401) 454-3434; www.englishcellaralehouse.com
Draft Beers: 12 **Bottled/Canned Beers:** Around 150

England is known for having one of the best pub cultures in the beer drinking world, but it also happens to be on the other side of the Atlantic Ocean. So to get your English pub fix, head to the English Cellar Alehouse in Providence. The bar has plenty of really good English beers, as well as beers from other parts of the world, too. The English Cellar Alehouse also features some traditional English-style pub food, as well as good ol' American cuisine.

The draft list features several English ales, including Newcastle, Old Speckled Hen, Young's Double Chocolate Stout, and Boddingtons. Other English ales are often available in bottles, including Hobgoblin, several beers from Well's and Young's, Fullers, and Samuel Smith's. Non-British beers often include Brooklyn Brewing, Flying Dog, and North Coast from the US; Warsteiner and Spaten from Germany; and Kasteel, Rochefort, and Maredous from Belgium. Along with beer, the English Cellar Alehouse has a large selection of single malt scotches; bourbons; and some interesting looking mixed drinks, many of which have very British-sounding names, such as Scotland Yard, Summer on the Thames, and Westminster Abbey.

The English influence carries on to the menu. Appetizers include such dishes as stout onion soup; Newcastle Steak on a Stick; and Scottish Eggs, which are soft-boiled eggs wrapped in bacon, breaded, and fried. The original James Bond was Scottish, not English, but the English Cellar Alehouse still offers a burger named after the famous movie spy. The James Bond Burger is an 8-ounce beef patty, topped with fried onions, barbecue sauce, and cheddar cheese. British classics like bangers and mash, fish and chips, chicken pot pie, and shepherd's pie are also available.

If you are a fan of the English Premier League, the English Cellar Alehouse is the place to go to watch football (soccer, to us). If there are no English games available, the New England Revolution will be on the screen. Head in for a beer and watch the game.

JULIANS
318 Broadway, Providence, RI; (401) 861-1770; www.juliansprovidence.com
Draft Beers: 20 **Bottled/Canned Beers:** About 50

If you happen to be a beer geek, Julians is the place to go in Providence. They may not have the largest beer selection in the city, but they do have the largest selection of hard-to-find beers, both in bottles and draft, with both rare and expensive beers not seen at many bars.

The draft list often includes beers from the Baladin brewery in Italy. Baladin makes some fantastic Belgian-style beers, but typically, even at a liquor store, the bottles can range from $25 to $45. Getting it on draft is a much better deal, because you can try one glass before making the commitment to such an expensive bottle. Typically, Julians will have beers from Belgium and Denmark on draft, as well as some great American craft beer like Bear Republic and Sixpoint. They also do not forget about the only production brewery in Rhode Island, usually having at least one Coastal Extreme beer on the list. The bottled list is much of the same. There are more Baladin beers, and some rare British beers such as several different versions of

Stout and Porter Dinner

Every year, Julians hosts several beer dinners, but our favorite is the Stout and Porter Dinner, held in December. Chef Michael McHugh prepares dinners that complement the bold flavors of coffee, chocolate, and often bourbon from barrel-aging, found in all the world-class dark beers paired with each dish. Past pairings include Smuttynose Brewing Company's Robust Porter with butternut squash ravioli and B.O.R.I.S., the Crusher Imperial Stout from Hoppin' Frog, with roasted duck.

the Harviestoun Old Dubh, Cantillon, and Mikkeller. American craft beers are also represented, with Ballast Point, Brooklyn Brewery, and Victory often available.

Julians also offers some pretty tasty food to go with their excellent beer selection. Popcorn and beer go together like peanut butter and jelly, but Julians' Bacon Fat Popcorn is an entirely different, albeit delicious, beast. Their version involves Parmesan cheese, smoked sea salt, pork cracklins, and crispy garlic gremolata. For an entree, try the excellent House Corned Beef, served with roasted fingerling potatoes, maple glazed carrots, and caraway stout braised cabbage. Desserts are a must at Julians. The Root Beer Roasted Sweet Potato Pie, the Deep Fried Cherry Cinnamon Buns, and Chocolate Marshmallow Pound Cake are all tasty. And if you are up early, Julians serves brunch daily. Brunch options included a scrambled egg pizza and Ilan's Israeli Breakfast, which is two eggs poached in a spicy house pomodoro with home fries and garlic bread.

POUR JUDGEMENT BAR & GRILL

32 Broadway, Newport, RI; (401) 619-2115; http://pourjudgement.com
Draft Beers: 18 **Bottled/Canned Beers:** 20

The Pour Judgement Bar & Grill is a neighborhood bar, always filled with locals. But, unlike many typical neighborhood bars, the Pour Judgement happens to pour a lot of great beer. The draft list usually includes beers from Clipper City Brewing Company, Coastal Extreme Brewing Company, Magic Hat Brewing Company, and Samuel Adams. Ithaca and Stone beers are also sometimes available. The bottled list is broken down between larger-format bottles and normal-sized 12-ounce bottles. The larger bottles are great for sharing (I don't share, but you can). There are typically beers from Unibroue, Lagunitas, and several of the 750 ml Dogfish Head beers.

Pour Judgement's food is pretty much straight-up pub fare; sometimes you just want a cold beer and a tasty, simple meal. Starters include chili, Southwest eggrolls, and steamed littleneck clams served in three different styles, including Italian with herbs, garlic, lemon, and dry vermouth. The lunch menu is packed with several grilled sandwiches, which include chicken salad with sliced almonds and dried apricots, as well as the black bean burger with guacamole and herb sour cream. Entrees are straightforward, but delicious. Try the Portuguese cod, which is cooked in white wine, fresh garlic, chourico, peppers, onions, tomatoes, and roasted potatoes. The Pour Judgement serves brunch on Sunday from 10 a.m. to 2 p.m. The brunch menu includes omelets, banana bread French toast, and several types of eggs Benedict, including regular, crab meat Benedict, sirloin Benedict, spinach Benedict, and surf and turf Benedict.

Beer Festivals

There simply isn't a better way to try a bunch of new beers at one time than going to a beer festival. Want to try a hard-to-find beer before buying it? Interested in sampling some quality craft brew that's not sold locally in your hometown? If you consider yourself a beer lover and you haven't been to a beer fest before, find the nearest event and go. Immediately.

New England is home to some fantastic beer festivals. Be it the wildly popular Extreme Beer Fest or the relatively new Massachusetts Brewer's Festival, there is something out there for everyone. This chapter profiles a 12-pack of the beer festivals everyone should go to at least once. The events are organized by month, but because some events take place more than once a year, and dates can change from year to year, it's best to check each event's website for up-to-date information on when the next festival is taking place.

February & March

BEER ADVOCATE'S EXTREME BEER FEST

The Cyclorama at the Boston Center for Arts, 539 Tremont St., Boston, MA; www.beer advocate.com

Have you ever had a beer brewed with tobacco? How about baby formula or jelly beans? Well, if you go to the Extreme Beer Fest, held every year in February or March at the Cyclorama in Boston, those are just a few of the odd creations that you may find. Brewers from around the country pull out all the stops for this beer festival. Sure, sometimes they don't work—tobacco probably doesn't belong in a beer—but when one of them does work, such as the Iced Coffee Stout from Hill Farmstead Brewery in Vermont (a 15 percent ABV beer that sports no alcohol flavor should be impossible), it can be amazing.

Tickets are $40 for each of the Saturday sessions, while the Night of the Barrels usually costs about $10 extra. The ticket gets you a tasting glass, a festival program, and unlimited 2-ounce samples. Food is sold separately. Keep an eye out for when tickets go on sale because they tend to sell out fast. There are three sessions: a Saturday afternoon session, a Saturday night session, and a special Friday session. The Friday sessions are usually called "Night of the Barrels" and include special beers not available on Saturday, and brewers mingle with the smaller crowd.

NEW ENGLAND REAL ALE EXHIBITION

VFW George Dilboy Post 529, 371 Summer St., Somerville, MA; www.nerax.org

The New England Real Ale Exhibition is a showcase of cask-conditioned beer, the traditional manner of serving real ale in England. The festival is held in the tiny Dilboy VFW Post in March over a four-day period, beginning on Wednesday and running through Saturday. Tickets are $15 for the first three days, and $10 on Saturday. The ticket gets you in, and then you pay $5 for a glass. You can either keep the glass or return it at the end to get your money back. You can also pick the size of beer you want—full pint, half-pint, or quarter-pint—and you pay a different price for each size. The New England Real Ale Exhibition, or NERAX, as it is known, is the best place to get rare English ales served in the manner they are supposed to be served—at the correct temperature and well-maintained. Along with the English ales, NERAX also features several American beers on cask, mainly from New England. Food from the nearby Redbones barbecue restaurant is available. The saddest moment of the festival is when the Grim Reaper comes out with his scythe, equipped with an eraser. When the Grim Reaper appears, that means one of the casks has been kicked and is no longer available. NERAX also hosts NERAX North in Haverhill in November, which typically features heavier, higher-alcohol winter beers. Both are great times.

April

GREAT INTERNATIONAL BEER FESTIVAL

Rhode Island Convention Center, Providence, RI; www.beerfestamerica.com

The Great International Beer Festival bills itself as the largest international beer festival in the US. I'm not sure if that is true, but it is huge. True to its size, the festival has a huge party atmosphere with food, unlimited beer, and music. This fest tends to attract a college crowd of newly legal drinkers looking to get drunk, so the afternoon session is more enjoyable for those not looking for a keg party. The night session, though, can still be fun. About 50 breweries from the US and beyond are in attendance at the festival, pouring nearly 200 beers. The festival features a wide range of breweries from New England, as well as pretty much anywhere else. You will also run into beers you normally do not see at festivals, such as Cottrell Brewing Company, Heineken, Innis and Gun, and even Guinness. The GIBF also hosts beer judging, with medals awarded in numerous beer styles, and breweries take great pride in the medals. Tickets are $40 each.

May

BRATTLEBORO BREWERS FESTIVAL

Chickering Road, Brattleboro, VT; www.brattleborobrewersfest.com

Outdoor festivals can be a joy, and there is no better host for outdoor beer festivals than Vermont. The Brattleboro Brewers Festival is one such event, held in a large field rain or shine—large tents are set up if there is inclement weather. Accompanied by live music, attendees get a chance to try beers from about 30 breweries, including Allagash Brewing Company, Bobcat Brewery, and Switchback Brewing Company. Non–New England beer producers represented include Brewery Ommegang and Brooklyn Brewing Company from New York, and Sierra Nevada Brewing Company and Stone Brewing Company from California. Tickets are $35 each and admission includes a 6-ounce tasting glass and eight beer tickets. More tickets are available for sale. Attendees also vote on the best brewery of the festival.

June

BEER ADVOCATE'S AMERICAN CRAFT BEER FEST

Seaport World Trade Center, 200 Seaport Blvd., Boston, MA; www.beeradvocate.com

Beer Advocate hosts three festivals throughout the year, and the American Craft Beer Fest is by far the largest. While the other two have about 30 breweries, this one has 100 breweries bringing more than 500 beers for excited beer fans. The American Craft Beer Fest, which runs three sessions—one on Friday night and one each on Saturday afternoon and night—is held inside the gigantic Seaport World Trade Center. After all, you need a lot of space for all these beers. The only problem with the festival—and it's a good problem to have—is that there are so many beers to choose from, you may get a brain cramp trying to decide which one you're going sample next. Nearly every popular craft brewery from New England and beyond attends this festival. Tickets are $45 online and $50 at the door. For that money you get an unlimited number of 2-ounce samples and a floor guide.

The American Craft Beer Fest is the culmination of Boston Beer Week, a celebration of Massachusetts breweries, brewpubs, and beer bars. With so many craft beer events in Boston and the surrounding areas leading up to the festival, there are usually a number of brewers on hand pouring samples, answering questions, and generally mingling with the crowd.

July

VERMONT BREWERS FESTIVAL
On the shores of Lake Champlain, Burlington, VT; http://vtbrewfest.com

No other beer festival in New England is in a more picturesque location than the Vermont Brewers Festival right on the shores of Lake Champlain. The festival, run by the Vermont Brewers Association, is a showcase of Vermont breweries, of which there are many. It's not limited to Vermont breweries, though—there are many hard-to-find breweries from Quebec, as well as some of the larger craft breweries from other regions in the US. Luckily for all of the festival-goers, the event is spread out in a large outdoor area with plenty of space and breathing room. Just make sure to bring some bug spray—mosquitoes definitely like beer fest attendees.

If you want a break from walking around, go to the Meet the Brewer Tent and attend one of the workshops, such as pairing beer and cheese or pairing beer with chocolate, or learn about sustainable brewing. The best thing about the festival is that after you're done, you're a 10-minute walk from downtown Burlington and great beer bars and brewpubs. Tickets cost $35 and there are three sessions: Friday night, Saturday afternoon, and Saturday night.

September

MASSACHUSETTS BREWERS FEST
Seaport World Trade Center; 200 Seaport Blvd., Boston, MA; www.massbrewersguild.com

The Massachusetts Brewers Festival is the best showcase of the truly amazing beers the state produces today. Sponsored by the Massachusetts Brewers Guild, the festival features nothing but Massachusetts breweries. The breweries pull out all the stops, bringing their flagship beers as well as hard-to-get or specially brewed beers. Don't expect to see just the longstanding in-state breweries, either; recent festivals have featured a handful of up-and-coming beer producers. There's a good mix of both breweries and brewpubs from every section of the state—east, west, central, and the coast—with unlimited sampling as part of the $35 ticket price. Lines can get long and sometimes you may not know which brewery you're in line for, but they move quickly and you're pretty much guaranteed to get a good beer when you finally get to the beer table. The festival is also held on the Trade Center's Concourse, so the festival is mostly outside, but with a partially roofed area. There's good food and equally good live music to be had as well. The parking is also some of the cheapest in Boston, $12 to $13, and there is plenty of public transportation in the area.

BEER ADVOCATE'S BELGIAN BEER FEST
The Cyclorama, 539 Tremont St., Boston, MA; www.beeradvocate.com

The Belgian Beer Fest is Beer Advocate's third beer festival of the year. As the name suggests, it is all about the Belgian ales. The beer is fantastic. The festival features beer from nearly every world-class brewery from Belgium, such as Cantillion, St. Bernardus, and De Struise. If there is an American brewery that specializes in Belgian-style ales, they will be at the festival. Breweries such as Allagash Brewing Company in Maine, Brewery Ommegang in New York, the Bruery in California, and Lost Abbey in California are almost always at the Belgian Beer Fest. There are three sessions of the Belgian Beer Fest. The two Saturday sessions, which cost $50 each, feature all sorts of Belgian ales. The Friday night session, called Night of the Funk, features sour ales, funky beers, and ales made with wild yeast creating unique and strange flavors that are sought out by hard-core beer lovers. The festival is one of the best in Boston every year.

BOSTON BEERSUMMIT
The Castle at Park Plaza, 130 Columbus Ave., Boston, MA; www.beersummit.com

If you can't get to Germany for Oktoberfest, the Samuel Adams Octoberfest at the Castle at Park Plaza is the closest thing to it in Boston. The Boston Beer Company, along with Beer Summit, hosts this 10-hour festival, which is more like a party, each and every September. The festival costs $20 and gets you a beer stein and your first Samuel Adams Octoberfest.

Although this is an Octoberfest event, there are plenty of other Samuel Adams beers to choose from. But unlike other festivals, this is about more than just the beer. This is all about fun. There are German bands playing oompah music and American bands playing more mainstream music. German food such as bratwursts and giant pretzels are good to nosh on, while people dressed in lederhosen take part in feats of strength as they see who can hold a full stein of beer the longest. There are other games and contests with plenty of prizes available.

There are not many festivals that are more fun than the Octoberfest. Try to get there and party like you are in Munich.

October

KILLINGTON BREWFEST
Killington Resort, Killington, VT; www.killington.com

The Killington Brewfest is not as well-known as some of the other beer festivals featured here, but it is still one of the best in New England. The festival is held at the base of the Killington Ski Resort, a beautiful scenic area. There are tons of hotels and restaurants in the area and it is a perfect place to spend the weekend. The festival begins Friday night at the Brewers Dinner with a specific brewery, and then the kickoff party. The actual festival is Saturday. For $25, you get 12 tasting tickets and a nice little sample beer glass. The samples are 3 ounces each. Most beers cost one ticket while some of the stronger beers, over 8 percent, take two tickets. If you want more tickets, you can buy them, so you do not have to worry about running out. There are usually about 20 breweries pouring about 75 different beers. The festival is big on local breweries, including some that are unavailable outside Vermont, like the Switchback Brewing Company and Northshire Brewing Company. There is plenty of food available, and plenty of live music. Definitely worth a trip.

NEW HAMPSHIRE BREW FEST
Redhook Brewery, Portsmouth, NH; http://brewnh.com

The New Hampshire Brew Fest is the largest yearly beer event in New Hampshire. Each October, thousands of people gather in the field outside the Redhook Brewery in Portsmouth to get a chance to sample beers from more than 30 different brewers who bring more than 100 beers. The tickets cost $25, and, for that money, you get unlimited beer samples in a 5-ounce tasting glass. Many of the participating breweries are smaller breweries, such as the Elm City Brewing Company, Moat Mountain Smokehouse and Brewery, Tuckerman Brewing Company, and Throwback Brewing Company, all from New Hampshire. Along with the beer, there is a ton of food to buy, and it is always a good idea to eat at a beer festival. A good base of food allows you to sample more beers. There is also live music. This is an outdoor festival, so make sure you dress appropriately in case of chilly weather. You cannot go out to your car to get a sweater and then come back. Once you are out, you are out.

Okay, you bought those tickets for the beer festival—now what?

Here are a few simple rules to help guide you through the festival experience. (I've followed them relatively closely throughout the years, with some trial and error.)

Always hydrate. Lack of hydration is always a killer at a festival. You're surrounded by hundreds of people in cramped quarters making you sweat and you're drinking beer—you will dehydrate if you don't drink water. Drink a couple glasses of water before the festival, and keep a bottle of water with you while at the festival. If you don't have water on you, drink the water that you rinse your glass with between tastings. It's a good way to keep your palate fresh and to stay hydrated.

Eat. Give yourself a good base before you start drinking a lot of beer. Eat a good breakfast and grab lunch before the festival, or eat something at the festival. Drinking on an empty stomach is never a good idea. You want to enjoy the different beers, and if you're drinking on an empty stomach, about halfway through you'll start forgetting what's in your glass.

Don't be stupid. Yeah, this sounds easy, but you'd be amazed by how some people act at a festival. It's a beer fest, not a drunk fest. Sure, beer gets you intoxicated, but don't get out of control, make a spectacle of yourself, and get dragged out by security. All your friends will know about it on Facebook before you even get over your hangover the next day.

Don't stand and talk to the brewer. One of the highlights of going to a beer festival is getting to meet the man or woman who brewed your favorite beer. I get that. But, while you're spending 15 minutes talking to the brewer and getting your glass refilled over and over, no one else can get his or her glass filled. Wait until there isn't much of a line, or if you really want to talk to the brewer, stand off to the side to let other people get their beer. Remember, if you want to meet him or her, there are probably dozens of others at the festival who also want to meet the brewer.

Have fun. That's the main part of a beer festival. Don't waste the whole time writing tasting notes on paper, or typing them into your iPhone. You can't judge a beer fully on a 2-ounce sample anyhow. I keep the brewery program handy and put a check next to a beer I like and want to try again. Review the beer later and enjoy it now.

November

MAINE BREWERS FESTIVAL
Portland Convention Center, Portland, ME; www.mainebrew.com

The Maine Brewers Festival is a showcase of the greatness of Maine breweries. The festival hosts nothing but Maine brewers, but rest assured, there is more than enough beer to go around. Maine has some fantastic breweries, and they all strive to bring their best beers to the Maine Brewers Festival. Tickets are $36 and get you a 6-ounce logoed beer glass and 12 beer sampling tickets. You cannot buy additional tickets, so choose wisely. It's a good idea to get a list of beers ahead of time so you can pick the ones you really want to try. The festival features the larger breweries, such as Allagash Brewing Company and Shipyard Brewing Company, as well as smaller ones such as Federal Jack's and the Oxbow Brewing Company. There is also plenty of food available. A nice feature at the Maine Brewers Festival is the fact they have designated driver tickets. The tickets are the same price, but instead of beer tickets, they get food and non-alcoholic beverage coupons to use.

BYOB:
Brew Your Own Beer

Are you sick of going to the liquor store and spending more and more money for beer? Do you want to unleash your inner brewer and concoct your own craft beer? Just make your own!

Homebrewing is a fun hobby, and it allows you to brew a beer exactly how you want it. The start-up cost is not cheap, but you will more than make up the difference when you are making beer for pennies at home.

This chapter includes profiles of several places where you can go to try brewing before making the investment, or if you want to brew your own beer but don't have the space at home. And for established homebrewers, there are a few homebrew recipes for you to try.

Brew-on-Premises

BARLEYCORN'S CRAFT BREW
21 Summer St., Natick, MA; (508) 651-8885; www.barleycorn.com

Barleycorn's is a brew-on-premises (BOP) business, which allows you to pick a type of beer you want and then brew it. Don't worry, owner Dan Eng or his assistants will lead you by the hand all the way from start to finish. Eng started Barleycorn's in 1990 after he was inspired by similar businesses on the west coast. It's a great way to get a taste of brewing without having to make your house smell like a brewery. Eng has dozens of different beer recipes with all of the ingredients on site. He is also quick to follow beer trends—if a particular style of beer is becoming popular, he will add a recipe to his portfolio. Eng will then lead you step by step through the brewing process, beginning with mixing the ingredients, grinding the malts, and then putting it in the kettle and adding all the ingredients at the exact time to get the beer you want. You then leave the beer at Barleycorn's and come back in a few weeks (the length of time depends on the style) to bottle the beer. A single bottling session yields about six cases of 12-ounce beers. Price-wise, brewing a batch of beer will range from $150 to about $200, although some batches will get as high as $250.

One exciting feature is that Eng invites professional brewers a few times a year to bring in specially created recipes. During these visits, the brewer leads a group of people through a collaborative brewing session where they brew all the different styles at once. Then, you come back a few weeks later to bottle the beers and get a mix of all the different beers. Barleycorn's also hosts collaborative brewing events where people come in and brew several batches of a popular beer, such as a pumpkin ale, and come back to bottle and buy as much as they want a few weeks later. In addition to beer, Barleycorn's also has wine-making and soda-making equipment.

CORK & BREW
35 North Main St., Southington, CT; (860) 863-5655; www.corkandbrew.com

Cork & Brew is a little different than other brew-on-premises businesses. While most BOPs have dozens of recipes, usually using all grain ingredients, Cork & Brew is more of a beginner's BOP. They have 10 different recipes, all made from Fiesta Brew kits. That makes it easier, because everyting is in one place, and easy to mix. The whole process takes about an hour to brew, and then you come back three weeks later and bottle your product. The beers available include a blonde ale, cream ale, red ale, brown ale, bock, pale ale, and stout. Along with the 10 base recipes, you can add extract flavors, such as various fruits, so you can have a raspberry stout or a number of other flavors. When you bottle the beer a few weeks later, you get about 60 12-ounce bottles. The price is right, too, ranging from $119 to $125 for a batch of beer. Along with beer, Cork & Brew also does wine and soda making. They also host homebrew parties where groups of people come in and do a group brew, sometimes of different types of beer, so each person can get a bigger variety.

DEJA BREW INC.
510B Boston Turnpike Rd., Shrewsbury, MA; (508) 842-8991; www.deja-brew.com

Brewing your own beer on-site at Deja Brew in Shrewsbury is a great experience. They have one of the most varied selections of beer recipes around, and they lead you through the entire process of brewing beer—from picking the right hops and grains, to mashing in, to putting the hops in at the right time during the boil, and, of course, the best part, bottling the beer. Deja Brew offers dozens of beer recipes (as well as 12 wine recipes, if you are so inclined) and has a more diverse selection of choices than many BOP buisinesses. They have beer for every taste, including mild, lower-alcohol beers such as bitters and brown ales, as well as lagers like Oktoberfests and pilsners. They also offer IPAs, pale ales, and speciality beers, including gluten-free beers.

They also offer many higher-octane beers, usually clones or approximations of famous craft beers. Are you a big fan of Dogfish Head's huge World Wide Stout (which comes in at 18 percent alcohol by volume)? Then brew the Deja Wide Stout.

Are you a hophead who absolutely loves Stone Brewing Company's Double Bastard Ale? Deja Brew has a version called Dave's Double Bastid. The costs range from a low $135 for one of the English bitter recipes to a high of $335 for a 9.5 percent alcohol by volume, 124 International Bittering Units double IPA.

For the money, you will get approximately 72 22-ounce bombers of beer. For $325 and the cost of bottles and labels (about $400 total), you would get 75 bottles of Deja Wide Stout. To buy the equivalent quantity of Dogfish Head World Wide Stout, it would cost more than $1,000. Quite the savings. When the beer is ready (usually in a couple of weeks), you go back and bottle the beer, which typically takes half an hour. You can also pick your own labels. Deja Brew also hosts several beer events a year, as well as a chili cookoff.

INCREDIBREW
112 Daniel Webster Hwy. South, Nashua, NH; (603) 891-2477; www.incredibrew.com

BOP businesses are now found almost everywhere throughout the country, but incrediBREW of Nashua, New Hampshire, was the first, founded in 1995. They are also the cheapest brew-on-premises business in New England. The cost to brew a beer ranges from $130 for a few recipes, such as the Beechwood Lager (a Budweiser-like beer), to the most expensive at $195 for a big, 11 percent alcohol by volume barleywine. In all, incrediBREW offers about 100 different recipes, ranging from low-alcohol bitters to Belgian-style quads, and pretty much everything in between. They also offer numerous clone recipes, or recipes inspired by commercial beers, including several beers you do not see at other brew-on-premises locations. Some of the clones include Amstel Light, Corona, Michelob, and Heineken. Other beers are inspired by craft beers, such as Arrogant Brewer, which is based on Stone Brewing Company's Arrogant Bastard Ale; Something Wicked, based on Pete's Wicked Ale; Catfish Head 60 Minute IPA, based on Dogfish Head's 60 Minute IPA; and Stella or Try, based on Stella Artois. Other recipes include Belgian whites, a wheat wine, and a barrel-aged porter. Also available are bitters, bocks, brown ales, several lagers, pale ales, IPAs, stouts, pilsners, and several honey beers.

The brewing can take an hour or two and you come back two weeks later to bottle the beer. For the money, it is a good deal. You brew 13.5 gallons of beer, which equals 72 22-ounce bottles. The bottles cost $12 for a case, so expect to add a few extra bucks to the final cost. Like other brew-on-premises businesses, incrediBREW offers several brewing nights where groups get together and brew several beers at once. They also offer wine and soda brewing sessions.

Beer Recipes

WILL MEYERS' SGT. PEPPER CLONE

There probably is not a better food beer brewed in New England than Cambridge Brewing Company's Sgt. Pepper, which is a saison brewed with peppercorns. When you drink this beer with a good meal, do not put pepper on the food, just take of sip of this. Cambridge Brewing Company's Brewmaster Will Meyers shared a homebrew clone recipe of his Sgt. Pepper. This recipe will make 5 gallons for all-grain homebrewers.

Grist

3.6 lbs. German pils
2.75 lbs. German wheat
2.75 lbs. North American pils
0.5 lbs. North American rye malt
0.5 lbs. Belgian Caravienne 20°L
Rice hulls

Mash with single-infusion to target conversion temp of 152°F; rest for 1 hour or until iodine test shows complete conversion. Sparge with 170°F water to collect 6.5 gallons in kettle.

At start of 90-minute boil add 0.25 ounce Magnum hops pellets at 13.5 percent alpha.

At 10 minutes remaining add 0.4 ounce Spalt pellets.

With 1 minute remaining add:*

0.5 ounce green peppercorns
0.06 ounce white peppercorns
0.3 ounce black peppercorns

Flameout and rest 5 minutes, then whirlpool by gently stirring kettle for 5 to 10 minutes. At end of whirlpool add:

0.13 ounce green peppercorns
0.06 ounce pink peppercorns

Immediately chill with wort chiller to 64°F, transfer gently to fermenter and aerate, and pitch yeast. We use a proprietary yeast strain, but recommend a well-attenuating saison yeast with considerable spicy flavor profile such as White Labs WLP566 Saison II or WLP 568 Saison Blend.

Target OG: 1.054/13.5°P

Target FG: 1.008/2.0°P

* Peppercorns should be purchased whole, then crushed in a spice mill moments before adding to kettle.

COURTESY OF WILL MEYERS, BREWMASTER AT CAMBRIDGE BREWING COMPANY (P. 47)

BEN ROESCH'S SWEET TAT'S CLONE

Wormtown Brewing Company's Sweet Tat's is one of the best beers brewed in New England. It has chocolate, coffee, vanilla, and oatmeal, all balanced nicely in this big beer, which is 9 percent ABV, 47 IBUs, and SG 21° Plato. Head Brewer Ben Roesch shares a homebrew clone of the beer. This is a 5-gallon extract recipe.

Grains
Steep at 154°F for 20 minutes:

8.8 ounces Dark Crystal
7.05 ounces 2-row pale
4.29 ounces black malt
8.8 ounces roasted barley
8.8 ounces chocolate malt
17.6 ounces flaked oats

Add mash liquid to 3.5 liters amber malt extract.

Boil for 60 minutes.

20 AAU Chinook hops boiled for 60 minutes

20 AAU Chinook hops boiled for 30 minutes

⅛ lb. cocoa nibs boiled for 5 minutes

¼ of a vanilla bean boiled for 5 minutes

¼ lb. cocoa nibs in secondary for 7 days

¼ of a vanilla bean in secondary for 7 days

1 ounce coffee in secondary for 24 hours

American ale yeast

COURTESY OF BEN ROESCH, HEAD BREWER AT WORMTOWN BREWING COMPANY (P. 43)

BRIAN FLACH'S SIMARILLO IPA

Brian Flach is the head brewer at the Tullycross Tavern & Microbrewery in Connecticut. Before that, he was a longtime homebrewer and entered numerous competitions throughout New England. This recipe is for Flach's Simarillo IPA, which came in second at a large homebrewing competition in 2010. The recipe yields 6 gallons.

90-minute boil:

> *9 lbs. Maris Otter*
> *3 lbs. US 2-Row*
> *0.5 lb Carapils*
> *0.5 lb C60*

0.70 ounce Columbus (14.2% AA) at 60 minutes

0.25 ounce Simcoe (12.2% AA) at 30 minutes

0.25 ounce Amarillo (8.2% AA) at 30 minutes

0.50 ounce Simcoe (12.2% AA) at 15 minutes

0.50 ounce Amarillo (8.2% AA) at 15 minutes

1 ounce Simcoe (12.2% AA) at 0 minutes

1 ounce Amarillo (8.2% AA) at 0 minutes

0.25 ounce Simcoe (dry hop 5 days)

0.25 ounce Amarillo (dry hop 5 days)

0.25 ounce Columbus (dry hop 5 days)

0.25 ounce Cascade (dry hop 5 days)

Mash at 149°F for 60 minutes

Yeast: 1,000 ml starter of White Labs WLP001 California Ale

Ferment at 65°F

OG: 1.060

FG: 1.010

COURTESY OF BRIAN FLACH, HEAD BREWER AT TULLYCROSS TAVERN (P. 199)

In the Kitchen

Pairing Beer with Food

Beer offers a wide variety of flavors, so you can actually match and contrast flavors with your food. Wine, on the other hand, is pretty much limited to contrasting flavors. Paring beer with a dish is not too difficult. Just remember a simple rule of thumb: Pair heavy foods with heavier beers, and lighter food with lighter beer. Below, we suggest some specific New England beers to pair with your meal.

Beef: A Belgian quad is good for beef, but if it is grilled, go with a brown ale. The caramelized meat and the caramel malts used in the brown ale will make your taste buds sing. **Pick:** *High & Mighty's Home for the Holidays*

Chicken/Turkey: Saisons are the easiest pairings for lighter meat like chicken and turkey. They just seem to be made for each other. **Pick:** *Pretty Things Beer & Ale Project's Jack D'Or*

Chocolate: You can go different directions with this. Grab a stout and the roasty chocolate and coffee malts can work perfectly. Or go with a really sweet fruit beer; it can taste like you are having a chocolate-covered fruit treat. **Pick:** *Samuel Adams Chocolate Bock*

Pasta with Red Sauce: Let wine have this one. It is not always about beer.

Pizza: Go with a good lager. The clean lager taste will not detract from the goodness that is pizza. **Pick:** *Cisco's Summer of Lager*

Pork: A German-style lager, or even a bock, always goes well with pork. This is a classic pairing. **Pick:** *Narragansett's Bock*

Salads: Choose a lighter Belgian ale. It will cut right through the vinegar used in most dressings, and it will not be too strong to overwhelm the veggies. **Pick:** *Harpoon's Belgian Pale Ale*

Seafood: Go with something light, maybe a hefeweizen or American wheat ale, with fish. With lobster and shrimp, the perfect beer is a Belgian-style witbier. **Pick:** *Allagash White*

Spicy Food: You can go two different ways with spicy foods. Go with a really hoppy beer to cut through the spice, or try something sweet to balance it all out. **Pick:** *Squam's Golden IPA*

Food Recipes

There are a lot of recipes that call for wine to be used as an ingredient, but more and more restaurants are using beer in their food. It just makes sense—beer adds a wider range of flavors than wine can. Depending on the style of beer you add to your recipe, you can get sweet, fruity, or bitter flavors, notes of chocolate or coffee, and anything and everything in between. Beer offers up more diversity than wine ever could.

This chapter offers several recipes that feature beer as an ingredient, ranging from classic New England dishes such as beer-battered fish and chips to desserts such as stout brownies. Enjoy!

BARRINGTON BREWERY'S CHEDDAR ALE SOUP

Beer and cheese, especially cheddar, is a great pairing. But what is even better is when both are combined into one bite. The Barrington Brewery's Cheddar Ale Soup is a perfect starter to any meal. It's not too heavy, but it has tons of flavor. Makes five gallons.

2 red peppers, diced
2 onions, diced
¼ cup Dijon mustard
1½ cups chicken stock
1½ pitchers blonde ale (6 to 8 cups)
Few dashes of Worcestershire sauce
1 handful chives
3 gallons milk
1-pound box cornstarch, mixed with water
2½ pounds American cheese
5 pounds white cheddar cheese

Mix peppers, onions, Dijon mustard, chicken stock, blonde ale, Worcestershire sauce, and chives together and bring to a boil.

Then add milk, cornstarch, American cheese, and cheddar cheese into the mix.

Heat until cheese is melted and then serve.

COURTESY OF BARRINGTON BREWERY (P. 46)

SHIPYARD BREWING COMPANY'S PEAKS ISLAND MUSSELS

The Shipyard Brewing Company is most known for its Portland brewery. But they also have several small brewpubs, and naturally they use beer in many of their recipes. Mussels, a New England staple, taste even better when cooked in a delcious beer-infused broth. Here is Shipyard's version of the dish.

2 tablespoons olive oil
1/2 cup diced onion
4 cloves chopped garlic
4 to 6 pounds mussels
8 ounces Shipyard Export Ale
2 tablespoons butter
10 basil leaves, sliced thin
10 to 12 chopped kalamata olives
1 cup diced tomatoes
2 tablespoons capers
Salt and pepper
Chopped parsley
4 to 6 lemon wedges
1/2 cup feta cheese

In a hot sauté pan, heat olive oil and cook the onions and garlic until they start to brown a bit.

Add mussels and Shipyard Export Ale, cover, and cook for 3 to 4 minutes.

Add butter, basil, olives, tomatoes, and capers, and toss in Export mix. Add salt and pepper to taste.

Put in serving bowl and garnish with parsley, lemon wedges, and feta cheese.

COURTESY OF SHIPYARD BREWING COMPANY (P. 103)

THE INN ON PEAKS ISLAND'S SHIPYARD PUMPKINHEAD ALE PANCAKES

The Inn on Peaks Island is part of the Shipyard Brewing Company's family of restaurants. Its chef, Chris Gordon (2008 Maine Chef of the Year), uses Shipyard's absurdly popular Pumpkinhead Ale to show that beer can be for breakfast, too, with this recipe for Pumpkinhead Ale Pancakes.

1 cup all-purpose flour
1/2 cup Shipyard Pumpkinhead Ale

½ teaspoon baking powder

½ teaspoon baking soda

½ teaspoon cinnamon

½ teaspoon nutmeg

½ cup pumpkin puree

½ cup milk

Pinch clove

2 eggs

¼ cup melted butter

1 teaspoon vanilla extract

Whisk all ingredients together until blended well. Spray non-stick frying pan with pan spray.

Place half cup batter in center of frying pan on medium heat.

Cook until bubbles form on pancake and flip (about 2 minutes on each side).

Serve with Reed's Maple Syrup.

COURTESY OF SHIPYARD BREWING COMPANY (P. 103)

SUNSET GRILL'S BEER STEAMED BURGERS

Sunset Grill & Tap is a certified Boston-area beer destination with around 380 different beers available. No wonder then that they also use beer in their kitchen to prepare some of their delicious dishes. Exhibit A: their beer steamed burgers. Sunset offers 10 variations on this burger in their restaurant, but they were kind enough to share the basic recipe below.

½ pound patty ⁸⁵/₁₅ high-quality ground beef

Sprinkle of kosher salt

Sprinkle of ground black pepper

Beer Baste Mix

4 ounces beer

1⅓ ounces water

2⅔ ounces middle-of-the-road beef

2 ounces Worcestershire sauce

Season ground beef with salt and pepper and form into a patty.

Place meat on a hot flat-top grill or pan and cover.

Splash 2 ounces of beer mix inside and re-cover.

When evaporated, flip over and repeat, adding 2 more ounces of beer mix and cooking to desired temperature. Do not overcook or press down on the patty. Let burger rest before eating or cutting.

COURTESY OF SUNSET GRILL & TAP (P. 73)

GARDNER ALE HOUSE FISH & CHIPS

There is no dish on more brewpub menus throughout New England than beer-battered fish and chips. The Gardner Ale House, even though nowhere near the ocean, makes some of the best fish and chips around.

2 5-ounce haddock fillets

Corn Flour
1/2 ounce corn flour
3 ounces of Old Bay seasoning

Beer Batter
1 gallon Gardner's Summer's End, or another kolsch beer
1 gallon white flour
2 ounces Old Bay seasoning

For the corn flour, blend corn flour and seasoning together.

For the batter, whisk beer, flour, and seasoning together until it forms into well-blended batter.

Coat both pieces of fish with corn flour. Shake off any extra flour.

Coat fish with beer batter, letting the extra batter run off.

After soybean oil reaches 350 degrees, slowly drop coated fish in the fryer (do not use a basket) or a pan. Let the fish cook for 3 or 4 minutes until golden brown.

Flip the fish over and let it cook the rest of the way, approximately another 3 minutes. When fully cooked, remove from the fryer with tongs and let it drain in a fryer basket.

Serve with fries, coleslaw, tartar sauce, and a lemon wedge.

COURTESY OF RICHARD WALTON, OWNER/PRESIDENT OF MOON HILL BREWING INC.
AND GARDNER ALE HOUSE (P. 49)

MILLY'S TAVERN OATMEAL STOUT BEEF STEW

Milly's Tavern of Manchester, New Hampshire, like all of New England, suffers through some harsh winters. What better way to warm up than a crock of beef stew? Milly's version of beef stew uses a hearty stout in its recipe. The roasted coffee flavors of the stout add just a little taste in the background to make you take notice of something different than you'd expect.

3 pounds stew beef
1 tablespoon olive oil
1 tablespoon chopped garlic
1/2 cup flour
2 pints Milly's Oatmeal Stout (or substitute), divided
3 large potatoes, chopped
3 large carrots, chopped
Water as needed
1/4 cup beef base
2 tablespoons black pepper
6 bay leaves
1 tablespoon dried thyme leaves
3 tablespoons dried rosemary leaves

Brown the beef in a mixture of the olive oil and garlic in a pot. Add flour and stir, browning the beef for another minute. After that minute add 1 pint of stout. Then add beef base, potatoes, and carrots. Bring to a boil.

In a sachet bag, add the herbs and black pepper. Simmer covered for an hour. Add remaining 1 pint of stout. Serve.

COURTESY OF MILLY'S TAVERN (P. 173)

PORTSMOUTH BREWERY'S OLD BROWN DOG HANGER STEAK

There is almost no better pairing than a nice slice of beef and really good brown ale. Portsmouth Brewery's Chef Todd Sweet takes that to the next level with his recipe for the Old Brown Dog Hanger Steak, for which he makes a marinade incorporating the brewery's Old Brown Dog beer. The nutty and caramel flavors latch right on to the caramelization of the beef to create a beautiful flavor combination.

1 cup Old Brown Dog
2 tablespoons tamari sauce

2 tablespoons Worcestershire sauce
2 tablespoons brown sugar
1 shallot, minced
2 stems fresh thyme, minced
2 stems rosemary, minced
1 clove garlic, minced
¼ cup olive oil
1 pinch red pepper flakes
1 tablespoon Dijon mustard
1 teaspoon black pepper
4 10-ounce hanger steaks (or substitute beef tips)

Combine all ingredients and pour over the steaks. Mix well, then marinate at least overnight before grilling to desired temperature.

When serving, cut against the grain. Serve with Gorgonzola Sauce (recipe follows).

Gorgonzola Sauce
2 cups heavy cream
¼ cup gorgonzola crumbles
Dash Worcestershire sauce
Dash Tabasco
Fresh ground black pepper to taste
1 teaspoon lemon juice

Reduce the heavy cream by half over medium heat in a small sauce pan.

Whisk in the cheese over the heat, removing it from the heat just as it is melted.

Add remaining ingredients and adjust seasoning.

COURTESY OF PORTSMOUTH BREWERY (P. 176)

THE CASK REPUBLIC'S GRILLED EXTRA-HOPPY-BEER-MARINATED HALF CHICKEN
The Cask Republic in New Haven, Connecticut, is one of the best beer destinations in the state—and the food is pretty darn tasty, too. The hops in an IPA or other hoppy beer in this recipe will combine nicely with the other ingredients to give this chicken an extra kick. Can be used for a half or full chicken.

2 quarts extra hoppy beer
1 tablespoons Dijon mustard

2 tablespoons honey
¼ bunch thyme
¼ bunch of rosemary
3 garlic gloves chopped
Juice of 1 orange
Juice of 1 lime
Juice of 1 lemon
½ or whole chicken
3 tablespoons butter
Salt and pepper to taste

Combine all ingredients except chicken, butter, salt, and pepper. Marinate the chicken in half the mixture for one day.

Remove chicken and pat dry. Season with salt and pepper and grill both sides.

In a sauté pan, bring the leftover marinade to a boil. Add the ckicken, skin side up, and finish in oven at 400°F for 10 to 12 minutes.

When chicken is done, remove to serving dish. Take the pan with the hot marinade and add butter, salt, and pepper until thickened. Pour over the chicken.

COURTESY OF THE CASK REPUBLIC (P. 201)

CITY STEAM BREWERY CAFE'S BEER-BRAISED POT ROAST

City Steam, a Hartford-based brewpub, is unique in that it brews beer and acts as the place to catch up-and-coming comedians. It also uses some of its house-made beers in many of its food recipes. The Beer-Braised Pot Roast is a restaurant favorite, using its popular Naughty Nurse amber ale as part of the recipe. The flavor of the amber ale does not overwhelm the taste of the meat, and vice versa. This recipe is for a large family gathering, not for a small meal.

2 bottom flat round cuts of beef
6 carrots
2 celery stalks
4 Spanish onions
4 quarts Naughty Nurse or another amber ale
8 ounces beef base
20 ounces tomato paste
8 quarts water
8 tablespoons cornstarch

Trim fat off beef. Slicing against the grain, cut the bottom flats into strips about 1½ inches thick. Cut the strips into cubes about 1 ½ to 2 inches thick.

Dice carrots, celery, and onions and add to the beef in the pan.

Combine remaining ingredients and place in the roast pan. Cover with foil and bake at 350°F for 4 hours.

COURTESY OF JAMES DUMOND, CO-OWNER OF CITY STEAM BREWERY CAFE (P. 197)

SEA DOG BREWING COMPANY'S BARBECUE BLUEPAW SHORT RIBS

The Sea Dog Brewing Company, a chain of brewpubs and restaurants in Maine and Massachusetts, has a twist on the traditional pairing of brown ales with beef. Instead, they use blueberry ale and real blueberries, giving these short ribs a unique flavor not found in any other dish.

6 to 8 pounds short ribs
1 cup diced onions
2 tablespoons chopped garlic
1 red pepper, diced
1 yellow pepper, diced
1 jalapeño chili pepper (no pith), diced
2 tablespoons olive oil
1 cup fresh or frozen blueberries
8 ounces Sea Dog Bluepaw Wheat Ale
16 ounces any barbecue sauce
1 bunch cilantro, chopped, divided
Salt and pepper

Season short ribs with salt and pepper. In a hot sauté pan (or grill) sear short ribs on all sides. Remove pan from heat and drain the grease. Remove ribs and set aside.

Sauté onions, garlic, and peppers in olive oil until brown. Put meat back in pan and add blueberries, Sea Dog Bluepaw, barbecue sauce, and half the cilantro. Cover and simmer for 1½ to 2 hours until the meat falls off the bone.

Serve with rice and vegetables and garnish with remaining fresh cilantro. Add salt and pepper to taste.

COURTESY OF SEA DOG BREWING COMPANY (P. 114)

CAMBRIDGE BREWING COMPANY'S YOU ENJOY MY STOUT BROWNIE

Beer, particularly imperial stout, is a fantastic pairing for dessert. Imperial stouts often have flavors of chocolate and coffee. Cambridge Brewing Company chef David Drew's You Enjoy My Stout Brownie is a fantastic and decadent dessert. Drew recommends avoiding cheap chocolate and splurging on the good stuff from a local chocolatier.

1/2 cup You Enjoy My Stout or any other big imperial stout

1/3 cup unsweetened cocoa powder

2 ounces chopped Taza 70% Semi-Sweet Baking Squares (or substitute)

1/2 stick butter, melted

1/2 cup canola oil

2 eggs

2 egg yolks

2 1/2 cups granulated sugar

1 3/4 cup all-purpose flour

1 teaspoon salt

2 ounces roasted cacao nibs (optional)

4 ounces chopped Taza 60% stone-ground dark chocolate (or substitute)

Preheat oven to 350°F. Heat beer in a small sauce pan on high until it comes to just a simmer.

In a large bowl, combine unsweetened cocoa powder and semi-sweet baking squares. Add warm beer to chocolate mix and stir until well incorporated. Next, add butter and oil and gently whisk. Add eggs, egg yolks, and sugar and whisk until fully incorporated.

Gently fold in flour, salt, nibs, and chopped chocolate. Dump into greased 9x13 baking pan and bake for about 30 minutes.

To check doneness, poke a toothpick into the center of brownies. The brownies are done when the toothpick comes out clean.

Be sure to experiment with different types of beers and chocolates to suit your taste.

COURTESY OF DAVID DREW, EXECUTIVE CHEF AT CAMBRIDGE BREWING COMPANY (P. 47)

Pub Crawls

The craft beer scene in New England grows more and more with each passing day. It's become easy to visit a craft brewery, take the tour, grab a bite to eat at a nearby brewpub, and if you haven't had your fill of good beer for the day, hit up the local beer bar, all within walking distance. Get together with some friends, develop an itinerary, and start walking, hitting up all the hot spots and trying your favorite beers as you go.

In this chapter, we highlight some of the best beer cities in New England in which to spend a day sampling the best brew the region has to offer. Just remember: Drink in moderation and take a cab if you get tired of walking from place to place, or assign a designated driver before heading out.

Boston, MA

Boston's Allston neighborhood has two of the best beer bars in all of New England. You will want to make three stops at three different venues—the Sunset Grill & Tap and Deep Ellum in Allston and the Publick House in nearby Brookline.

Sunset Grill & Tap, 130 Brighton Ave., Allston. The Sunset Grill & Tap is where I cut my teeth on my early journey into beer geekdom. It has the largest beer selection in the greater Boston area, with 113 beers on tap and several hundred bottles and cans. Pretty much every good brewery in the US, and many from other parts of the country and Europe, has at least one beer available, either on draft or in bottles. New England is always well represented, with many beers from Clown Shoes and Rapscallion usually available. They also update the seasonal list quite often, so always make sure to take a look before ordering. And you can't leave without having a burger. The burgers are steamed in beer and are the best in the state. The best of the burgers is the Viva La France, which is topped with boursin and grilled portobello mushrooms.

From there, walk west on Brighton Avenue for about 0.3 miles and take a quick right onto Cambridge Street, where you will see:

Deep Ellum, 477 Cambridge St., Allston. Deep Ellum may not have the huge draft list of the Sunset Grill, but the 28 beers on draft and the 80 bottled and canned beers are all fantastic. They always seem to have some hard-to-find imported beers, such as one of the best lagers brewed today, the Bryggeri Oppigards Well-Hopped

Boston Pub Crawl

Braintree St.
Penniman Road Play Area
Harvard Ave.
Linden St.
90
Pratt St.
Ashford St.
N. Beacon St.
Hitchborn St.
Arthur St.
Harvey
Steel Rd.
Emery Rd.–
Rugg Rd.
Farrington Ave.
Gardner St.
Erna St.
Murdock St.
Dustin St.
North Beacon Allee
20
Saunders St.
Cambridge St.
Deep Ellum
Brighton Ave.
Sunset Grill & Tap
Brighton Ave.
Reedsdale St.
Chester St.
St. Luke Rd.
Linden St.
Cambridge St.
Ridgemont St.
Innie Rd.
Armington St.
Allston St.
Quint Ave.
Park Vale Ave.
Linden St.
30
Lawton Playground
Warren St.
Ringer Playground
Gordon St.
Greylock Rd.
Glenville Ave.
Commonwealth Ave.
Harvard St.
Lawton St.
Brighton High Park
Brainerd Rd.
Verndale St.
Kenwood St.
Russel St.
Columbia St.
Thorndike St.
Coolidge St.
Fuller St.
Centre St.
Fidelis Way Park
Commonwealth Ave.
Kelton St.
Walbridge St.
Coolidge Pake
Washington St.
Allston St.
Corey Rd.
Winchester St.
Mason Terrace
Monastery Rd.
Claymoss Rd.
Fidelis Way
Summit Ave.
Jordan Rd.
Colborne Rd.
Euston Rd.
Ransom Rd.
Claymoss Rd.
30
Brian Honan Park
Corey Hill Outlook Park
Summit Ave.
Euston Path Rock Park
Commonwealth Ave.
Mt. Hood Rd.
Washington St.
Westbourne Terrace
Lancaster Terrace
York Terrace
Mason Terrace
Mason Path
Wilson Park
Egremont Rd.
Orchard Rd.
Williston Rd.
Evans Rd.
Cummings Rd.
Windsor R d.
Corey Rd.
Salisbury Rd.
The Publick House
Washington St.
Beacon St.
Griggs Rd.
Griggs Park
Kilsyth Rd.
University Rd.
N
Eaglewood Ave.
Beacon St.
Jean B. Waldstein Playground
Garrison Rd.
Winthrop Rd.
Addington St.
Colbourne Crescent
0   0.1   0.2 mile

Lager from Sweden, which is a treat for lager lovers. They also have some good German beers, such as the Aecht Schlenkerla Helles Bock or some Belgian goodies such as the St. Louis Gueuze from Brouwerij Van Honsebrouk. If you want something to munch on, grab a deviled egg, which is pretty much the quintessential pub food, or a giant steamed pretzel.

When you leave Deep Ellum, either be prepared for a walk, or grab a cab. Your next stop is 1.4 miles away. Just follow Commonwealth Avenue until you reach Washington Street and you will be at:

The Publick House, 1648 Beacon St., Brookline. The Publick House is probably the best beer bar in the greater Boston area. Each beer is hand-picked to give you the best drinking experience possible, the staff is knowledgeable and the beer is served in the proper glassware at all times. The draft list is heavy on Belgian ales, such as N'Ice Chouffe, as well as some fine American craft beer, such as Sixpoint's Gorilla Warfare and Boulevard Brewing Company's Chocolate Ale. The food is nearly as good as the beer selection. Starters include Moules Frites (available in full meal and appetizer sizes), available in four styles, and the potato and cheese croquettes are fabulous. For a meal, go with the grilled marinated steak tips or the spicy pulled pork sandwich.

Cambridge, MA

Cambridge is perfect for a pub crawl. The city is full of great bars and brewpubs, all within walking distance of one another. This pub crawl incorporates the area's newest beer bar, a brewpub that brews some of the best beer in Massachusetts, and a beer geek haven.

Meadhall, 4 Cambridge Center. This new bar features more than 100 beers on tap and a small but well-crafted food menu. Even on a busy Saturday night, you should still expect good service. Start with some snacks like the House Made Pork Rinds or the House Made Giant Pretzels—the best in greater Boston. The House Made Long Island Duck Sausage is amazing, but if you want a bigger meal go with the Braised Niman Ranch Lamb Shoulder. Pair it with a number of New England beers they always have on tap, such as Jack's Abby Brewing's Hoponius Union or a nice Allagash White Ale.

Head down Broadway until it turns into Hampshire Street, and you will see the Cambridge Brewing Company on your right.

Cambridge Brewing Company, 1 Kendall Sq., Building 100. While at the Cambridge Brewing Company, make sure to look for one of their two barleywines, the Blunderbuss

Cambridge Pub Crawl

Lord Hobo

Cambridge Brewing Company

Meadhall

John A. Ahern Field

Donnelly Park

Squirrel Brand Park

Green Rose Heritage Park

0   0.1 mile

N

or the Arquebus. If you don't want such a big beer, go with the Tall Tale Pale Ale, or if you're there during the summer, order a pint of Spring Training IPA, a great India pale ale. Don't forget to eat. Go with the always table-pleasing nachos or the charcuterie plate to start. Follow that up with the Lobster and Chorizo Pizza or the fabulous Atlantic salmon.

Leave Cambridge Brewing Company and get on Hampshire Street. Walk for about 5 minutes until you reach:

Lord Hobo, 92 Hampshire St. They might have a small sign, but you can't miss it. The food is excellent at Lord Hobo and the beer selection is top-of-the-line. Grab a fine Belgian ale or maybe a good German lager. A good start is the House Made Turkey Chili, or maybe a plate of artisan cheeses. If you go with the shaved prime rib sandwich or the pork schnitzel for dinner, you will have a very happy stomach. A High & Mighty XPA or maybe the Maine Beer Company's Peeper Ale would go great with those meals.

Burlington, VT

There may not be a better pub crawl in all of New England than downtown Burlington. All three of the city's brewpubs are close to each other, as well as two excellent beer bars. And there are plenty of hotels to stay at nearby.

Das Bierhaus, 175 Church St. The Das Bierhaus specializes in German beers, which is perfect for a pub crawl. You don't want to start with a high-alcohol extreme beer. Instead, grab a half-liter of a nice authentic German kolsch, such as the Reissdorf Kolsch, or one of the finest wheat beers in the world, the Weihenstephan Hefeweis. Pacing yourself is important, particularly when there are five stops in this crawl. You can't leave a German-style bar without getting some food, but don't go overboard. Grab a Bavarian pretzel or maybe some Schnitz on a Stick.

After leaving Das Bierhaus, take the 0.10-mile walk to:

American Flatbread, 115 Saint Paul St. American Flatbread is not only home of the best pizzas in Vermont, they also host the Zero Gravity Pub. The brewmasters produce great beer there, such as the Ripley, a Belgian-style tripel, and the London Calling, a low-alcohol (3.9 percent ABV) session beer, and if nothing on draft catches your eye, they do have a large bottle list, so you should be able to find something you like. If you like pizza, you'll love American Flatbread's selection; they use nothing but local ingredients. Personal favorite: the sausage.

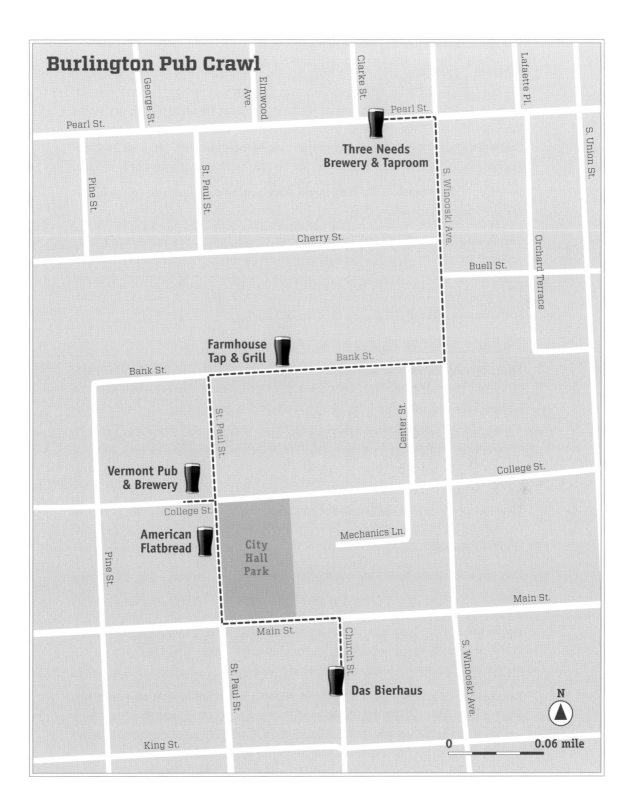

Burlington Pub Crawl

Pearl St.

George St.

Elmwood Ave.

Clarke St.

Pearl St.

Lafaette Pl.

Pine St.

St. Paul St.

Three Needs
Brewery & Taproom

S. Winooski Ave.

S. Union St.

Cherry St.

Buell St.

Orchard Terrace

Farmhouse
Tap & Grill

Bank St.

Bank St.

St. Paul St.

Center St.

College St.

Vermont Pub
& Brewery

College St.

American
Flatbread

City
Hall
Park

Mechanics Ln.

Pine St.

Main St.

Main St.

Church St.

Das Bierhaus

S. Winooski Ave.

St. Paul St.

King St.

N

0   0.06 mile

The next destination is less than one football field away from American Flatbread:

Vermont Pub & Brewery, 144 College St. The Vermont Pub & Brewery is one of the old-time New England brewpubs, so stop there for some New England classics, such as the Burley Irish Stout, one of the best and most traditional Irish dry stouts available in new England. Want to be a little more adventurous? If so, grab the Forbidden Fruit, a tart but extremely refreshing beer brewed with 500 pounds of real raspberries. A plate of local cheeses would be nice to share with someone, or order the portobello mushroom sandwich for yourself.

It's less than a 0.10-mile walk to:

Farmhouse Tap & Grill, 160 Bank St. Take advantage of the Farmhouse's truly amazing bottle list, or grab some Hill Farmstead on draft, not an easy beer to find. Make sure to order something to eat, because the final stop of the night does not have food. The Vermont Chicken & Biscuits and the Maple Wind Farm Meatloaf are both winners and will fill you up for your last stop.

The longest walk of the night, less than 10 minutes to:

Three Needs Brewery & Taproom, 185 Pearl St. Three Needs doesn't offer food. But when they brew beer this good, you don't really want anything to get in the way between you and your glass. It has the feel of a dive bar, but that adds to the charm. The Dortmunder-style Lager and Milo's IPA are both good, solid beers, but for something a little more exciting, go with the Ich Bin Ein Berliner Weiss.

New Haven, CT

The craft beer scene is really growing in Connecticut, with new bars and breweries popping up all the time. Nowhere in the state is craft beer as well represented as it is in New Haven.

Delaney's Restaurant & Tap Room, 882 Whalley Ave. Delaney's has by far the biggest and best beer selection of any bar in town, so you have to go there. The problem is it is far away from every other location; grab a couple of beers there—maybe the Innis & Gunn Rum Barrel-aged beer, which is very rarely found on draft, or a New England Brewing Company Imperial Stout Trooper—and then jump into a cab and tell the driver to drop you off at 254 Crown St.

Bru Room at Bar, 254 Crown St. It kind of has a nightclub-type of feel to it, but what is important is that they brew good beer and have good food. Food is always key on a pub crawl, so grab a white pizza topped with bacon and mushrooms and wash it down with a house-brewed pale ale or the AmBAR Ale.

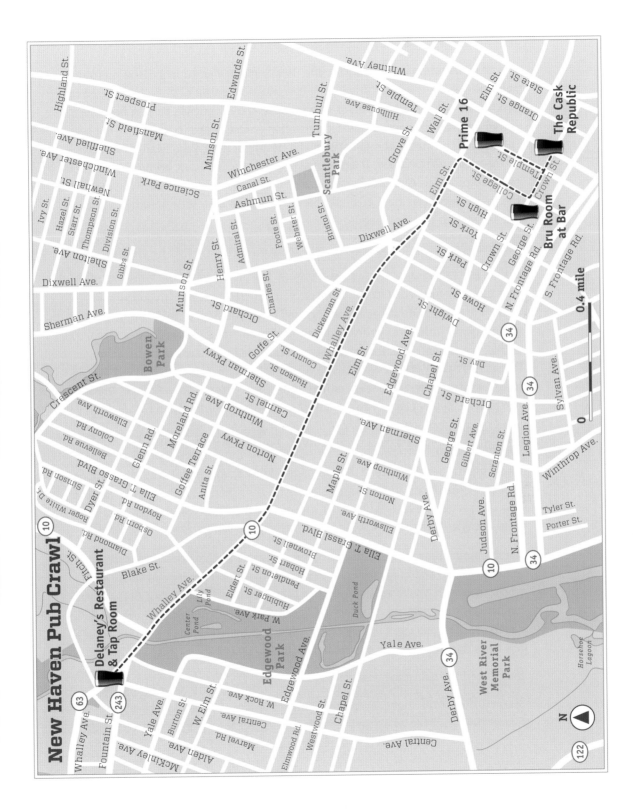

Walk about 0.1 mile down the street, and stop in at:

The Cask Republic, 179 Crown St. The Cask Republic has an impressive draft and bottle list. There is always at least one beer available on cask. If you're not used to cask beers, it's a totally different way to serve and experience beer. A beer that's served on cask will have different carbonation—some people might think the beer is flat—but the bubbles bring out some interesting flavors, particularly if its served at the proper temperature. Don't worry, if you're not into cask beer, they have 53 other beers on tap. The Cask Republic also holds numerous beer dinners throughout the year, when beers from a certain brewery, such as Blue Hills Brewing Company, are paired with specific dishes.

The final destination is less than 0.1-mile away at:

Prime 16, 172 Temple St. The final stop of the night should be Prime 16. Make sure you still have room for food when you get here, because they specialize in gourmet burgers made of beef from grass-fed cows. The Honey Truffle Burger, a beef patty topped with Swiss cheese, applewood bacon, roasted tomatoes, and honey truffle, is excellent, as is the Smoker, which is topped with smoked Canadian bacon, a fried egg, and Vermont cheddar. To wash those burgers down, you need a good beer. Luckily, Prime 16 delivers on that front, too. Try the New England Brewing Company's Elm City Lager or the Victory Brewing Company Headwaters Pale Ale.

Northampton, MA

Massachusetts beer geeks tend to center around Boston and its suburbs when talking about beer, beer bars, and brewpubs. However, they should not forget the western part of the state, which is home to Amherst, a true craft beer mecca and small college community.

Northampton Brewery, 11 Brewster Court. It is one of the oldest brewpubs in all of New England, and they do a great job of brewing beer. They brew beers for pretty much anyone. If you're a fan of lighter beers, try the Paradise City Gold. If you happen to be a fan of big, hop-forward beers, order a Double Take, a 9 percent ABV double IPA. The pub itself is very comfortable, and there is a large bar area. After a few beers there, you'll be in the mood for dinner.

Take a short 0.3-mile stroll down to:

Sierra Grille, 41A Strong Ave. The Sierra Grille is a combination beer geek and foodie dream. All the available beer is fantastic, and the food is world class—they

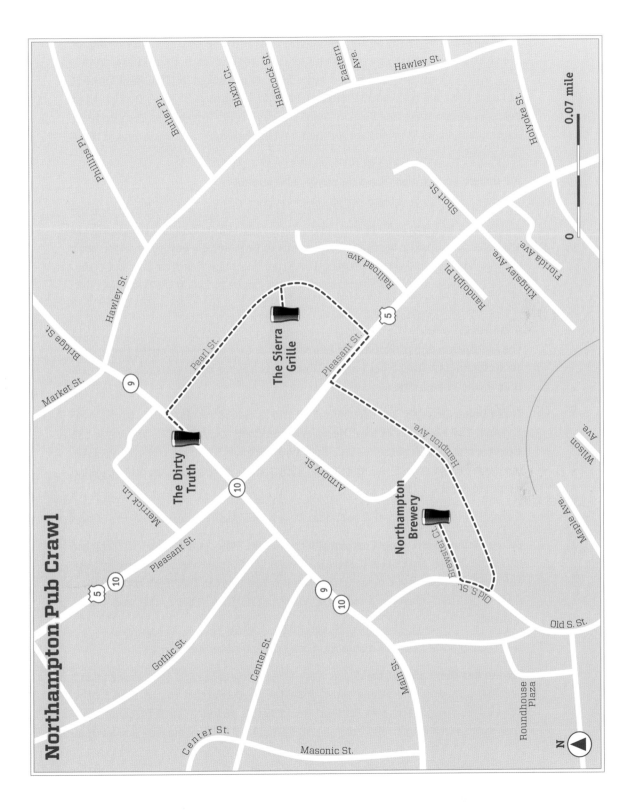

Northampton Pub Crawl

The Dirty Truth

The Sierra Grille

Northampton Brewery

0.07 mile

N

stand up favorably to any Boston restaurant. Start with the smoked chicken wings or the shrimp in chocolate sauce. Move on to an entree. You start by picking a protein (I go with duck usually) and then a sauce for it to be cooked in (Thai Basil Coconut or Citrus Salsa are both good choices). The draft list always includes Dogfish Head beers, as well as some fine Belgian lambics such as Echte Kriekenbier. It's rare when a restaurant shows as much care for their food as their beer, and this is one of those rare places.

A 2-minute walk straight down the street leads you to:

Dirty Truth, 29 Main St. The beer selection is huge, the crowd can get loud, and it's a great way to party and end the night. The crowd is a mixture of college stuents and some townies. The beer list always seems to be heavy on west coast beers, such as Bear Republic and Stone Brewing Company, but some fine New England beers, such as Allagash Black and Smuttynose's Porter, can be found on the large draft list.

Portland, ME

The Old Port section of Portland is full of small antiques shops, touristy stores, and good restaurants. It also has its good share of places for beer lovers, all within less than a mile of each other.

Three Dollar Dewey's, 241 Commercial St. This is one of the oldest beer bars in New England. There are tons of local Maine beers on draft, the beer is cheap, and it has a townie feel to it. A pint of Geary's Brewing Company's IPA or a Bar Harbor Real Ale is always a good start to a night. Or go with Maine's best stout, Atlantic's Cadillac Mountain Stout.

A short, 5-minute walk from Three Dollar Dewey's will lead you to:

Gritty McDuff's Brewing Company, 396 Fore St. Here, order some of the most authentic British-style beers brewed in New England, and make sure to get at least one on cask. They do a great job of serving the beer at the right temperature. Also, do yourself a favor and order the sweet potato fries—they're the best in New England.

Take a quick stroll to the next stop for a truly different beer experience:

Novare Res Bier Cafe, 4 Canal Plaza. Novare Res is one of the five great New England beer bars. They do everything right, from the beer selection to the food to the knowledgable staff. A trip to Portland would not be complete without going here. They specialize in Belgian ales, so grab a St. Bernardus Abt 12, or maybe a Rochefort 8.

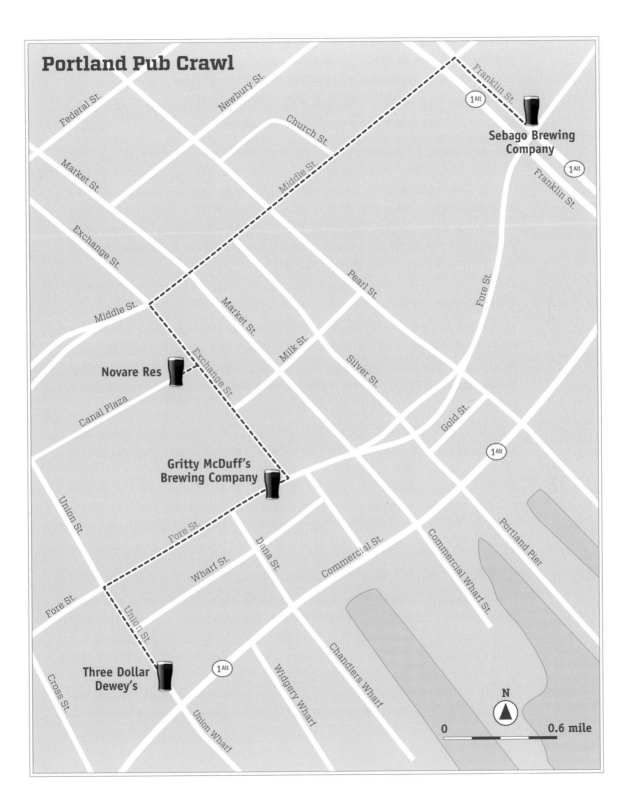

Portland Pub Crawl

Federal St.

Newbury St.

Church St.

Franklin St.

1 Alt

Market St.

Middle St.

**Sebago Brewing
Company**

Franklin St.

1 Alt

Exchange St.

Pearl St.

Fore St.

Middle St.

Market St.

Novare Res

Exchange St.

Milk St.

Silver St.

Canal Plaza

Gold St.

1 Alt

**Gritty McDuff's
Brewing Company**

Union St.

Portland Pier

Fore St.

Commercial St.

Commercial Wharf St.

Wharf St.

Dana St.

Commercial St.

Cross St.

**Three Dollar
Dewey's**

Union St.

1 Alt

Chandlers Wharf

Widgery Wharf

N

Union Wharf

0   0.6 mile

They make sure to take care of Maine breweries, too. Marshall Wharf, one of the best breweries not a lot of people know about, always seems to be on tap here, and it would be a shock if there isn't an Allagash beer or two available.

This next walk will be the longest one of the night at a little more than 0.5 mile, but it should build up your appetite by the time you get to:

Sebago Brewing Company, 211 Fore St. Here, grab some of the fine Sebago beers on draft, and maybe a burger or some nachos to share. Sebago's two best beers are its IPAs. The Frye's Leap IPA is the "regular" IPA, while the Full Throttle is the big, burly, west coast double IPA. At this point you're probably in the mood for some food, so share some pork dumplings or Cajun-dusted Haddock Bites for an appetizer. You can't go wrong with the beer-battered fish and chips or the New York center sirloin if you're hungry enough for a full meal.

Portsmouth, NH

Portsmouth is a great little beer city. It is by far the best beer destination in the whole Granite State, with the best selection of bars and one of the best brewpubs in all of New England in the Portsmouth Brewery. Portsmouth is also one of those picturesque New England cities, right on the coast of the Atlantic Ocean, with numerous little shops perfect for a day of window-shopping.

RiRa Irish Pub, 22 Market Square. Don't skip RiRa just because it is a chain. They do things right here. The Portsmouth location is housed in a bank that was built in 1809, and you can still see the vault from the seating area. The food is heavy on Irish specialties, so either start with an appetizer like some lamb sliders, or go with a hearty meal of shepherd's pie or corned beef and cabbage. Wash it down with a bomber of Rogue Brewing Company's Dead Guy Ale or grab a Guinness Stout.

After you leave RiRa, walk by the many small shops, even a store that specializes in the sale of various salts, about 100 feet to:

The Portsmouth Brewery, 56 Market St. The Portsmouth Brewery, the sister brewpub to the Smuttynose Brewing Company, is a world class brewpub. The beers are phenomenal. The Oatmeal Stout is divine, and the Belgian-style Tripel is out of this world. If you happen to be there on a certain day during the winter, either in February or early March, you may get a chance to try Kate the Great, a Russian imperial stout that happens to be one of the best beers in the world. Of course, you will have to wait in line for hours to try it. They also always have some Smuttynose

Portsmouth Pub Crawl

Bow Street

Penhallow Street

Daniel Street

Market Street

Market Street

Portsmouth Gas
Light Co.

Portsmouth
Brewery

RiRa Irish Pub

Pleasant
Street

Ladd Street

West City Avenue

High Street

Hanover St.

Haven Street

High Street

High Street

High Street

Hanover Street

Fleet Street

Blue Mermaid
Island Grill

N

0   0.3 miles

beers on tap, as well as guest taps for various breweries from around the country. The food is also top-notch. The Ploughman's Plate and the Hummus and Baba Ghanoush are both good for sharing. If you or one of your fellow pub crawlers is a vegetarian, this is the place for you because there are many veggie options.

After you leave the Portsmouth Brewery, turn right and walk approximately 10 feet to your next destination:

The Portsmouth Gas Light Co., 64 Market St. If you haven't filled up before you get here, the Portsmouth Gas Light Co. has some fantastic food. The appetizers include a personal favorite, the Wood Fired Chicken Legs, as well as a large order of fried calamari. Want something more substantial? Go for the lobster-stuffed haddock or the braised short ribs. If you are in the mood for pizza, grab one from Downtown Pizza, which is located within the Gas Light Company. The Congress Street, topped with pepperoni, sausage, onions, green peppers, mushrooms, and black olives, is nice and filling. With all that good food, you need good beer to wash it down. The Portsmouth Gas Light Company has plenty of good beers, such as the Berkshire Brewing Company's Steel Rail Extra Pale Ale or the Hinterland Cherry Wheat.

There's one more stop on this pub crawl. Just head on to Hanover Street and walk about 400 feet to High Street, before crawling about another 200 feet to The Hill and a little piece of the Caribbean in Portsmouth:

Blue Mermaid Island Grill, 409 The Hill. The Blue Mermaid is a standout in Portsmouth because it is just so much different than the other locations. While all three of the other destinations feel like beer bars, this has a much brighter and more sunny feel to it. However, they still have really good beer. Most of the Blue Mermaid's eight draft lines are reserved for New England beers. You are likely to find a Peak Organic Local Harvest or Throwback Brewing Company Love Me Long Time Pilsner on draft. Both of those go swimmingly with the islands-inspired menu. If you still have room for food, the Bermuda Triangles Beef Patties and Lobster Quesadillas are fantastic. If you have had enough beer, they also have a large drink menu, which features such tropical coolers as the Mermaid Mai Tai, made with light and dark rums, Triple Sec, orange juice, mango juice, pineapple juice, and sour mix; or the Cocomojorinha, made with Bacardi coconut rum, fresh lime, mint, and simple syrup with a splash of pineapple.

Providence, RI

Providence may not have the beer reputation of some of the other New England cities featured in this book, but you would be surprised. Craft beer appreciation is growing there, and for those who don't want to travel outside of Rhode Island, this is a nice little pub crawl.

English Cellar Ale House, 165 Angell St. As the name implies, this is an English-centric pub, although beer from the US, Germany, and Belgium are well-represented. A good starter would be an Old Speckled Hen—low alcohol, high in flavor, and just a good beer.

Get ready for some fresh air, because you will have your longest walk of the pub crawl heading to your second stop, a 0.7-mile walk that should only take you about 15 to 20 minutes.

Union Station Brewery, 36 Exchange Terrace. The walk is worth it once you try some of Union Station's house-brewed beers. It is part of the John Harvard's chain of brewpubs, so the beers are all solid and well-made. Grab dinner there if you're hungry, because the food is excellent. The nachos smothered with cheese and pulled pork are gigantic, and great for a group. If you want a sandwich, the fontina and grape grilled cheese is fantastic, while the lobster mac and cheese is a meal that will leave you stuffed and ready to move to your next bar.

A 0.25-mile walk will lead you to:

Trinity Brewhouse, 186 Fountain St. The Trinity Brewhouse always has a wide variety of beers, so grab your favorite style, or maybe two. The Rhode Island IPA would go perfectly with a bowl of the Spicy Trinity Chili, and is there a food that says beer more than a grilled sausage platter? Pair it with Trinity's well-done Kolsch.

The final stop on the crawl is Julians, which is a little over 0.5 mile from Trinity. At this point in the crawl, the walk will do you good.

Julians, 318 Broadway. Once at Julians, take advantage of the top-notch draft list or large bottle selection. They have a list of larger-format bottles, such as 750 ml, perfect for sharing at the end of the night.

Providence Pub Crawl

English Cellar Alehouse

Union Station Brewery

Trinity Brewhouse

Julians

N

0   0.3 mile

How to Taste a Beer

Tasting beer is not as easy as you may think. Sure, you can grab a bottle, pop the top, and take a sip and taste it, but you won't get the whole experience that way.

First off, pour your beer into a glass. A pint glass is fine, or if you're drinking a stronger beer, such as an imperial stout or a Belgian tripel, pull out a brandy snifter or a wine glass.

Now stick your nose in there, almost touching the beer. Notice how it smells. You lose the aroma when drinking from a bottle, and you can't appreciate anything, food or beer, without being able to smell it.

What does it smell like? Is it bready or doughy? That could be from the malts in a lager. Are there aromas of grapefruits or pine? That could be the hops in an IPA. Coffee? Roasted barley malt in a stout could be the cause of that. There are hundreds of aromas you could be detecting.

Look at the beer. Is it dark, light, cloudy? Different beers look different. A cloudy appearance could mean the beer is unfiltered.

Now, the most important part of tasting a beer is actually tasting it. Take a sip. Not a huge one, but not a dainty sip—enough to fill your mouth. Let it sit on your tongue for a second to see what flavors you will pick up. Don't spit it out like wine. You actually need to swallow it. The taste receptors for bitterness are on the back of the tongue, so you can't fully taste a beer without swallowing.

Okay, the next step is to take another sip, and another, and a few more. Have fun—it's beer. Enjoy.

Appendix

Beer Lover's Pick List

Archer's Ale, Sherwood Forest Brewers, English Pale Ale, 39

Baby Tree, Pretty Things Beer & Ale Project, Belgian Quad, 36

Berliner Weisse, White Birch Brewing, Berliner Weisse, 166

Big Wally Porter, Cavalry Brewing, Porter, 186

Black Bear Stout, Black Bear Microbrewery, American Stout, 87

Brother Adam's Bragget, Atlantic Brewing Company, Braggot, 82

Cadillac Mountain Stout, Bar Harbor Brewing Company, American Stout, 83

Cape Cod Red, Cape Cod Beer, Red Ale, 9

Chocolate Oatmeal Stout, Lefty's Brewing Company, Oatmeal Stout, 25

Chocolate Oatmeal Stout, Trout River Brewing Company, Oatmeal Stout, 140

Coffeehouse Porter, Berkshire Brewing Company, Coffee Porter, 3

Curieux, Allagash Brewing Company, Tripel, 79

Damariscotta Double Brown, Sheepscot Valley Brewing Company, Brown Ale, 102

Daymark, Rising Tide Brewing Company, Rye Pale Ale, 99

Dirty Penny Ale, Olde Burnside Brewing Company, Black and Tan, 193

Doppelbock, Pioneer Brewing Company, Doppelbock, 34

Double Black Stout, Redhook Ale Brewery, American Double Stout, 159

Eagle Claw Fist, Clown Shoes Beer, Imperial Amber Ale, 12

Effinghamburgherbrau, Prodigal Brewing Company, Lager, 157

Equinox Pilsner, Northshire Brewery, Czech Pilsner, 134

Extra Special Oak (Cask), Element Brewing Company, English Strong Ale, 15

Farmhouse Pale Ale, Oxbow Brewing Company, Saison, 95

Fat Alberta, Throwback Brewery, Imperial Stout, 163

Frosty Knuckle Ale, Frosty Knuckle Brewing Company, Hybrid, 17

Frye's Leap India Pale Ale, Sebago Brewing Company, IPA, 101

Gandhi-Bot Double IPA, New England Brewing Company, Double IPA, 191

Golden Flounder, Just Beer Brewing Company, Pale Wheat Ale, 23

Golden IPA, Squam Brewing Company, Double IPA, 162

Gonzie, Lawson's Finest Liquids, Pale Ale, 129

Grateful Harvest Cranberry Ale, Harpoon Brewery, Fruit Beer, 18

Halloween Ale, Gritty McDuff's Brewery, Extra Special Bitter, 91

Headwall Alt, Tuckerman Brewing Company, Alt, 165

Home for the Holidays, High & Mighty Beer Company, American Brown Ale, 20

Hop Monster, Paper City Brewing Company, Double IPA, 33

Hoponius Union, Jack's Abby Brewing, India Pale Lager, 21

Howl, Magic Hat Brewing Company, Schwarzbier, 132

Hurricane Amber Ale, Coastal Extreme Brewing Company, Amber Ale, 209

Iced Coffee Stout (Iced Earl), Hill Farmstead Brewery, Imperial Stout, 127

Ipswich Dark Ale, Mercury Brewing Company, Brown Ale, 28

Kanc Country Maple Porter, Woodstock Inn Brewery, Porter, 168

Lager, Rapscallion, American Pale Lager, 37

Laughing Loon Lager, Oak Pond Brewing Company, Munich Dunkel Lager, 93

Liberator Doppelbock, Thomas Hooker Brewing Company, Doppelbock, 194

Lobster Ale, Belfast Bay Brewing Company, Amber/Red Ale, 86

Long Trail Ale, Long Trail Brewing Company, Altbier, 130

Mild at Heart, Wandering Star Brewing Company, English Dark Mild, 42

Milk Stout, Wachusett Brewing Company, Milk Stout, 41

Narragansett Bock, Narragansett Beer, Bock, 210

Notch Session Pils, Notch Brewing, Pilsner, 31

Nut Brown Ale, Peak Organic Brewing Company, Brown Ale, 96

Oaktoberfest, Nashoba Valley Winery, Oktoberfest, 30

The Old Factory Whistle, Penobscot Bay Brewery, Scottish Ale, 98

Old Yankee Ale, Cottrell Brewing Company, Pale Ale, 188

OktoBrau, Blue Hills Brewery, Oktoberfest, 4

Otter Creek Black IPA, Otter Creek Brewing, Black IPA, 135

Pechish Woods, Cisco Brewers, American Wild Ale, 10

Peeper Ale, Maine Beer Company, Pale Ale, 92

Praying Mantis Porter, The Hartford Better Beer Company, Porter, 189

Index